WORLD SOCCER
INFOGRAPHICS
The Beautiful Game in Vital Statistics

opta
The World's Leading Football Data Provider

PUBLISHER'S NOTES

All European domestic league infographic data runs up until the end of the 2016–17 season.
All European team names printed in accordance with UEFA.

First published in the United States of America in 2018 by
UNIVERSE PUBLISHING
A Division of Rizzoli International Publications, Inc.
300 Park Avenue South
New York, NY 10010
www.rizzoliusa.com

Originally published in the United Kingdom in 2016 (updated in 2017) by
Carlton Books Limited

Infographic statistical data © Perform Media Channels Limited 2016, 2017
All other text, graphics, and design © Carlton Books Limited 2016, 2017

2018 2019 2020 2021 / 10 9 8 7 6 5 4 3 2 1

ISBN: 978-0-7893-3426-8
Library of Congress Control Number: 2017952765

Printed in China

Numbers, Statistics, and
Trends of the Players, Teams,
Stadiums, and more

WORLD SOCCER
INFOGRAPHICS
The Beautiful Game in Vital Statistics

The World's Leading Football Data Provider

UNIVERSE

CONTENTS

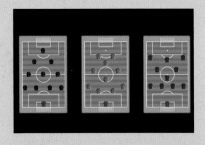

WORLD SOCCER

FIFA WORLD CUP

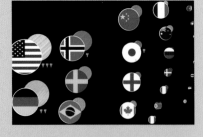

FIFA WOMEN'S WORLD CUP

DOMESTIC CLUB SOCCER

MISCELLANEOUS

CONTINENTAL CHAMPIONSHIPS

CONTINENTAL CLUB SOCCER

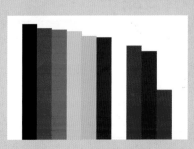

DOMESTIC CLUB SOCCER

opta

Foreword

It is now 20 years since Opta started collecting soccer data and in that time the popularity of the information produced has gone from being a curiosity in a newspaper or TV feature to an integral part of sports coverage in every type of media.

Data was long seen as the home of the stats geek, only accessible to those willing to pore through statistical tomes to find "interesting" snippets of information. Today it's consumed by ordinary soccer fans through a variety of methods. You'll still see tables of numbers and hear facts and figures spoken by commentators, pundits, or by people to their friends on their way to matches, but you're now just as likely to see a graphical interpretation of that information.

From pie charts and bar charts, to radars and word clouds, numbers are regularly turned into easily understandable graphics, where the viewer can see what you're trying to tell them instantly. Added to that, the positional and tracking data available within sports allows tactical insight to be communicated easily through heat maps, average formation graphics, or expected goals visualizations, which show at a glance the chance of scoring from a particular position on the pitch relative to other types of shots.

Infographics have become one of the most quickly developing trends in sports data analysis. As datasets become more complex, infographics are an invaluable way of displaying complex information in a clear, concise, attractive way. The unique infographics created for the second edition of this book, incorporating comparisons between players, teams, and leagues for almost every continent, showcases the mass of detailed data now available from right across the world of sports.

Enjoy the book,

Rob Bateman, Global Director of Content (@Orbinho)

Introduction

Statistics are an integral part of modern soccer—pored over by coaches, analysts, and armchair fans alike. Rarely though, have the thrills and skills, triumphs and trophies of the global game been transformed into such thought-provoking graphs, diagrams, and charts as those presented on the pages that follow. You'll be amazed at what emerges from these technicolor infographics. From the statistics that illuminate the Messi–Ronaldo rivalry to the evolution of team formations, right through to the different parts of the body used to score World Cup goals—it's all here… and more.

Our fascination with football takes many forms. We can admire the breathtaking skills of stars such as Mesut Özil, Eden Hazard, or Neymar; the performances of great teams like Bayern München and Real Madrid; and the strategies of coaches such as José Mourinho and Antonio Conte. However, in recent years, statistics, trends, and data collection have added to our interest in top-level soccer. And, where there are numbers, there can be infographics capable of unlocking the power of big data and presenting it in a brilliant, captivating way.

This invaluable book uses imaginative infographics to take a topical look at the trends and data in top-class soccer. It compares the top leagues and players across Europe and assesses the performances in the Champions League, Europa League, and Copa Libertadores. At the international level, we see the domination and surprises of the nation's tournaments around the world. And, of course, the greatest soccer show on earth, the FIFA World Cup, is represented in vibrant infographics that include analysis on goalkeepers, goal re-creations, and perfect penalty placements. Intriguing charts and maps also reveal other facets such as club rivalries, stadium sizes, MLS, the FIFA World Player of the Year and where to find the most shots from distance or dribbles.

Thanks to the rich and compelling information supplied by data providers such as Opta, soccer is no longer just a simple game of two halves. The doors have been blown open and the beautiful game is just a little bit more beautiful.

FIFA SOCCER NATIONS

FIFA's six confederations represent different regions of the world: UEFA (Europe), CAF (Africa), CONCACAF (North and Central America), CONMEBOL (South America), OFC (New Zealand and South Pacific island nations) and AFC (Asia). FIFA was founded on May 21, 1904 in Paris by delegates from Belgium, Denmark, France, the Netherlands, Spain, Sweden and Switzerland. It now has more member countries than the United Nations – 211 to the UN's 193. The British nations, acting in unison, had a checkered relationship with the world body in its early years, joining in 1906 but leaving on two occasions before re-joining permanently in 1946.

NATIONAL ASSOCIATIONS:
YEAR FOUNDED

- UEFA
- OFC
- AFC
- CONMEBOL
- CONCACAF
- CAF

1863	England
1873	Scotland
1876	Wales
1880	Northern Ireland
1889	Denmark
1889	Netherlands
1891	New Zealand
1892	Singapore
1893	Argentina
1895	Belgium
1895	Chile
1895	Gibraltar
1895	Switzerland
1898	Italy
1900	Germany
1900	Malta
1900	Uruguay
1901	Czech Republic
1901	Hungary
1902	Guyana
1902	Norway
1904	Austria
1904	Haiti
1904	Sweden
1906	Paraguay
1907	Finland
1907	Phillipines
1908	Luxembourg
1908	Trinidad and Tobago
1909	Romania
1910	Barbados
1910	Jamaica
1912	Canada
1912	Croatia
1912	Russia
1913	Spain
1913	USA
1914	Brazil
1914	Hong Kong
1914	Kazakhstan
1914	Portugal
1916	Thailand
1919	Belgian Congo
1919	France
1919	Guatemala
1919	Poland
1919	Serbia
1920	Iran
1920	Slovenia
1920	Suriname
1921	Costa Rica
1921	Curaçao
1921	Egypt
1921	Estonia
1921	Japan
1921	Latvia

1921	Republic of Ireland
1922	Afghanistan
1922	Lithuania
1922	Peru
1923	Bulgaria
1923	Turkey
1924	China PR
1924	Colombia
1924	Cuba
1924	Grenada
1924	Uganda
1925	Bolivia
1925	Ecuador
1926	Greece
1926	Venezuela
1927	Mexico
1928	Antigua and Barbuda
1928	Bermuda
1928	Israel
1928	New Caledonia
1929	Zambia
1930	Albania
1930	Indonesia
1930	Tanzania
1931	Montenegro
1931	Nicaragua
1931	San Marino
1932	Aruba
1932	Lesotho
1932	St. Kitts and Nevis
1933	Cambodia
1933	Korea Republic
1933	Lebanon
1933	Malaysia
1934	Cyprus
1934	Liechtenstein
1934	Vanuatu
1935	El Salvador
1935	Honduras
1936	Chinese Tapei
1936	Liberia
1936	Sudan
1936	Syria
1936	Tajikistan
1937	India
1937	Panama
1938	Fiji
1938	Slovakia
1939	Macau
1939	Sri Lanka
1940	Puerto Rico
1943	Ethiopia
1945	Korea DPR
1945	Nigeria
1946	Kosovo

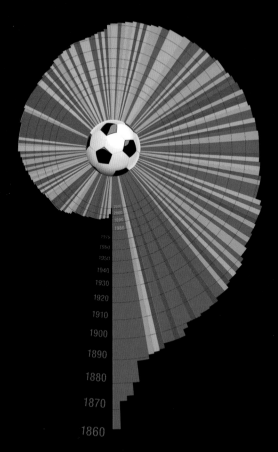

1946	Uzbekistan
1947	Iceland
1947	Myanmar
1948	Burundi
1948	FYR Macedonia
1948	Iraq
1948	Pakistan
1949	Jordan
1951	Laos
1951	Nepal
1951	Somalia
1952	Gambia
1952	Kuwait
1952	Mauritius
1953	Dominican Republic
1955	Morocco
1956	Saudi Arabia
1957	Bahrain
1957	Equatorial Guinea
1957	Ghana
1957	Tunisia
1959	Brunei Darussalam
1959	Cameroon
1959	Mongolia
1960	Burkino Faso
1960	Côte D'ivoire
1960	Guinea
1960	Kenya
1960	Mali
1960	Qatar
1960	Senegal
1960	Sierra Leone
1960	Togo
1961	Australia
1961	Central African Republic
1961	Madagascar
1961	Mauritania
1961	Niger
1962	DR Congo
1962	Algeria
1962	Benin
1962	Chad
1962	Gabon
1962	Libya
1962	Palestine
1962	Papua New Guinea
1962	Vietnam
1962	Yemen
1965	Tonga
1965	Zimbabwe
1966	Cayman Islands
1966	Malawi

1967	Bahamas
1968	Samoa
1968	Swaziland
1970	Botswana
1970	Dominica
1971	Cook Islands
1971	United Arab Emirates
1972	Bangladesh
1972	Rwanda
1974	British Virgin Islands
1974	Guinea-Bissau
1975	Guam
1975	São Tomé e Príncipe
1976	Mozambique
1978	Oman
1978	Solomon Islands
1979	Angola
1979	Comoros
1979	Djibouti
1979	Faroe Islands
1979	Seychelles
1979	St. Lucia
1979	St. Vincent and the Grenadines
1980	Belize
1982	Cape Verde Islands
1982	Maldives
1983	Bhutan
1984	American Samoa
1989	Belarus
1989	Tahiti
1990	Anguilla
1990	Georgia
1990	Moldova
1990	Namibia
1991	South Africa
1991	Ukraine
1992	Armenia
1992	Azerbaijan
1992	Bosnia and Herzegovina
1992	Kyrgystan
1992	Turkmenistan
1992	US Virgin Islands
1994	Andorra
1994	Montserrat
1996	Eritrea
1996	Turks and Caicos Islands
2002	Timor-Leste
2011	South Sudan

NATIONAL ASSOCIATIONS:
YEAR AFFILIATED WITH FIFA

⚽ **WORLD CUP**

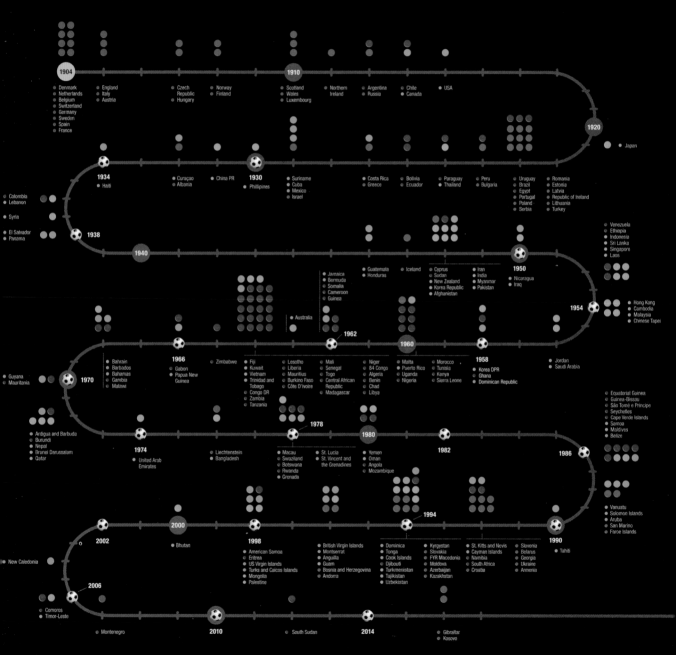

1904
Denmark, Netherlands, Belgium, Switzerland, Germany, Sweden, Spain, France — England, Italy, Austria — Czech Republic, Hungary — Norway, Finland — Scotland, Wales, Luxembourg — Northern Ireland — Argentina, Russia — Chile, Canada — USA

1910

1920 — Japan

1934 — Haiti

1930 — Curaçao, Albania — China PR — Phillipines — Suriname, Cuba, Mexico, Israel — Costa Rica, Greece — Bolivia, Ecuador — Paraguay, Thailand — Peru, Bulgaria — Uruguay, Brazil, Egypt, Portugal, Poland, Serbia — Romania, Estonia, Latvia, Republic of Ireland, Lithuania, Turkey

Colombia, Lebanon — Syria — El Salvador, Panama

1938

1940

1950 — Nicaragua, Iraq

Venezuela, Ethiopia, Indonesia, Sri Lanka, Singapore, Laos

Guatemala, Honduras — Iceland — Cyprus, Sudan, New Zealand, Korea Republic, Afghanistan — Iran, India, Myanmar, Pakistan

1954

Hong Kong, Cambodia, Malaysia, Chinese Tapei

Jamaica, Bermuda, Somalia, Cameroon, Guinea — Australia

1962

1960

1966 — Gabon, Papua New Guinea — Zimbabwe — Fiji, Kuwait, Vietnam, Trinidad and Tobago, Congo DR, Zambia, Tanzania — Lesotho, Liberia, Mauritius, Burkino Faso, Côte D'ivoire — Mali, Senegal, Togo, Central African Republic, Madagascar — Niger, 84 Congo, Algeria, Benin, Chad, Libya — Malta, Puerto Rico, Uganda, Nigeria — Morocco, Tunisia, Kenya, Sierra Leone

Bahrain, Barbados, Bahamas, Gambia, Malawi

1958 — Korea DPR, Ghana, Dominican Republic — Jordan, Saudi Arabia

Guyana, Mauritania

1970

Equatorial Guinea, Guinea-Bissau, São Tomé e Principe, Seychelles, Cape Verde Islands, Samoa, Maldives, Belize

Antigua and Barbuda, Burundi, Nepal, Brunei Darussalam, Qatar

1978

1980

1982

1986

1974 — United Arab Emirates — Liechtenstein, Bangladesh — Macau, Swaziland, Botswana, Rwanda, Grenada — St. Lucia, St. Vincent and the Grenadines — Yemen, Oman, Angola, Mozambique

Vanuatu, Solomon Islands, Aruba, San Marino, Faroe Islands

1994

1990

New Caledonia

2000

2002 — Bhutan

1998 — American Samoa, Eritrea, US Virgin Islands, Turks and Caicos Islands, Mongolia, Palestine — British Virgin Islands, Montserrat, Anguilla, Guam, Bosnia and Herzegovina, Andorra — Dominica, Tonga, Cook Islands, Djibouti, Turkmenistan, Tajikistan, Uzbekistan — Kyrgystan, Slovakia, FYR Macedonia, Moldova, Azerbaijan, Kazakhstan — St. Kitts and Nevis, Cayman Islands, Namibia, South Africa, Croatia — Slovenia, Belarus, Georgia, Ukraine, Armenia — Tahiti

2006 — Comoros, Timor-Leste — Montenegro

2010 — South Sudan

2014 — Gibraltar, Kosovo

Source: Opta (June 2017)

9

SOCCER STADIUMS BY SIZE

The soccer world may still mourn the loss of iconic grounds such as Arsenal's Highbury stadium, Benfica's Estádio da Luz, and Athletic Bilbao's La Catedral at San Mamés, but the stadiums that replaced them and other new venues such as the Allianz Arena in Munich, Juventus' stadium in Turin, and Atlético Madrid's Wanda Metropolitano look set to join Camp Nou, Old Trafford, and La Bombonera on the list of the world's most hallowed grounds. This infographic illustrates the world's biggest soccer stadiums (on this page) and the homes of leading soccer clubs and major national teams (facing)—and, for comparison, includes two of the smallest.

Source: Google (May 2017)

RUNGRADO MAY DAY STADIUM
Pyongyang, North Korea

DPR KOREA NATIONAL FOOTBALL TEAM
150,000

CAMP NOU
Barcelona, Spain

BARCELONA
99,354

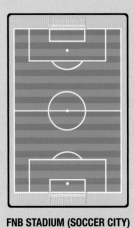

FNB STADIUM (SOCCER CITY)
Johannesburg, South Africa

SOUTH AFRICA NATIONAL TEAM,
KAIZER CHIEFS, 2010 WORLD CUP
94,736

WEMBLEY STADIUM
London, England

ENGLAND NATIONAL
FOOTBALL TEAM
90,000

ESTADIO AZTECA
Mexico City, Mexico

MEXICO NATIONAL FOOTBALL TEAM,
CLUB AMÉRICA
87,000

BORG EL ARAB STADIUM
Alexandria, Egypt

EGYPT NATIONAL
FOOTBALL TEAM
86,000

SALT LAKE STADIUM
Kolkata, India

INDIA NATIONAL
FOOTBALL TEAM
85,000

**SIGNAL IDUNA PARK
(WESTFALENSTADION)**
Dortmund, Germany
BORUSSIA DORTMUND
81,359

STADE DE FRANCE
Saint-Denis, France
FRANCE NATIONAL FOOTBALL TEAM
81,338

SANTIAGO BERNABÉU STADIUM
Madrid, Spain
REAL MADRID
81,044

LUZHNIKI STADIUM
Moscow, Russia
**RUSSIA NATIONAL FOOTBALL TEAM,
2018 WORLD CUP FINAL**
81,000

**STADIO GIUSEPPE MEAZZA
(SAN SIRO)**
Milan, Italy
INTERNAZIONALE MILANO, AC MILAN
80,018

MARACANÃ STADIUM
Rio De Janeiro, Brazil
**BRAZIL NATIONAL TEAM,
CR FLAMENGO, FLUMINENSE FC,
BOTAFOGO FR**
78,383

OLD TRAFFORD
Manchester, England
MANCHESTER UNITED F.C.
75,643

ALLIANZ ARENA
Munich, Germany
**BAYERN MÜNCHEN,
TSV 1860 MUNICH**
75,024

**PRINCIPALITY (MILLENNIUM)
STADIUM**
Cardiff, Wales
WALES NATIONAL FOOTBALL TEAM
74,500

STADIO OLIMPICO
Rome, Italy
A.S. ROMA, S.S. LAZIO
72,630

**OLYMPIC STADIUM ATHENS
(SPIROS LOUIS)**
Athens, Greece
**GREECE NATIONAL FOOTBALL TEAM,
AEK ATHENS, PANATHINAIKOS FC**
69,618

ESTÁDIO DA LUZ
Lisbon, Portugal
**S.L. BENFICA, UEFA EURO 2004 FINAL,
2014 UEFA CHAMPIONS LEAGUE FINAL**
65,647

CELTIC PARK
Glasgow, Scotland
CELTIC FC
60,832

EMIRATES STADIUM
London, England
ARSENAL
60,432

AMSTERDAM ARENA
Amsterdam, Netherlands
**AJAX, NETHERLANDS NATIONAL
FOOTBALL TEAM**
54,033

STADE LOUIS II
Monaco
AS MONACO
18,500

VICTORIA STADIUM
Gibraltar
GIBRALTAR NATIONAL TEAM
5,000

**ESTADI COMUNAL
D'ANDORRA LA VELLA**
La Vella, Andorra
ANDORRA NATIONAL TEAM
1,300

EVOLUTION OF FORMATIONS
1872–1967

Every team has 10 outfield players. What has proved critical over the years is not just how those players perform, but where. Formation is a key tactical element and, as these diagrams show, it is continually evolving. We can see the attack-heavy teams that dominated the early years of the game gradually becoming more balanced, with stronger midfields and defense.

1872
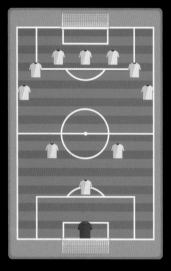
1-2-7 Formation
England

1889

The Pyramid (2-3-5)
Preston North End

1930
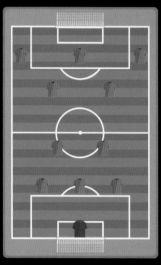
The WM Formation
Arsenal

" [Going behind] didn't bother us at all... We just knew we could turn the game around. "

Djalma Santos, Brazil's
1958 FIFA World Cup defender

Brazil's employment of a 4-2-4 formation helped them to victory in the 1958 FIFA World Cup.

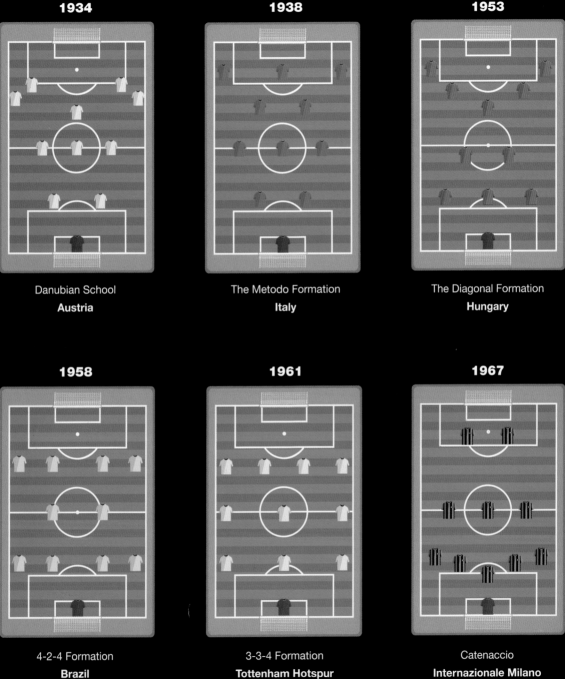

1934

Danubian School
Austria

1938

The Metodo Formation
Italy

1953

The Diagonal Formation
Hungary

1958

4-2-4 Formation
Brazil

1961

3-3-4 Formation
Tottenham Hotspur

1967

Catenaccio
Internazionale Milano

EVOLUTION OF FORMATIONS
1971–2017

1971

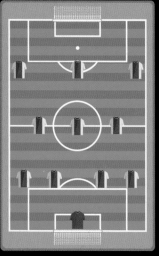

4-3-3 Formation

Ajax

1990

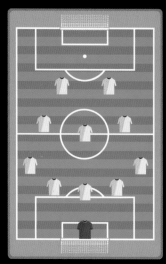

Wing-backs Formation

Germany

1998

4-4-2 Formation

Manchester United

2003

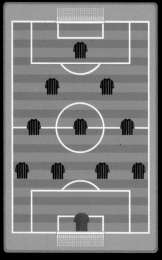

4-3-2-1 Christmas Tree

AC Milan

2006

Diamond Formation

Ghana

2012

The "False 9" Formation

Spain

From the 1970s onwards, the 4-4-2 formation became synonymous with the modern game. Here was a system that focused on passing and tackling in the central zones of the pitch and enabled increasingly fit midfielders to bolster both attacks and defenses. It seemed the evolution had reached its conclusion. However, the search for any slight advantage meant coaches kept on tinkering. "Wingless wonder" teams and fluid "total football" line-ups were followed by wing-backs, "false 9s", pyramids, and Christmas trees. Brazilian coach Carlos Alberto Parreira once predicted 4-6-0 as the "formation of the future"—and some might claim we are edging ever closer to that prophecy.

The pace and attacking skills of Tottenham Hotspur and England's Danny Rose (on left) were integral to the success of the club's wing-back formation in 2017.

2014

4-5-1 Formation

Chelsea

2017

3-4-1-2 Formation

Tottenham Hotspur

" When you have full-backs like ours, Danny Rose or Kyle Walker, they can play forward as offensive players. We tried to put them in a better position to try and play more like wing-backs. That was our idea, and then to play with two strikers. "

Mauricio Pochettino, manager Tottenham Hotspur

FIFA WORLD CUP WINS BY COUNTRY

Brazil truly are the World Cup kings. Not only are they the most successful nation, they also top the chart of World Cup wins, have registered the most consecutive wins (from 2002 vs Turkey to 2006 vs Ghana) and they are the only team to have won all their matches in two tournaments (1970 and 2002). At the other end of the scale, Bulgaria failed to win in five finals from 1962 to 1986, before finally beating Greece in their second game in 1994.

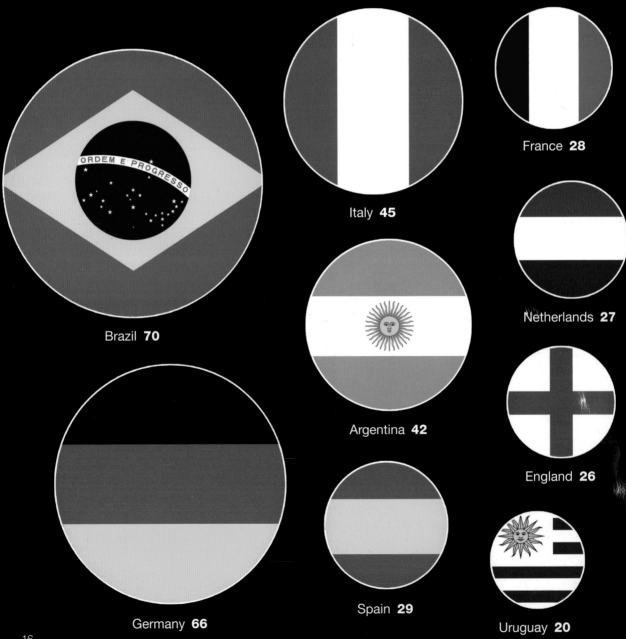

France 28

Italy 45

Netherlands 27

Brazil 70

Argentina 42

England 26

Germany 66

Spain 29

Uruguay 20

Source: Opta (August 2015)
Data relates to individual games won per team, 1930–2014

Yugoslavia **16**

Denmark **8**

Belgium **14**

Nigeria **5**

Northern Ireland **3**

East Germany **2**

Czech Republic **1**

Peru **4**

Greece **2**

Tunisia **1**

Romania **8**

Ghana **4**

Morocco **2**

Jamaica **1**

Mexico **14**

USA **8**

Japan **4**

Ukraine **2**

Slovenia **1**

Belgium **14**

Portugal **13**

Colombia **7**

Ecuador **4**

Republic of Ireland **2**

Bosnia and Herzegovina **1**

Sweden **16**

Croatia **7**

Scotland **4**

Senegal **2**

DPR Korea **1**

Hungary **15**

Paraguay **7**

Cameroon **4**

Saudi Arabia **2**

Cuba **1**

Chile **11**

Costa Rica **5**

Algeria **3**

Russia **2**

Iran **1**

Poland **15**

Switzerland **11**

Turkey **5**

Ivory Coast **3**

Norway **2**

Slovakia **1**

USSR **15**

Czechoslovakia **11**

Korea Republic **5**

Bulgaria **3**

Australia **2**

Wales **1**

South Africa **2**

Serbia **1**

Austria **12**

17

WORLD CUP FINALS RESULTS 1930–2014

The FIFA World Cup has grown from a small tournament comprising 13 teams from Europe and South America (US and Mexico participated, too) to 32 nations from five continents battling it out in the most widely followed sporting event in the world. There have been 20 to date, each one as spectacular as the last. Every tournament has had its amazing stories, controversies, moments that took our breath away, and heartbreak that saw us plunge into despair. Behind all these iconic events, what remains (apart from memories) are these simple facts—the statistics that mark each country's triumphs and disappointments in black and white. Make of these what you will…

Source: Google (October 2015)

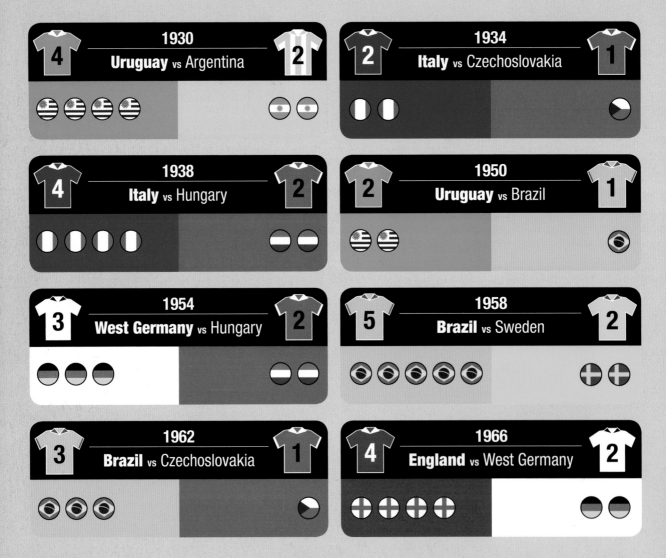

1930 — 4 **Uruguay** vs Argentina 2

1934 — 2 **Italy** vs Czechoslovakia 1

1938 — 4 **Italy** vs Hungary 2

1950 — 2 **Uruguay** vs Brazil 1

1954 — 3 **West Germany** vs Hungary 2

1958 — 5 **Brazil** vs Sweden 2

1962 — 3 **Brazil** vs Czechoslovakia 1

1966 — 4 **England** vs West Germany 2

4 1970 Brazil vs Italy **1**

2 1974 West Germany vs Netherlands **1**

3 1978 Argentina vs Netherlands **1**

3 1982 Italy vs West Germany **1**

3 1986 Argentina vs West Germany **2**

1 1990 West Germany vs Argentina **0**

0 1994 Brazil vs Italy **0**
PENALTIES

3 1998 France vs Brazil **0**

2 2002 Brazil vs Germany **0**

1 2006 Italy vs France **1**
PENALTIES

1 2010 Spain vs Netherlands **0**

1 2014 Germany vs Argentina **0**

WORLD CUP GOALSCORERS BY COUNTRY

It was Lucien Laurent, for France, who scored the first World Cup finals goal at the 1930 competition. Since then over 2,300 goals have been scored by 80 different countries in 20 finals tournaments. Germany and Brazil have both been tournament top scorers on four occasions,

GERMANY

Miroslav Klose **16**

Jürgen Klinsmann **11**

Thomas Müller **10**

Helmut Rahn **10**

Uwe Seeler **9**

Rudi Völler **8**

Max Morlock **6**

Helmut Haller **6**

Gerd Müller **14**

Karl-Heinz Rummenigge **9**

Hans Schäfer **7**

Lothar Matthäus **6**

Lukas Podolski **5**

Franz Beckenbauer **5**

ITALY

Roberto Baggio **9**

Paolo Rossi **9**

Salvatore Schillaci **6**

Christian Vieri **9**

Alessandro Altobelli **5**

Silvio Piola **5**

ARGENTINA

Gabriel Batistuta **10**

Diego Maradona **8**

Mario Alberto Kempes **6**

Guillermo Stábile **8**

Lionel Messi **5**

Gonzalo Higuaín **5**

BRAZIL

Ronaldo **15**

Vavá **9**

Rivaldo **8**

Ademir **8**

Jairzinho **9**

Careca **7**

Bebeto **6**

Garrincha **5**

Pelé **12**

Leônidas da Silva **8**

Rivellino **6**

Zico **5**

Romário **5**

NETHERLANDS

Johnny Rep **7**

Wesley Sneijder **6**

Robin van Persie **6**

Dennis Bergkamp **6**

Arjen Robben **6**

Rob Rensenbrink **6**

Johan Neeskens **5**

Hungary have the highest strike rate at 2.72 goals scored per match (helped by their record 27 goals in 1954), while Canada, China, Dutch East Indies, Trinidad and Tobago, and Zaire all have reached the finals but failed to register a single goal—a notable achievement in itself.

Source: Opta (August 2015)

SPAIN

David Villa
9

Fernando Morientes
5

Fernando Hierro
5

Basora
5

Emilio Butragueño
5

Raúl
5

FRANCE

Just Fontaine
13

Thierry Henry
6

Michel Platini
5

Zinedine Zidane
5

HUNGARY

Sándor Kocsis
11

Lajos Tichy
7

György Sárosi
6

Gyula Zsengellér
5

URUGUAY

Óscar Míguez
8

Diego Forlán
6

ENGLAND

Gary Lineker
10

Geoff Hurst
5

CZECHOSLOVAKIA

Oldřich Nejedlý
7

Tomáš Skuhravý
5

AUSTRIA

Erich Probst
6

Hans Krankl
5

Juan Alberto Schiaffino
5

Luis Suárez
5

Pedro Cea
5

PERU

Teófilo Cubillas
10

BULGARIA

Hristo Stoichkov 6

COLOMBIA

James Rodríguez 6

CROATIA

Davor Šuker 6

POLAND

Grzegorz Lato
10

Andrzej Szarmach
7

SWEDEN

Henrik Larsson
5

Kennet Andersson
5

GHANA

Asamoah Gyan 6

RUSSIA

Oleg Salenko 6

AUSTRALIA

Tim Cahill
5

BELGIUM

Marc Wilmots 5

CAMEROON

Roger Milla
5

DENMARK

Jon Dahl Tomasson 5

USA

Landon Donovan 5

Zbigniew Boniek 6

PORTUGAL

Eusébio 9

SWITZERLAND

Josef Hügi 6

NORTHERN IRELAND

Peter McParland 5

USSR

Valentin Ivanov 5

THE PERFECT WORLD CUP PENALTY

To place or to blast? That is the question facing World Cup penalty-takers under the intense pressure of the glaring floodlights, thousands of expectant fans and their teammates unable to look away. In a World Cup tie the hopes of a nation lie on the quality of the execution. Some, like Andreas Brehme in 1990, have the steady composure to help their sides lift the Jules Rimet, whereas others, such as England's Chris Waddle's high-and-wide miss in 1990, led only to the shattering of millions of hearts. So where would you aim *your* penalty kick?

TOP LEFT

96% SCORED

49 GOALS SCORED
2 PENALTIES SAVED

HIGH CENTER

94% SCORED

BOTTOM LEFT

80% SCORED

104 GOALS SCORED
26 PENALTIES SAVED

LOW CENTER

69% SCORED

68 Left-footed penalty goals

245 Right-footed penalty goals

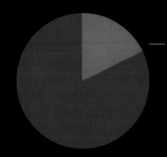

313 Penalty goals in total
68 Penalty saves in total

Source: Opta (October 2015)
Percentages relate to penalties on target.

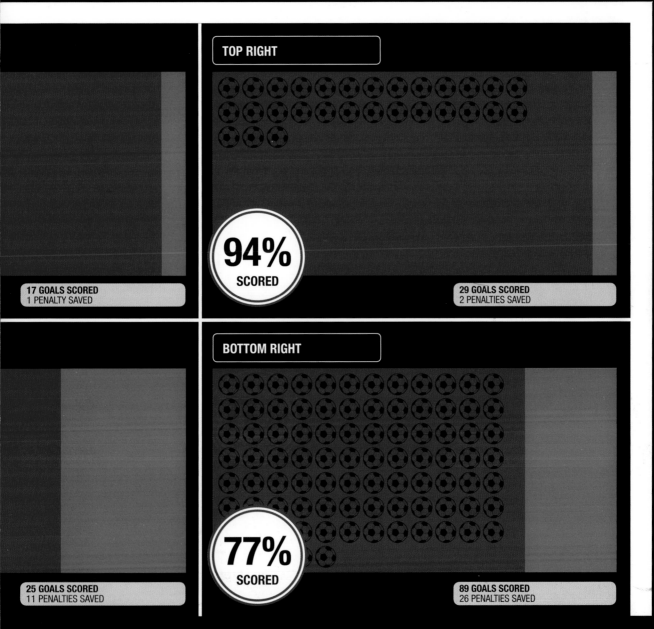

TOP RIGHT

94%
SCORED

17 GOALS SCORED
1 PENALTY SAVED

29 GOALS SCORED
2 PENALTIES SAVED

BOTTOM RIGHT

77%
SCORED

25 GOALS SCORED
11 PENALTIES SAVED

89 GOALS SCORED
26 PENALTIES SAVED

23

LONG-RANGE WORLD CUP GOALS

Everyone loves a shot at goal from far out, especially if it's on target and struck with an awesome power to match. In particular, long-range goals during World Cups are even more wondrous to behold because they instantly take on legendary status. Those long-rangers that live forever in the memory include Bobby Charlton's 25-yard strike against Mexico, which fired up England's 1966 campaign, Arie Haan's 40-yard lightning-bolt as the Netherlands defeated Italy in 1978, and James Rodríguez's sensational chest and volley against Uruguay in 2014. All excellent goals, but where do they map in the long-range pantheon?

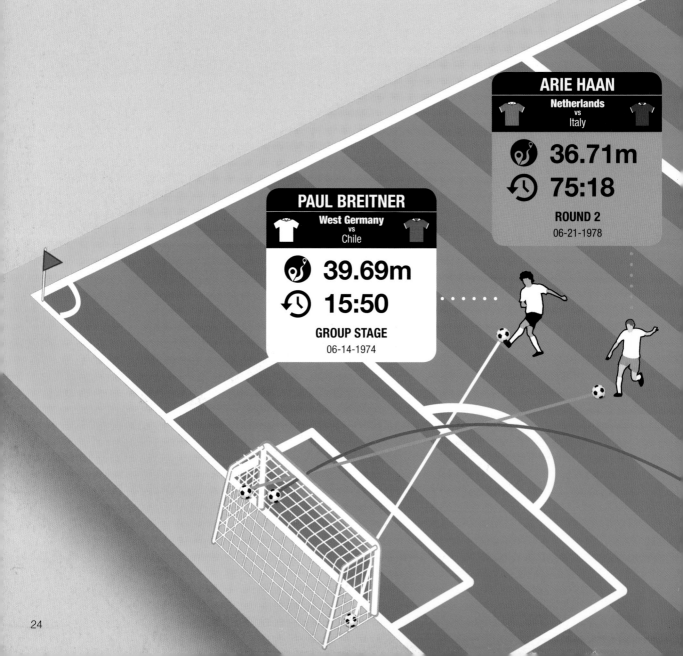

ARIE HAAN

Netherlands
vs
Italy

36.71m

75:18

ROUND 2
06-21-1978

PAUL BREITNER

West Germany
vs
Chile

39.69m

15:50

GROUP STAGE
06-14-1974

Source: Opta (October 2015)

LOTHAR MATTHÄUS

West Germany
vs
Yugoslavia

31.93m

62:51

GROUP STAGE
06-10-1990

ARIE HAAN

Netherlands
vs
West Germany

31.41m

26:40

ROUND 2
06-18-1978

JOE COLE

England
vs
Sweden

33.2m

33:04

GROUP STAGE
06-20-2006

RONALDINHO

Brazil
vs
England

40.08m

49:02

QUARTER-FINAL
06-21-2002

NELINHO

Brazil
vs
Italy

31.86m

63:35

3RD PLACE MATCH
06-24-1978

25

WORLD CUP GOALS BY BODY PART

"They all count!" It may be an old soccer cliché but it is as true in World Cup finals as it is anywhere else. For every exquisite shot curled in from the edge of the penalty area, there is a ricochet off the shin from two yards. For every perfectly timed scissor-kick, there is a vicious and ugly toe-punt just to make sure the ball goes in. When it comes down to the wire in a World Cup match, any goal will do.

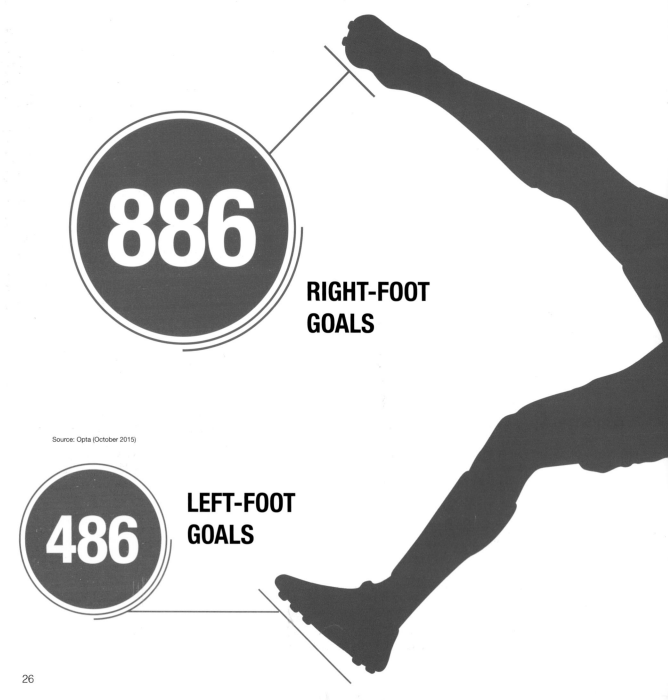

886

RIGHT-FOOT GOALS

Source: Opta (October 2015)

486

LEFT-FOOT GOALS

300 HEADED GOALS

10 OTHER GOALS

The most notorious scoring body part belongs to Maradona's "Hand of God" against England in 1986. Also worthy of a mention are Clint Dempsey's "Groin Goal" for the US against Portugal in 2014 and the great Jairzinho "chesting" the ball in to score Brazil's second goal in the 1970 final.

30 OWN GOALS

Of the 1,712 goals scored in the World Cup only 30 have been own goals—less than two percent. Perhaps the strangest own goal ever scored, so far, belongs to Greece's Vasilis Torosidis during the World Cup qualifying game against Romania in 2014, whose intended left-foot clearance from inside the penalty box ended up being fished out from the back of his own net.

WORLD CUP GOALKEEPERS

The Golden Glove Award, introduced in 1994 (and named the Yashin Award until 2010), is awarded to the best goalkeeper of the World Cup finals. Gianluigi Buffon, Iker Casillas, and Manuel Neuer are recent winners in 2006, 2010, and 2014, respectively. At the 2002 FIFA World Cup, German keeper Oliver Kahn became the first and so far only goalkeeper in the tournament's history to win the Golden Ball, the award given to the player voted as the most outstanding at the FIFA World Cup finals.

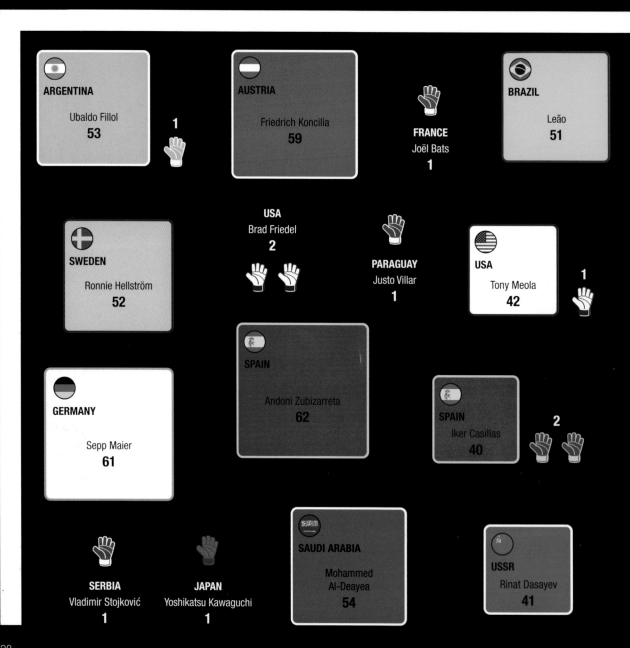

ARGENTINA

Ubaldo Fillol
53

1

AUSTRIA

Friedrich Koncilia
59

FRANCE
Joël Bats
1

BRAZIL

Leão
51

SWEDEN

Ronnie Hellström
52

USA
Brad Friedel
2

PARAGUAY
Justo Villar
1

USA

Tony Meola
42

1

GERMANY

Sepp Maier
61

SPAIN

Andoni Zubizarreta
62

SPAIN
Iker Casillas
40

2

SERBIA
Vladimir Stojković
1

JAPAN
Yoshikatsu Kawaguchi
1

SAUDI ARABIA

Mohammed
Al-Deayea
54

USSR
Rinat Dasayev
41

Source: Opta (October 2015)
All data from 1966–2014.

SAVES

PENALTY SAVES
(excluding penalty shootouts)

GHANA
Richard Kingson
42

POLAND
Jan Tomaszewski
2

NIGERIA
Vincent Enyeama
46

COLOMBIA
René Higuita
1

USA
Tim Howard
41

SWITZERLAND
Diego Benaglio
1

SWEDEN
Thomas Ravelli
42

ITALY
Dino Zoff
67

SWEDEN
Magnus Hedman
1

JAPAN
Eiji Kawashima
1

ITALY
Gianluigi Buffon
48

1

POLAND
Józef Młynarczyk
48

URUGUAY
Ladislao Mazurkiewicz
51

PERU
Ramón Quiroga
60

1

ENGLAND
Peter Shilton
55

GERMANY
Manuel Neuer
44

WORLD CUP FOULS AND CARDS

Behind these figures lie some of the most controversial and downright disgraceful moments in World Cup history. They include the South Africa vs Denmark tie in 1998, which resulted in seven yellow and three red cards, plus the three yellows in one match collected by Josip Šimunić for Croatia against Australia in 2006. If you thought that was bad, let's not forget the final itself, which saw two Argentinians sent off in 1990 and Zinedine Zidane seeing red after a confrontation with Marco Materazzi in 2006.

ARGENTINA 112	GERMANY 110	BRAZIL 95	ITALY 89	NETHERLANDS 89	MEXICO 67	
SPAIN 65	URUGUAY 61	KOREA REPUBLIC 60	FRANCE 56	ENGLAND 50	USA 48	
CAMEROON 45	CHILE 43	POLAND 40	PORTUGAL 40	PARAGUAY 39	SWEDEN 38	
BELGIUM 37	GHANA 33	CROATIA 33	BULGARIA 33	ROMANIA 32	DENMARK 31	
JAPAN 31	SWITZERLAND 31	COSTA RICA 30	TUNISIA 28	YUGOSLAVIA 27	NIGERIA 27	
AUSTRIA 24	ECUADOR 23	AUSTRALIA 23	COLOMBIA 22	SAUDI ARABIA 22	USSR 21	
SOUTH AFRICA 20	GREECE 19	SLOVENIA 19	MOROCCO 19	IVORY COAST 19	RUSSIA 19	
IRAN 18	SERBIA 18	TURKEY 17	SCOTLAND 17	CZECHOSLOVAKIA 17	REPUBLIC OF IRELAND 16	
ALGERIA 14	SENEGAL 14	HONDURAS 13	NORWAY 13	UKRAINE 12	SLOVAKIA 11	
PERU 10	EAST GERMANY 10	ANGOLA 9	NORTHERN IRELAND 9	EL SALVADOR 9	TOGO 8	
IRAQ 8	TRINIDAD AND TOBAGO 8	UNITED ARAB EMIRATES 6	BOLIVIA 6	NEW ZEALAND 6	CHINA PR 5	
CZECH REPUBLIC 5	JAMAICA 4	EGYPT 4	HUNGARY 4	ISRAEL 4	HAITI 3	
KUWAIT 3	BOSNIA AND HERZEGOVINA 3	DPR KOREA 2	ZAIRE 2	CANADA 1		

ARGENTINA 10 CAMEROON 8 URUGUAY 8 NETHERLANDS 7 ITALY 6 PORTUGAL 6

BRAZIL 6 MEXICO 6 FRANCE 6 GERMANY 5 CROATIA 4 USA 4

AUSTRALIA 4 ENGLAND 3 DENMARK 3 BELGIUM 3 BULGARIA 3 SWEDEN 3

SERBIA 3 ALGERIA 2 CHILE 2 TURKEY 2 KOREA REPUBLIC 2 BOLIVIA 2

PARAGUAY 2 HUNGARY 2 USSR 2 HONDURAS 2 CZECHOSLOVAKIA 2 SOUTH AFRICA 2

CZECH REPUBLIC 2 TUNISIA 1 CANADA 1 POLAND 1 JAMAICA 1 GREECE 1

SLOVENIA 1 TOGO 1 ANGOLA 1 UNITED ARAB EMIRATES 1 COSTA RICA 1 UKRAINE 1

IVORY COAST 1 SENEGAL 1 GHANA 1 IRAQ 1 YUGOSLAVIA 1 TRINIDAD AND TOBAGO 1

ZAIRE 1 SAUDI ARABIA 1 RUSSIA 1 ECUADOR 1 SCOTLAND 1 ROMANIA 1

SWITZERLAND 1 NORTHERN IRELAND 1 CHINA PR 1 AUSTRIA 1 NIGERIA 1 SPAIN 1

Total Fouls 1966–2014

GERMANY 1339	SWEDEN 467	SWITZERLAND 291	ALGERIA 205	TURKEY 117	TOGO 56
BRAZIL 1212	CAMEROON 438	COLOMBIA 284	MOROCCO 202	EL SALVADOR 109	EGYPT 52
ARGENTINA 1153	USSR 421	AUSTRIA 277	CZECHOSLOVAKIA 197	UKRAINE 108	CZECH REPUBLIC 52
ITALY 1147	PORTUGAL 399	ROMANIA 270	SAUDI ARABIA 184	SLOVENIA 103	ZAIRE 51
NETHERLANDS 996	USA 396	DENMARK 269	ECUADOR 184	SENEGAL 100	TRINIDAD AND TOBAGO 50
FRANCE 781	BULGARIA 383	COSTA RICA 252	SOUTH AFRICA 157	SERBIA 89	UNITED ARAB EMIRATES 48
ENGLAND 773	CHILE 357	AUSTRALIA 249	IVORY COAST 151	NEW ZEALAND 88	CANADA 45
SPAIN 735	PARAGUAY 348	IRAN 246	GREECE 150	DPR KOREA 86	BOSNIA AND HERZEGOVINA 41
MEXICO 683	YUGOSLAVIA 343	REPUBLIC OF IRELAND 238	NORTHERN IRELAND 150	ANGOLA 73	BOLIVIA 40
URUGUAY 652	JAPAN 319	TUNISIA 237	RUSSIA 141	SLOVAKIA 69	CHINA PR 40
BELGIUM 592	SCOTLAND 312	GHANA 233	HONDURAS 135	ISRAEL 68	HAITI 34
POLAND 574	NIGERIA 296	PERU 215	NORWAY 126	IRAQ 61	KUWAIT 32
KOREA REPUBLIC 516	CROATIA 291	HUNGARY 206	EAST GERMANY 119	JAMAICA 56	

1966 WORLD CUP GOALS

Many nations thought they had a chance of winning the World Cup in 1966: West Germany, Argentina, Brazil, and England were all confident it would be their turn to lift the Jules Rimet trophy. Despite being blighted by the barbaric treatment of Pelé and some controversial refereeing, the tournament was enlightened by the giant-slaying North Korea, the brilliance of Eusébio, and a nail-biting, but triumphant, final for the host nation. The 1966 World Cup also saw goals that would become legendary, including the lung-bursting run from West Germany's Franz Beckenbauer, an outside-of-the-foot free kick from Brazil's Garrincha, and Geoff Hurst's monumental hat trick in the final—the first ever in a World Cup final.

GEOFF HURST – England vs West Germany

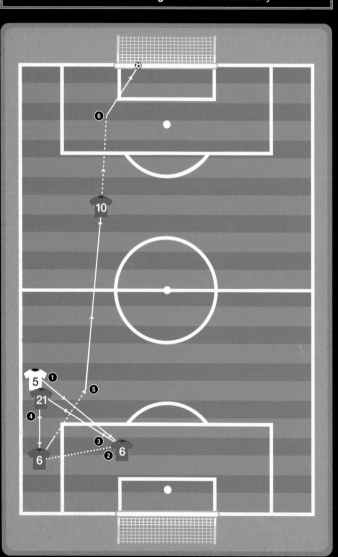

England's Geoff Hurst scores that famous fourth goal to put England 4–2 up against West Germany after extra time, July 30, 1966.

1. Pass (chipped, cross) **Schulz**
2. Ball recovery **Moore**
3. Pass **Moore**
4. Pass **Hunt**
5. Pass (chipped, long ball) **Moore**
6. Goal **Hurst**

KEY

Ball movement	Player with ball
Shot	Player without ball

LUIS ARTIME – **Argentina** vs Spain

1. Interception **Más**
2. Pass **Más**
3. Pass **Solari**
4. Pass **Rattín**
5. Pass **Onega**
6. Pass **Solari**
7. Goal **Artime**

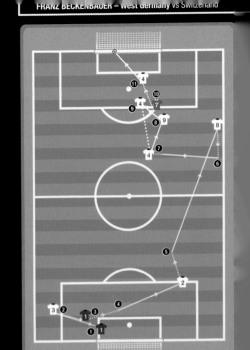

FRANZ BECKENBAUER – West Germany vs Switzerland

JÁNOS FARKAS – **Hungary** vs Brazil

1. Pass **Gérson**
2. Pass **Mátrai**
3. Pass **Mészöly**
4. Pass **Káposzta**
5. Pass **Albert**
6. Pass (cross, chipped, long ball) **Bene**
7. Goal **Farkas**

EDUARD MALOFEYEV – **USSR** vs DPR Korea

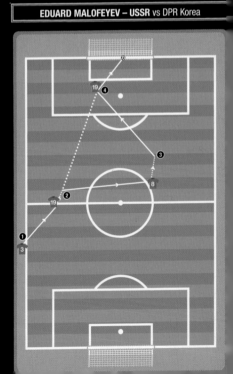

1970 WORLD CUP GOALS

Many pundits, players, and fans still regard the 1970 World Cup in Mexico as the finest World Cup tournament of all. Reigning champions England played Brazil in a scintillating group game, Italy met Germany in the "Game of the Century"—Italy won 4–3 after five goals were scored in extra time, the only FIFA World Cup game when this has happened—and the final was a masterclass in demolition by the Brazilian squad. It was Carlos Alberto's perfect strike that was the nail in the coffin for Italy, and arguably one of the greatest goals ever scored, helping to create Brazil's glorious 4–1 win.

CARLOS ALBERTO – Brazil vs Italy

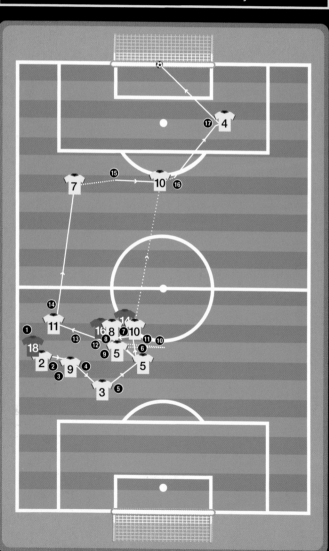

Brazil captain Carlos Alberto celebrates his team's fourth goal against Italy goalkeeper Enrico Albertosi. Final score: Brazil 4 Italy 1, June 21, 1970.

1. Take on **Juliano**
2. Tackle **Brito**
3. Ball recovery **Tostão**
4. Pass **Tostão**
5. Pass **Piazza**
6. Pass **Clodoaldo**
7. Pass **Pelé**
8. Pass **Gérson**
9. Take on **Clodoaldo**
10. Good skill **Clodoaldo**
11. Challenge **Rivera**
12. Challenge **De Sisti**
13. Pass **Clodoaldo**
14. Pass **Rivelino**
15. Pass **Jairzinho**
16. Pass **Pelé**
17. Goal **Alberto**

KEY

Ball movement

Shot

Player with ball

Player without ball

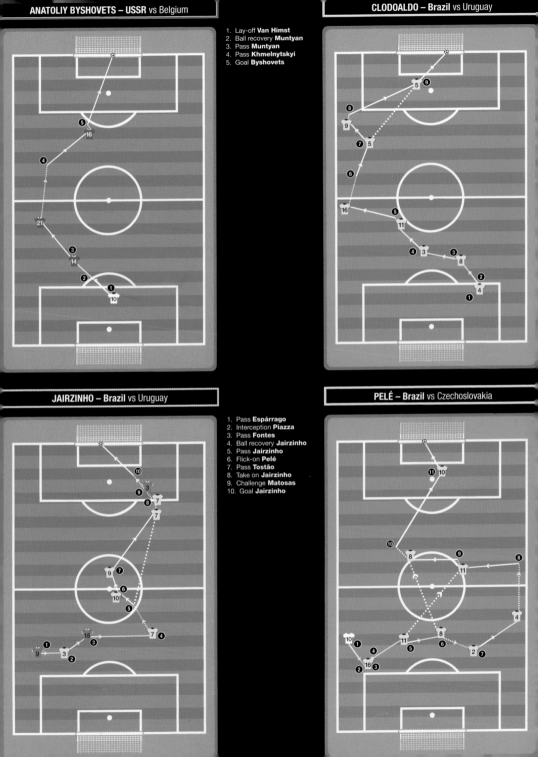

ANATOLIY BYSHOVETS – USSR vs Belgium

1. Lay-off **Van Himst**
2. Ball recovery **Muntyan**
3. Pass **Muntyan**
4. Pass **Khmelnytskyi**
5. Goal **Byshovets**

CLODOALDO – Brazil vs Uruguay

JAIRZINHO – Brazil vs Uruguay

1. Pass **Espárrago**
2. Interception **Piazza**
3. Pass **Fontes**
4. Ball recovery **Jairzinho**
5. Pass **Jairzinho**
6. Flick-on **Pelé**
7. Pass **Tostão**
8. Take on **Jairzinho**
9. Challenge **Matosas**
10. Goal **Jairzinho**

PELÉ – Brazil vs Czechoslovakia

WORLD CUP GOALS

rmany hosted (and won) a memorable World Cup that first gave us the Cruyff
e the first African team to qualify, a Cold War classic between East and
d the "total soccer" displayed by the Netherlands. Goals came in all shapes
all remember the two belters from West Germany's Paul Breitner, Peter
r Scotland against Zaire, Haiti's Emmanuel Sanon outpacing the Italian
an Cruyff's stunner against Brazil—a goal that crowned the Dutchman Player
t.

N CRUYFF – **Netherlands** vs Brazil

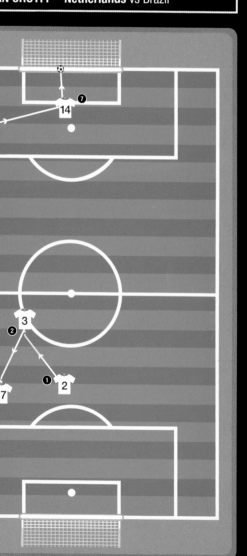

*Fifty-two thousand fans watched Johan Cruyff score his second goal
for the Netherlands against Brazil, July 3,1974.*

1. Free kick taken **Haan**
2. Pass **van Hanegem**
3. Pass (chipped) **Rijsbergen**
4. Pass **Krol**
5. Pass **Rensenbrink**
6. Pass (cross, chipped, long ball) **Krol**
7. Goal **Cruyff**

KEY

Ball movement

Shot

Player with ball

Player without ball

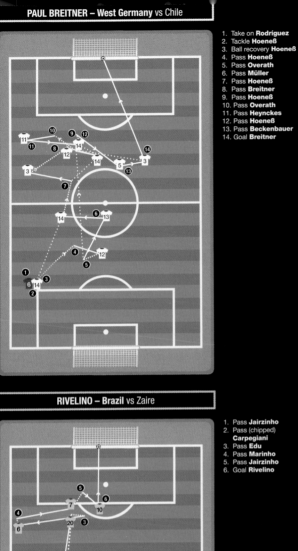

PAUL BREITNER – West Germany vs Chile

1. Take on **Rodriguez**
2. Tackle **Hoeneß**
3. Ball recovery **Hoeneß**
4. Pass **Hoeneß**
5. Pass **Overath**
6. Pass **Müller**
7. Pass **Hoeneß**
8. Pass **Breitner**
9. Pass **Hoeneß**
10. Pass **Overath**
11. Pass **Heynckes**
12. Pass **Hoeneß**
13. Pass **Beckenbauer**
14. Goal **Breitner**

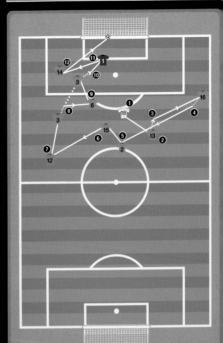

JOHAN CRUYFF – Netherlands vs Argentina

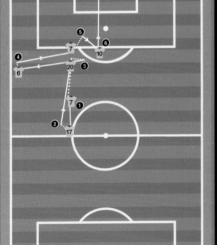

RIVELINO – Brazil vs Zaire

1. Pass **Jairzinho**
2. Pass (chipped) **Carpegiani**
3. Pass **Edu**
4. Pass **Marinho**
5. Pass **Jairzinho**
6. Goal **Rivelino**

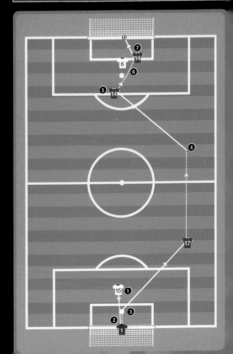

JÜRGEN SPARWASSER – East Germany vs West Germany

1978 WORLD CUP GOALS

The "Tickertape Tournament" in 1978 was a bittersweet affair. It was set against an unsavory political background, boycotted by Johan Cruyff (rated as the world's best player at the time) and disgraced by Scotland's Willie Johnston, who was sent home after a positive drug test. However, the tournament also gave us some unforgettable goals, including a magical finish by Scotland's Archie Gemmill, screamers from the Netherlands' Arie Haan and Brazil's Nelinho, and a much-needed, morale-boosting triumph for the host nation, Argentina, when they defeated the Netherlands 3–1, thanks to the tournament's top scorer, Mario Kempes, and his second goal of the day.

ARIE HAAN – Netherlands vs West Germany

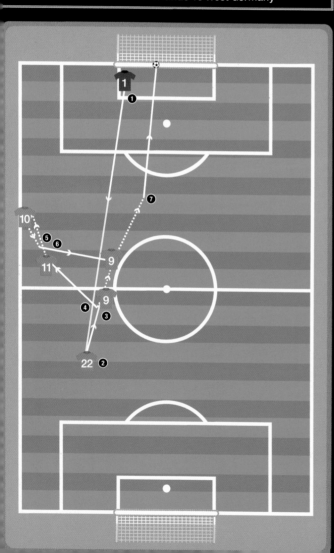

Arie Haan's goal against West Germany helped the Dutch national team reach the 1978 World Cup final, where they were beaten by Argentina 3–1 in extra time, June 18, 1978.

1. Goal kick (long ball) **Maier**
2. Head pass **Brandts**
3. Ball recovery **Haan**
4. Pass **Haan**
5. Pass **Willy van de Kerkhof**
6. Pass **René van de Kerkhof**
7. Goal **Haan**

KEY

Ball movement ——————
Shot
Player with ball ············
Player without ball ············

ARCHIE GEMMILL – Scotland vs Netherlands

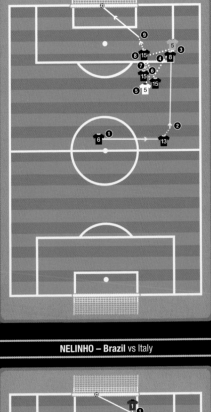

1. Free kick taken **Rioch**
2. Pass **Kennedy**
3. Take on **Dalglish**
4. Take on **Gemmill**
5. Tackle **Krol**
6. Good skill **Gemmill**
7. Challenge **Krol**
8. Take on **Gemmill**
9. Goal **Gemmill**

LEOPOLDO LUQUE – Argentina vs France

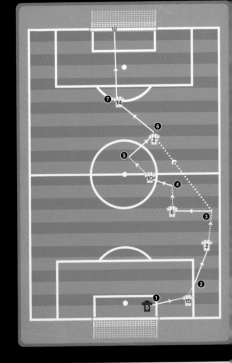

NELINHO – Brazil vs Italy

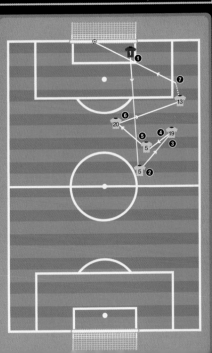

1. Goal kick (long ball) **Zoff**
2. Interception **Cerezo**
3. Ball recovery **Mendonça**
4. Pass **Mendonça**
5. Pass **Cerezo**
6. Pass **Dinamite**
7. Goal **Nelinho**

KARL-HEINZ RUMMENIGGE – West Germany vs Mexico

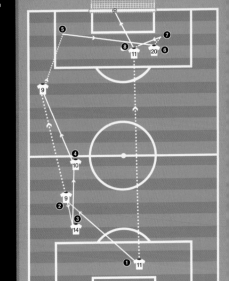

WORLD CUP GOALS

d Cup finals saw 24 teams play in a format involving two group stages.
again. The tournament became the battleground for two of the greatest matches ever
up history. Italy's Paolo Rossi hit a hat trick in an amazing 3–2 defeat of Brazil and, after a
ermany overcame France in the first ever World Cup penalty shootout. Memorable goals
ead bicycle kick by Germany's Klaus Fischer, a sublime chip from Brazil's Éder and a
mpatriot, Sócrates, which proved completely unstoppable. However, it was Tardelli's goal
n) against West Germany in the final that we all remember the most.

0 TARDELLI – Italy vs West Germany

Italy's Marco Tardelli celebrates scoring his goal against West Germany during the 1982 World Cup final. Italy won the match 3–1, July 11, 1982.

1. Pass **Conti**
2. Pass **Rossi**
3. Pass **Scirea**
4. Pass **Bergomi**
5. Pass **Scirea**
6. Goal **Tardelli**

KEY

Ball movement ──────

Shot ──────⚽

Player with ball ••••••••••••

Player without ball ••••••••••••

ZBIGNIEW BONIEK – Poland vs Belgium

1. Goal kick **Młynarczyk**
2. Pass **Janas**
3. Pass **Żmuda**
4. Pass **Buncol**
5. Pass **Majewski**
6. Pass (long ball) **Buncol**
7. Pass **Janas**
8. Pass (chipped, long ball) **Buncol**
9. Pass **Dziuba**
10. Take on **Lato**
11. Challenge **Millecamps**
12. Pull-back **Lato**
13. Goal **Boniek**

BRUNO CONTI – Italy vs Peru

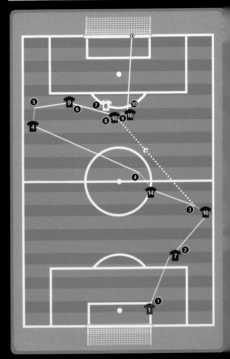

KLAUS FISCHER – West Germany vs France

1. Corner taken **Kaltz**
2. Clearance **Platini**
3. Pass **Breitner**
4. Pass (chipped, cross) **Kaltz**
5. Head pass **Kaltz**
6. Pass (long ball) **Rummenigge**
7. Pass **Förster**
8. Pass (chipped, cross, long ball) **Littbarski**
9. Head pass **Rummenigge**
10. Goal **Fischer**

SÓCRATES – Brazil vs Italy

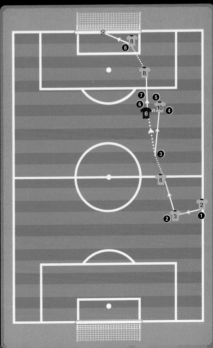

1986 WORLD CUP GOALS

Mexico may have hosted the 1986 World Cup, but the tournament was all about one man—Argentina's Diego Maradona. The 25-year-old's goals against England and Belgium were described by many pundits, players and fans alike as "pure genius". In the now famous quarterfinal match against England, Maradona's unforgettable "Hand of God" goal was (almost) forgotten when he scored his "Goal of the Century" just four minutes later. His achievements would dwarf the World Cup's other magical moments, which included six goals from England's Gary Lineker (the tournament's top scorer), a screamer from Brazil's Josimar and an ambitious scissor-kick from the Mexican player Manuel Negrete.

DIEGO MARADONA – Argentina vs England

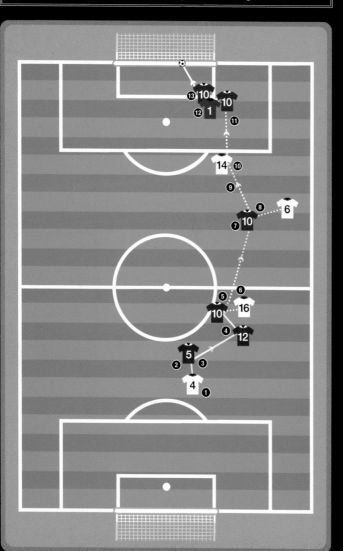

Diego Maradona dribbles the ball beyond England goalkeeper Peter Shil to score the "Goal of the Century". Argentina won 2–1, June 22, 1986.

1. Pass **Hoddle**
2. Pass **Brown**
3. Ball recovery **Brown**
4. Pass **Enrique**
5. Take on **Maradona**
6. Challenge **Reid**
7. Take on **Maradona**
8. Challenge **Butcher**
9. Take on **Maradona**
10. Challenge **Fenwick**
11. Take on **Maradona**
12. Challenge **Shilton**
13. Goal **Maradona**

KEY

Ball movement ————
Shot ————⚽
Player with ball ············
Player without ball ············

CARECA – Brazil vs France

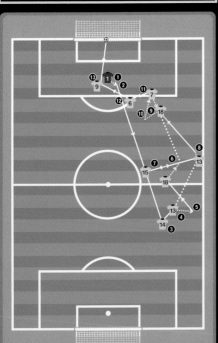

1. Keeper pick-up **Bats**
2. Keeper kick from hands (long ball) **Bats**
3. Clearance **César**
4. Ball recovery **Josimar**
5. Pass (chipped) **Josimar**
6. Pass **Sócrates**
7. Pass **Alemão**
8. Pass **Josimar**
9. Pass **Sócrates**
10. Pass **Müller**
11. Pass **Müller**
12. Pass **Júnior**
13. Goal **Careca**

MICHAEL LAUDRUP – Denmark vs Uruguay

1. Pass **Lerby**
2. Pass **Andersen**
3. Pass **Bertelsen**
4. Pass **Andersen**
5. Good skill **Laudrup**
6. Pass **Laudrup**
7. Pass **Andersen**
8. Pass **Laudup**
9. Pass **Olsen**
10. Pass (crossed, chipped) **Arnesen**
11. Pass (chipped) **Lerby**
12. Clearance **Batista**
13. Pass **Busk**
14. Pass **Lerby**
15. Take on **Laudrup**
16. Take on **Laudrup**
17. Take on **Laudrup**
18. Good skill **Laudrup**
19. Goal **Laudrup**

GARY LINEKER – England vs Poland

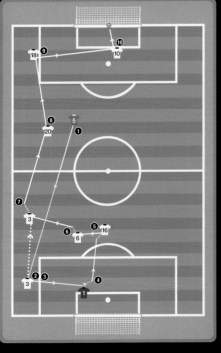

1. Pass (chipped, long ball) **Wójcicki**
2. Ball recovery **Sansom**
3. Pass **Sansom**
4. Pass **Shilton**
5. Pass **Reid**
6. Pass **Butcher**
7. Pass **Sansom**
8. Pass **Beardsley**
9. Pass (cross, long ball) **Hodge**
10. Goal **Lineker**

JEAN TIGANA – France vs Hungary

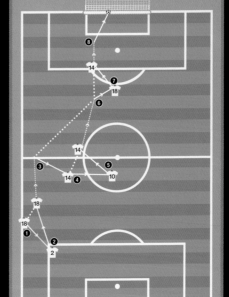

1. Pass **Rocheteau**
2. Pass **Amoros**
3. Pass **Rocheteau**
4. Pass **Tigana**
5. Pass **Platini**
6. Pass **Tigana**
7. Through ball **Rocheteau**
8. Goal **Tigana**

Source: Opta (October 2015)

1990 WORLD CUP GOALS

The negativity surrounding the soccer performances of the 1990 World Cup finals in Italy was alleviated by Luciano Pavarotti's singing of the tournament anthem "Nessun Dorma", the energy and spirit of Roger Milla and his Cameroon teammates, the passion and drama of England's Paul Gascoigne, and the superboots of Italy's Salvatore "Totò" Schillaci. There were outstanding goals galore too, including a surging run and knockout shot from Germany's Lothar Matthäus, an over-the-shoulder volley from England's David Platt, and virtuoso brilliance by Italy's one-and-only *Il Divin Codino* (The Divine Ponytail)—Roberto Baggio.

ROBERTO BAGGIO – **Italy** vs Czechoslovakia

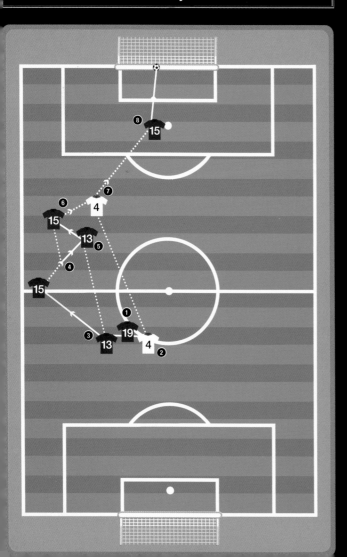

Roberto Baggio on his way to scoring Italy's second goal. Italy won 2–0 against Czechoslovakia, June 19, 1990.

1. Take on **Schillaci**
2. Tackle **Hašek**
3. Pass **Giannini**
4. Pass **Baggio**
5. Pass **Giannini**
6. Take on **Baggio**
7. Challenge **Hašek**
8. Goal **Baggio**

KEY

Ball movement	▬▬▬	Player with ball	··············
Shot	▬▬⚽	Player without ball	··············

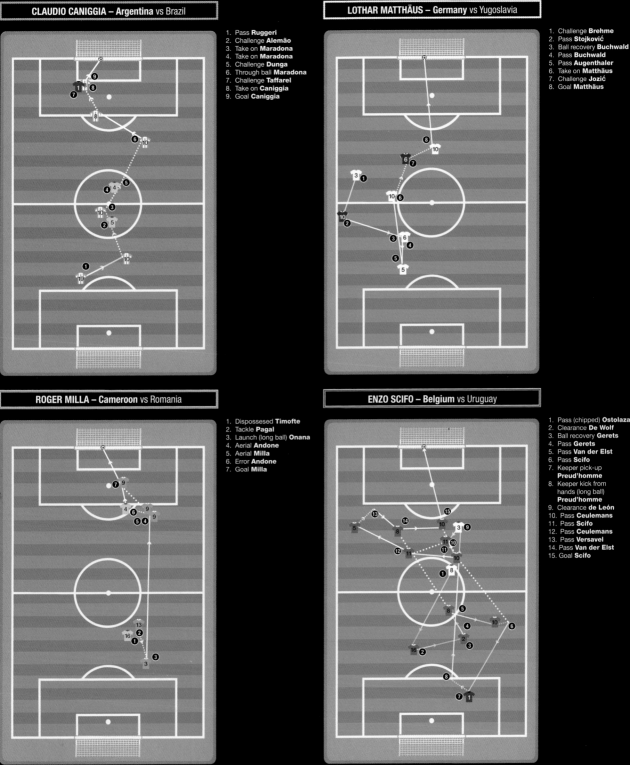

CLAUDIO CANIGGIA – Argentina vs Brazil

1. Pass **Ruggeri**
2. Challenge **Alemão**
3. Take on **Maradona**
4. Take on **Maradona**
5. Challenge **Dunga**
6. Through ball **Maradona**
7. Challenge **Taffarel**
8. Take on **Caniggia**
9. Goal **Caniggia**

LOTHAR MATTHÄUS – Germany vs Yugoslavia

1. Challenge **Brehme**
2. Pass **Stojković**
3. Ball recovery **Buchwald**
4. Pass **Buchwald**
5. Pass **Augenthaler**
6. Take on **Matthäus**
7. Challenge **Jozić**
8. Goal **Matthäus**

ROGER MILLA – Cameroon vs Romania

1. Dispossesed **Timofte**
2. Tackle **Pagal**
3. Launch (long ball) **Onana**
4. Aerial **Andone**
5. Aerial **Milla**
6. Error **Andone**
7. Goal **Milla**

ENZO SCIFO – Belgium vs Uruguay

1. Pass (chipped) **Ostolaza**
2. Clearance **De Wolf**
3. Ball recovery **Gerets**
4. Pass **Gerets**
5. Pass **Van der Elst**
6. Pass **Scifo**
7. Keeper pick-up **Preud'homme**
8. Keeper kick from hands (long ball) **Preud'homme**
9. Clearance **de León**
10. Pass **Ceulemans**
11. Pass **Scifo**
12. Pass **Ceulemans**
13. Pass **Versavel**
14. Pass **Van der Elst**
15. Goal **Scifo**

1994 WORLD CUP GOALS

Despite America's lack of a national top-level league, the 1994 World Cup is remembered for breaking average attendance records with almost 70,000 fans per game—a feat that still stands today. Played in nine cities across the US, this World Cup saw Italy lose 3–2 to Brazil in a penalty shootout—the first-ever World Cup final to be decided by penalties. Roberto Baggio's wild penalty miss will long be remembered. The flick, spin and volley by Germany's Jürgen Klinsmann, the 65-yard run to score by Saudi Arabia's Saeed Al-Owairan and the diving header by Bulgaria's Yordan Letchkov were all wonderful goals, but it's Hagi's strike against Colombia that we'll never forget...

GHEORGHE HAGI – Romania vs Colombia

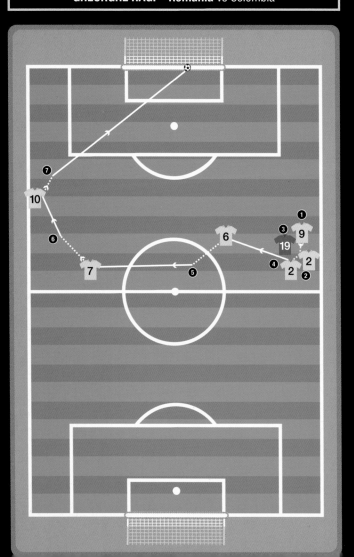

Romania's Gheorghe Hagi celebrates after scoring his unforgettable left-foot lob over the top of Colombian keeper Óscar Córdoba, June 18, 1994.

1. Tackle **Râducioiu**
2. Ball recovery **Petrescu**
3. Dispossesed **Rincón**
4. Pass **Petrescu**
5. Pass **Popescu**
6. Pass **Munteanu**
7. Goal **Hagi**

KEY

Ball movement	▬▬▬	Player with ball	▪▪▪▪▪▪▪
Shot	▬▬⚽	Player without ball	●●●●●●

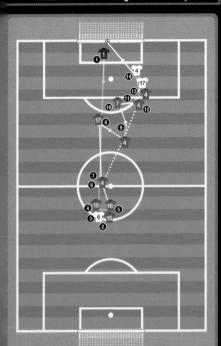

PHILIPPE ALBERT – Belgium vs Germany

1. Goal kick (long ball) **Illgner**
2. Aerial **Emmers**
3. Aerial **Buchwald**
4. Head pass **Emmers**
5. Head pass **Boffin**
6. Pass **Albert**
7. Ball recovery **Albert**
8. Lay-off (chipped) **Weber**
9. Pass **Albert**
10. Challenge **Wagner**
11. Pass **Van der Elst**
12. Challenge **Kohler**
13. Take on **Albert**
14. Goal **Albert**

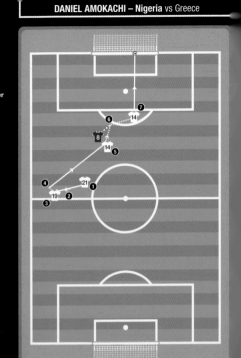

DANIEL AMOKACHI – Nigeria vs Greece

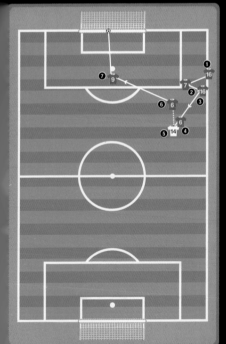

YORDAN LETCHKOV – Bulgaria vs Germany

1. Throw in **Kiriakov**
2. Pass **Kostadinov**
3. Pass **Kiriakov**
4. Take on **Yankov**
5. Challenge **Berthold**
6. Pass (cross, chipped) **Yankov**
7. Goal (head) **Letchkov**

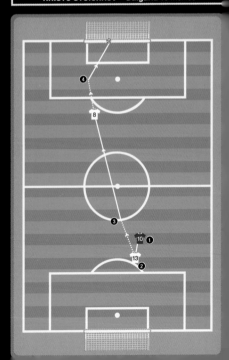

HRISTO STOICHKOV – Bulgaria vs Mexico

1998 WORLD CUP GOALS

Host nation France lit up their own World Cup in 1998, and finished the tournament with the greatest triumph of all—defeating Ronaldo's Brazil in the final. England met Argentina in Saint-Étienne, unarguably the match of the tournament, while five goals secured the Golden Boot for Davor Šuker of Croatia. Rivaldo hit the winner as Brazil and Denmark shared five goals in a riveting quarterfinal, while goals such as Michael Owen's run-and-shoot, and Dennis Bergkamp's control-and-finish for the Netherlands—both against Argentina— highlighted that world-class soccer at its best can transcend any country's border.

DENNIS BERGKAMP – Netherlands vs Argentina

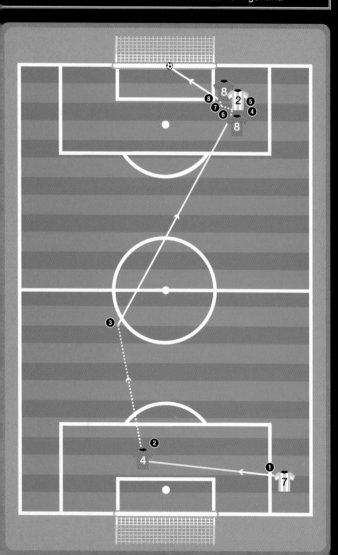

Dennis Bergkamp clips it beautifully past Argentinian goalkeeper Carlos Roa, July 4, 1998.

1. Pass (cross, long ball, chipped) **López**
2. Ball recovery **de Boer**
3. Pass (long ball, chipped) **de Boer**
4. Take on **Bergkamp**
5. Challenge **Ayala**
6. Good skill **Bergkamp**
7. Good skill **Bergkamp**
8. Goal **Bergkamp**

KEY

Ball movement ————

Shot ————⚽

Player with ball ·············

Player without ball ··············

MICHAEL OWEN – England vs Argentina

1. Take on **López**
2. Tackle **Ince**
3. Ball recovery **Ince**
4. Pass **Ince**
5. Pass **Beckham**
6. Good skill **Owen**
7. Take on **Owen**
8. Challenge **Chamot**
9. Take on **Owen**
10. Goal **Owen**

EMMANUEL PETIT – France vs Brazil

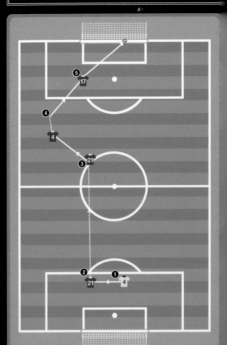

RONALDO – Brazil vs Morocco

1. Pass (chipped) **Bassir**
2. Head pass **Cafu**
3. Ball recovery **Sampaio**
4. Pass **Sampaio**
5. Launch **Aldair**
6. Head pass **Rossi**
7. Pass **Dunga**
8. Lay-off **Rivaldo**
9. Pass **Dunga**
10. Pass **Bebeto**
11. Through ball (chipped) **Rivaldo**
12. Goal **Ronaldo**

BOUDEWIJN ZENDEN – Netherlands vs Croatia

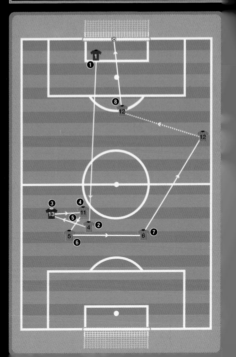

2002 WORLD CUP GOALS

Japan and South Korea co-hosted Asia's first World Cup in 2002 and it is a tournament remembered for being full of surprises. Reigning champions France and preferred favorites Argentina went home after the group stage and South Korea beat Spain, Italy, and Portugal on their way to the semifinals. Few fans were shocked, however, by Brazil's clear run to victory, powered by a player at the top of his game—Ronaldo. The chest and volley by Uruguay's Diego Forlán, Matt Holland's superstrike for Ireland and the overhead kick by Brazil's Edmílson are goals also still regularly voted in World Cup Greatest Goals lists, along with these ones too...

JARED BORGETTI – Mexico vs Italy

Mexico's Jared Borgetti scored the first goal against Italy with a knockout strike past goalkeeper Gianluigi Buffon, June 13, 2002.

1. Clearance **Vidrio**
2. Tackle **Carmona**
3. Take on **Inzaghi**
4. Ball recovery **Torrado**
5. Pass **Torrado**
6. Pass **Márquez**
7. Pass **Luna**
8. Pass **Márquez**
9. Pass **Carmona**
10. Pass **Rodríguez**
11. Pass **Blanco**
12. Pass **Arellano**
13. Pass **Blanco**
14. Pass **Torrado**
15. Pass **Vidrio**
16. Pass (long ball) **Torrado**
17. Pass **Morales**
18. Pass **Luna**
19. Pass (chipped) **Blanco**
20. Goal **Borgetti**

KEY

Ball movement

Shot

Player with ball

Player without ball

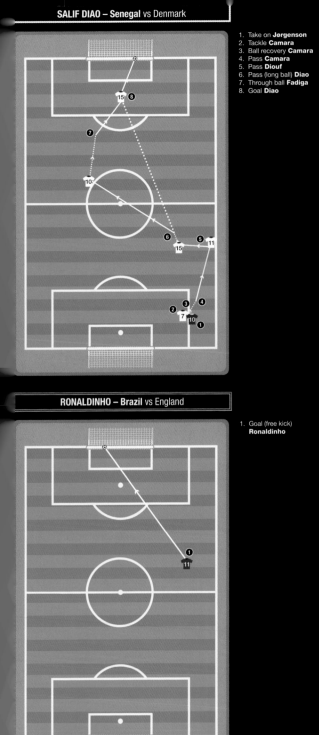

SALIF DIAO – Senegal vs Denmark

1. Take on **Jørgenson**
2. Tackle **Camara**
3. Ball recovery **Camara**
4. Pass **Camara**
5. Pass **Diouf**
6. Pass (long ball) **Diao**
7. Through ball **Fadiga**
8. Goal **Diao**

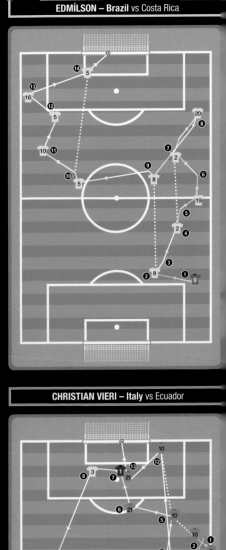

EDMÍLSON – Brazil vs Costa Rica

RONALDINHO – Brazil vs England

1. Goal (free kick)
   Ronaldinho

CHRISTIAN VIERI – Italy vs Ecuador

2006 WORLD CUP GOALS

The 2006 World Cup, hosted by Germany, will forever be dominated by one image: the world's greatest soccer player, Zinedine Zidane, playing his last game ever, headbutting Italy's Marco Materazzi in the chest. In a low-scoring tournament, five goals were enough to reward Germany's Miroslav Klose the Golden Boot, while Philipp Lahm's wonderstrike in the opening game, Bakari Koné's solo effort for the Ivory Coast and Argentina's Cambiasso finishing an exquisite 24-pass movement stood out as the tournament's best goals.

ESTEBAN CAMBIASSO – Argentina vs Serbia & Montenegro

Esteban Cambiasso celebrates in style after scoring the second goal against Serbia & Montenegro, June 16, 2006.

1. Dispossesed **Kežman**
2. Challenge **Mascherano**
3. Tackle **Rodríguez**
4. Ball recovery **Heinze**
5. Pass **Heinze**
6. Pass **Mascherano**
7. Pass **Riquelme**
8. Pass **Rodríguez**
9. Pass **Sorín**
10. Pass **Rodríguez**
11. Pass **Sorín**
12. Pass **Mascherano**
13. Pass **Riquelme**
14. Pass **Ayala**
15. Pass **Cambiasso**
16. Pass **Mascherano**
17. Pass **Rodríguez**
18. Pass **Sorín**
19. Pass **Rodríguez**
20. Pass **Cambiasso**
21. Pass **Riquelme**
22. Pass **Mascherano**
23. Pass **Mascherano**
24. Pass **Saviola**
25. Pass **Riquelme**
26. Pass **Saviola**
27. Pass **Cambiasso**
28. Pass **Crespo**
29. Goal **Cambiasso**

KEY

Ball movement ⎯⎯⎯ Player with ball ⋯⋯⋯⋯

Shot ⎯⚽ Player without ball ••••••••

JOE COLE – England vs Sweden

1. Clearance **Alexandersson**
2. Good skill **Cole**
3. Goal **Cole**

DECO – Portugal vs Iran

MAXI RODRÍGUEZ – Argentina vs Mexico

1. Pass **Pineda**
2. Pass **Ayala**
3. Pass **Aimar**
4. Pass **Scaloni**
5. Pass **Messi**
6. Pass **Riquelme**
7. Pass (long ball) **Messi**
8. Pass (chipped, long ball) **Sorin**
9. Goal **Rodríguez**

FERNANDO TORRES – Spain vs Ukraine

WORLD CUP GOALS

Cup in South Africa was the first to be hosted on African soil. To the
t of thousands of vuvuzelas, it was Ghana and Uruguay who were the
es—separated only by penalties in the quarterfinal, after Luis Suárez's
nute handball save. Spain would triumph over the Netherlands in the final of
minated by goals such as the incredible effort from an impossible angle by
a precision chip from Italy's Fabio Quagliarella and, most memorable of all,
foot punt from South Africa's Siphiwe Tshabalala...

TSHABALALA – **South Africa** vs Mexico

*Siphiwe Tshabalala belts the ball hard from the 18-yard box to take
South Africa into the lead against Mexico, June 11, 2010.*

1. Flick-on **dos Santos**
2. Interception **Mokoena**
3. Ball recovery **Letsholonyane**
4. Pass **Letsholonyane**
5. Pass **Dikgacoi**
6. Pass **Mphela**
7. Through ball **Dikgacoi**
8. Goal **Tshabalala**

KEY

Ball movement	━━━━	Player with ball	▪▪▪▪▪▪▪▪▪
Shot	━━━⚽	Player without ball	••••••••••

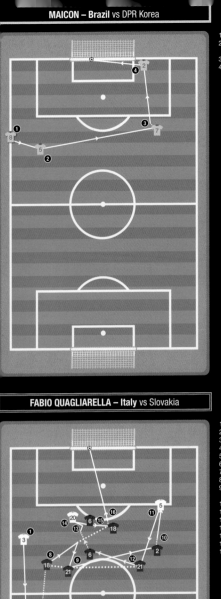

MAICON – Brazil vs DPR Korea

1. Throw in **Silva**
2. Pass (long ball, chipped) **Melo**
3. Pass **Elano**
4. Goal **Maicon**

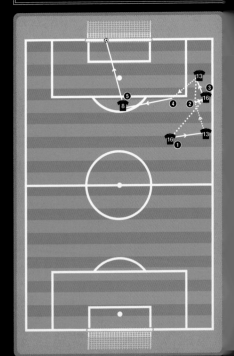

MESUT ÖZIL – Germany vs Ghana

FABIO QUAGLIARELLA – Italy vs Slovakia

1. Launch (long ball) **Škrtel**
2. Ball recovery **Chiellini**
3. Pass **Chiellini**
4. Pass **Marchetti**
5. Lay-off **Cannavaro**
6. Pass **Chiellini**
7. Pass **Pirlo**
8. Lay-off **Quagliarella**
9. Pass (chipped, long ball) **Pirlo**
10. Pass **Maggio**
11. Clearance **Zabavnik**
12. Pass **Pirlo**
13. Blocked **De Rossi**
14. Block **Kopúnek**
15. Pass **De Rossi**
16. Goal **Quagliarella**

GIOVANNI VAN BRONCKHORST – Netherlands vs Uruguay

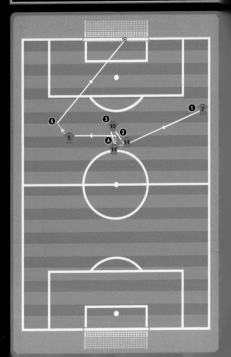

2014 WORLD CUP GOALS

There were too many unforgettable stories in Brazil's 2014 World Cup: reigning champions Spain crashing out in the group stage; the attacking zest displayed by Mexico, Costa Rica, US, and Colombia; Brazil's semifinal capitulation; and the superb soccer played by worthy winners Germany. Miroslav Klose became the competition's all-time top scorer, Colombia's James Rodríguez scored from a top-class chest, swivel, and volley smash, Robin van Persie perfected a diving header, and Mario Götze hit a volley worthy of winning a World Cup final.

ROBIN VAN PERSIE – Netherlands vs Spain

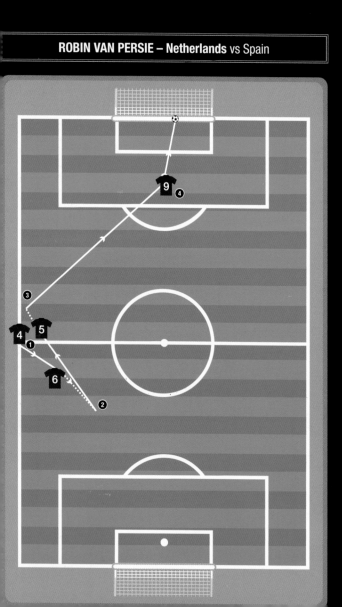

The Netherlands' Robin van Persie scores with his head to equalize in the match against Spain, June 13, 2014.

1. Throw in **Martins Indi**
2. Pass **De Jong**
3. Through ball (chipped, long ball) **Blind**
4. Goal (head) **Van Persie**

KEY

Ball movement ▬▬▬▬   Player with ball ▪▪▪▪▪▪▪▪▪▪▪▪

Shot ▬▬▬⚽   Player without ball ••••••••••••

MARIO GÖTZE – Germany vs Argentina

1. Free kick taken **Lahm**
2. Pass **Schweinsteiger**
3. Pass **Boateng**
4. Pass **Hummels**
5. Pass **Kroos**
6. Pass **Schürrle**
7. Pass **Kroos**
8. Pass (cross, chipped) **Schürrle**
9. Goal **Götze**

LIONEL MESSI – Argentina vs Bosnia

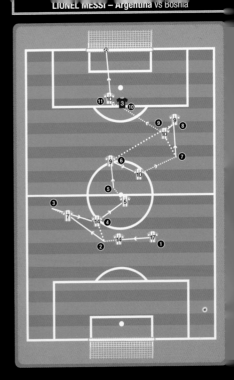

JAMES RODRÍGUEZ – Colombia vs Uruguay

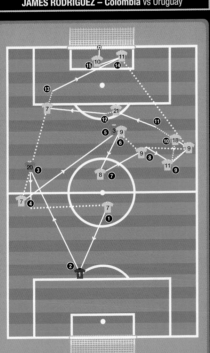

1. Pass **Armero**
2. Launch (long ball) **Ospina**
3. Head pass **González**
4. Pass (chipped, long ball) **Armero**
5. Head pass **Godín**
6. Pass (chipped) **Gutiérrez**
7. Pass **Aguilar**
8. Pass **Gutiérrez**
9. Pass **Cuadrado**
10. Pass **Zúñiga**
11. Pass **Gutiérrez**
12. Pass **Martínez**
13. Pass (cross, chipped) **Armero**
14. Head pass **Cuadrado**
15. Goal **Rodríguez**

DAVID VILLA – Spain vs Australia

WOMEN'S WORLD CUP TROPHIES AND GOALS

first official Women's World Cup took place in China in 1991. There were 12 teams but no
ners' prize money and no sponsor, while the matches lasted just 80 minutes. Since then, the
men's game and the competition have grown beyond recognition and, still played every four
rs, there have now been seven tournaments. In Canada, in 2015, the qualifying rounds saw
nations compete for 24 places; 26.7 million TV viewers made the final the most-watched
cer game in American history and the victorious US team won $2 million in prize money.

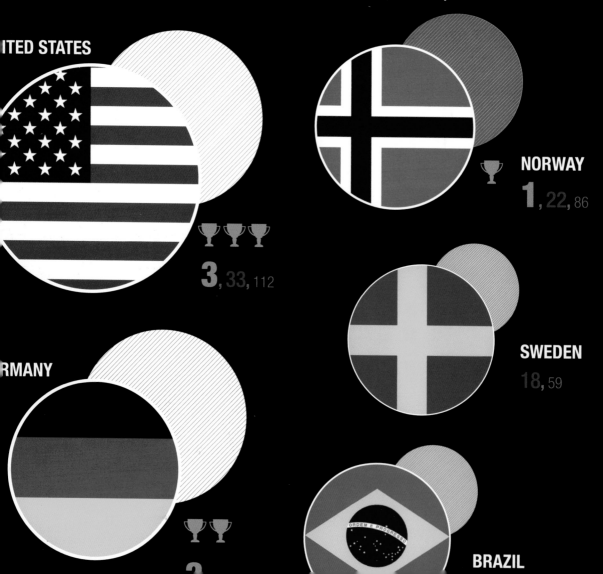

ITED STATES

3, 33, 112

NORWAY

1, 22, 86

SWEDEN

18, 59

RMANY

BRAZIL

Source: Opta (October 2015)

PR CHINA
15, 52

FRANCE
6, 22

CAMEROON
2, 9

SWITZERLAND
1, 11

AUSTRALIA
5, 29

GHANA
1, 6

JAPAN
1, **13,** 36

RUSSIA
4, 16

KOREA REPUBLIC
1, 5

COLOMBIA
1, 4

ENGLAND
10, 30

DENMARK
3, 19

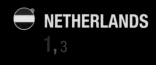

THAILAND
1, 3

NIGERIA
3, 18

NETHERLANDS
1, 3

CHINESE TAIPEI
1, 2

CANADA
6, 30

DPR KOREA
3, 12

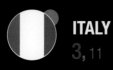

ITALY
3, 11

🏆 1 **TOURNAMENTS WON**
◉ 1 **MATCHES WON**
● 1 **GOALS SCORED**

59

WOMEN'S WORLD CUP GOALSCORERS

Since Chinese defender Ma Li scored the first goal in Women's World Cup history, 770 goals have been scored in the finals. Among these are memorable strikes such as the stunning volley by Germany's Birgit Prinz in 2003 and Brazilian Marta's unstoppable flick and finish in 2007. The 2015 World Cup competition was graced by fabulous long-range shots from

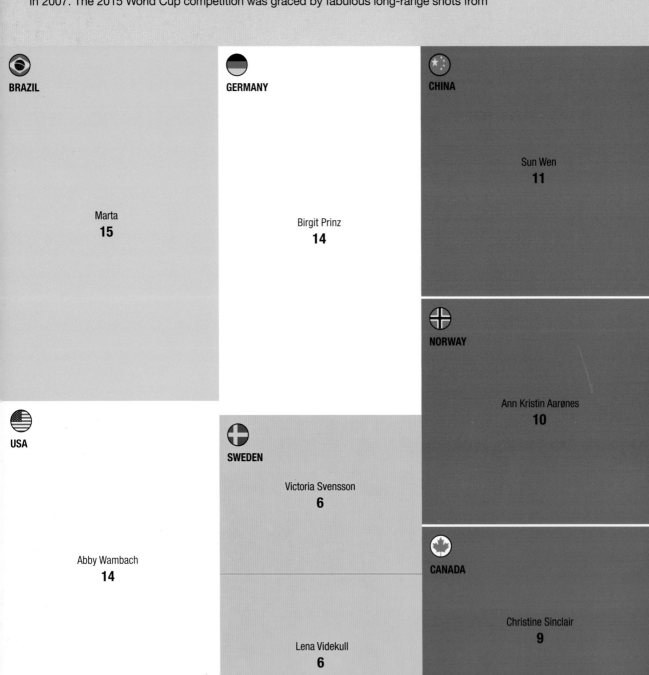

BRAZIL

Marta
15

GERMANY

Birgit Prinz
14

CHINA

Sun Wen
11

NORWAY

Ann Kristin Aarønes
10

USA

Abby Wambach
14

SWEDEN

Victoria Svensson
6

Lena Videkull
6

CANADA

Christine Sinclair
9

England's Lucy Bronze and France's Amandine Henry, but will surely be remembered most for the hat trick by the USA's Carli Lloyd in the final, capped by a sensational right-foot strike (and lob) from the halfway line. The goal was awarded Goal of the Tournament.

Source: Opta (August 2015)

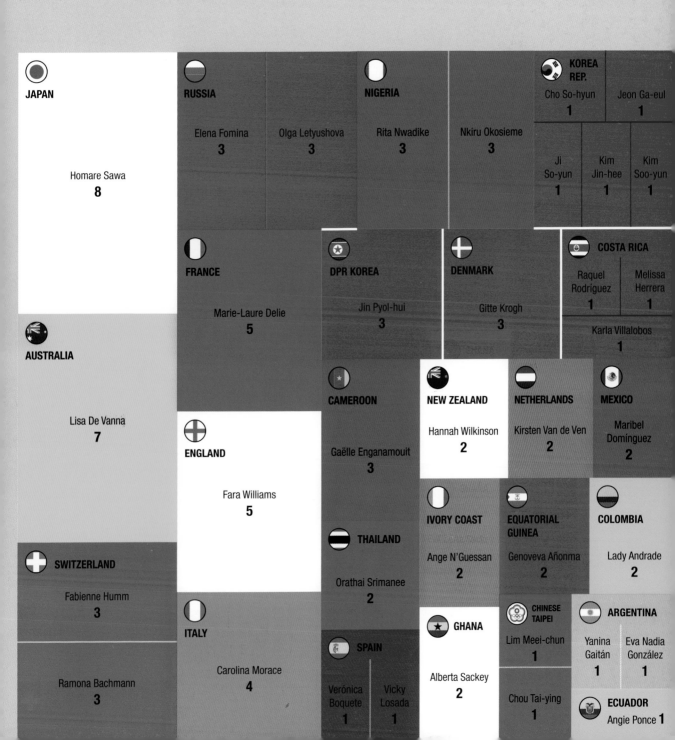

JAPAN
Homare Sawa
8

RUSSIA
Elena Fomina **3**
Olga Letyushova **3**

NIGERIA
Rita Nwadike **3**
Nkiru Okosieme **3**

KOREA REP.
Cho So-hyun **1**
Jeon Ga-eul **1**
Ji So-yun **1**
Kim Jin-hee **1**
Kim Soo-yun **1**

FRANCE
Marie-Laure Delie **5**

DPR KOREA
Jin Pyol-hui **3**

DENMARK
Gitte Krogh **3**

COSTA RICA
Raquel Rodríguez **1**
Melissa Herrera **1**
Karla Villalobos **1**

AUSTRALIA
Lisa De Vanna **7**

CAMEROON
Gaëlle Enganamouit **3**

NEW ZEALAND
Hannah Wilkinson **2**

NETHERLANDS
Kirsten Van de Ven **2**

MEXICO
Maribel Domínguez **2**

ENGLAND
Fara Williams **5**

IVORY COAST
Ange N'Guessan **2**

EQUATORIAL GUINEA
Genoveva Añonma **2**

COLOMBIA
Lady Andrade **2**

SWITZERLAND
Fabienne Humm **3**

THAILAND
Orathai Srimanee **2**

ITALY
Carolina Morace **4**

GHANA
Alberta Sackey **2**

CHINESE TAIPEI
Lim Meei-chun **1**
Chou Tai-ying **1**

ARGENTINA
Yanina Gaitán **1**
Eva Nadia González **1**

Ramona Bachmann **3**

SPAIN
Verónica Boquete **1**
Vicky Losada **1**

ECUADOR
Angie Ponce **1**

EUROPEAN CHAMPIONSHIP RECORDS BY NATION

Brainchild of Henri Delaunay, the secretary of the French Football Federation, the European Championship has been held every four years since 1960. Qualification for the first two finals was conducted on a home-and-away knockout basis, with the group qualification format beginning in 1968. Originally only four teams qualified for the finals. This was extended to eight teams in 1980, to 16 in 1996 and further expanded to include 24 nations in 2016. To mark 60 years of the tournament, the 2020 finals will be held in 13 different cities across the continent.

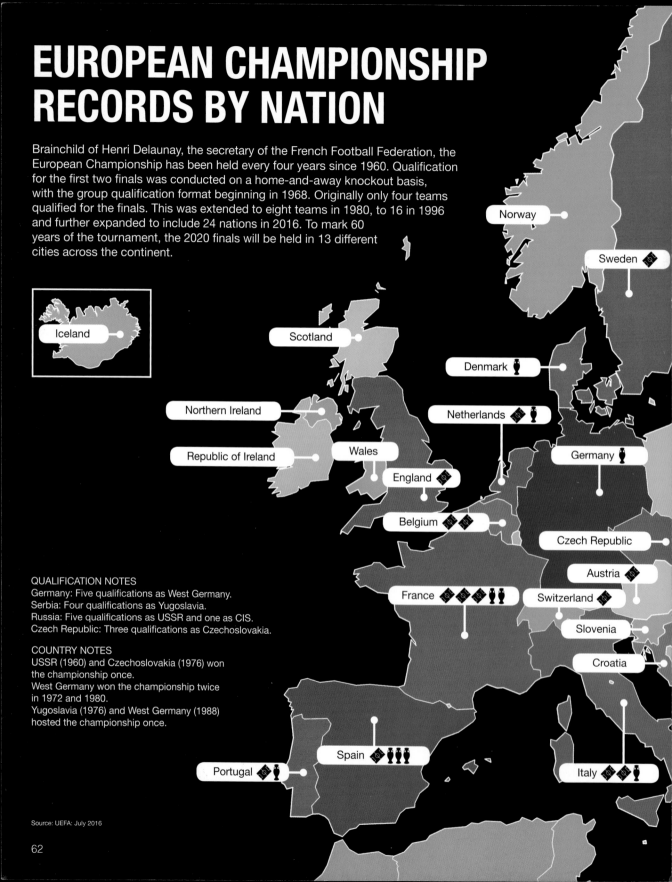

QUALIFICATION NOTES
Germany: Five qualifications as West Germany.
Serbia: Four qualifications as Yugoslavia.
Russia: Five qualifications as USSR and one as CIS.
Czech Republic: Three qualifications as Czechoslovakia.

COUNTRY NOTES
USSR (1960) and Czechoslovakia (1976) won the championship once.
West Germany won the championship twice in 1972 and 1980.
Yugoslavia (1976) and West Germany (1988) hosted the championship once.

Source: UEFA: July 2016

Qualified

0
1
2
3
4
5
6
7
8
9
10
11
12

Finland

Estonia

Latvia

Lithuania

Russia

Belarus

Poland

Ukraine

Slovakia

Kazakhstan

Hungary

Moldova

Romania

Bosnia and Herzegovina

Serbia

Bulgaria

Georgia

Albania

Armenia

Azerbaijan

Turkey

Greece

Cyprus

Winner

Host

EUROPEAN CHAMPIONSHIP TROPHIES, WINS, AND GOALS

It's an old soccer cliché, but it is certainly true that there have been no easy games in the European Championship. The format of this much-revered event has historically led to a select and elite group of nations reaching the finals, so this data is not distorted by easy wins and goal feasts. While Germany are top in the all-time Euro table, the other leading nations have similar records—except for England, whose lack of success in the competition is starkly obvious.

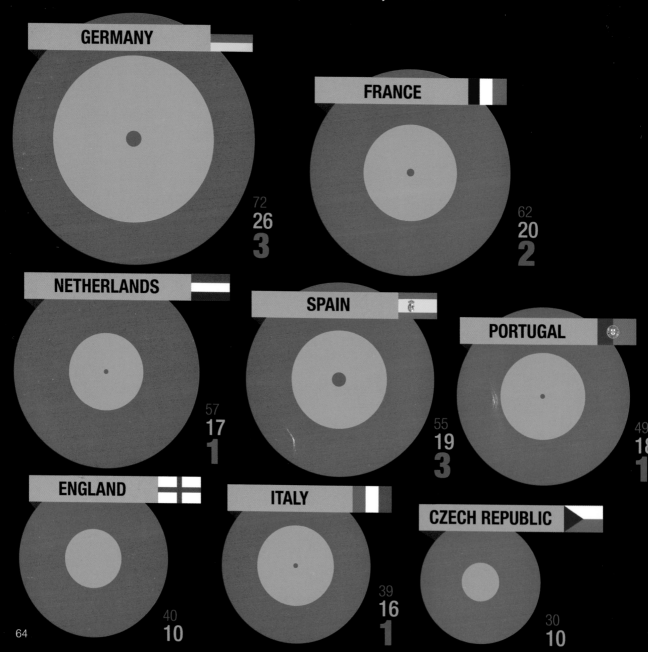

GERMANY
72
26
3

FRANCE
62
20
2

NETHERLANDS
57
17
1

SPAIN
55
19
3

PORTUGAL
49
18
1

ENGLAND
40
10

ITALY
39
16
1

CZECH REPUBLIC
30
10

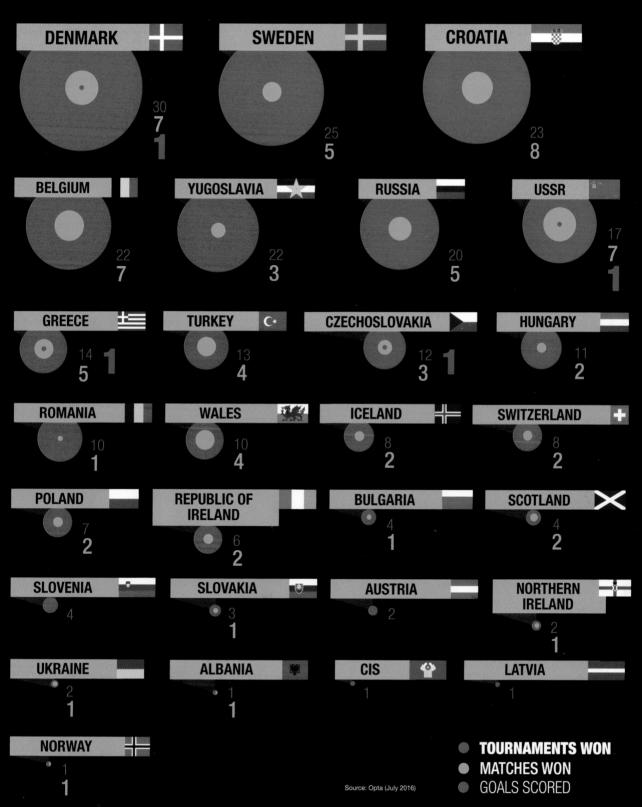

DENMARK ⊕
30
7
1

SWEDEN ⊕
25
5

CROATIA
23
8

BELGIUM
22
7

YUGOSLAVIA ★
22
3

RUSSIA
20
5

USSR
17
7
1

GREECE ≡
14 **1**
5

TURKEY ☾★
13
4

CZECHOSLOVAKIA
12 **1**
3

HUNGARY
11
2

ROMANIA
10
1

WALES
10
4

ICELAND
8
2

SWITZERLAND ✚
8
2

POLAND
7
2

REPUBLIC OF IRELAND
6
2

BULGARIA
4
1

SCOTLAND ✕
4
2

SLOVENIA
4

SLOVAKIA
3
1

AUSTRIA
2

NORTHERN IRELAND
2
1

UKRAINE
2
1

ALBANIA
1
1

CIS
1

LATVIA
1

NORWAY
1
1

● **TOURNAMENTS WON**
● **MATCHES WON**
● **GOALS SCORED**

Source: Opta (July 2016)

UEFA EURO 2016 GOALS

Despite a record 108 goals being scored in the 2016 European Championship, the matches were not a feast of goals. With a ratio of just 2.12 a game, Euro 2016 was the lowest-scoring European Championship for 20 years. However, there certainly was drama: 18 goals (seven winners and three equalizers) were scored in the last five minutes or later, including Dimitri Payet's majestic 89th-minute winner against Romania in the opening game and Northern Ireland's Niall McGinn setting the record for latest goal ever in a European Championship at 96 minutes.

XHERDAN SHAQIRI – Switzerland vs Poland

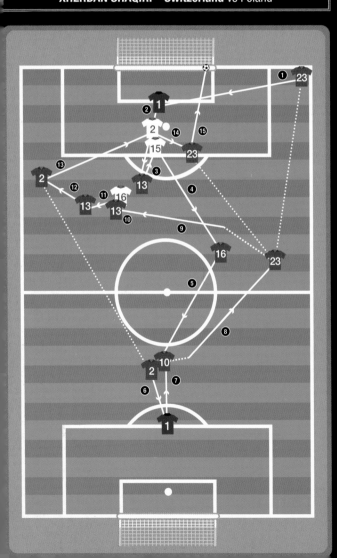

Many believed Xherdan Shaqiri's acrobatic strike for Switzerland in their last-16 match against Poland to be the Goal of the Tournament.

1. Corner kick **Shaqiri**
2. Punch **Fabianski**
3. Blocked shot **Rodriguez**
4. Defensive block **Glik**
5. Pass **Fernandes**
6. Pass **Lichtsteiner**
7. Pass **Sommer**
8. Pass **Xhaka**
9. Pass **Shaqiri**
10. Unsuccessful pass **Rodriguez**
11. Blocked pass **Blaszczykowski**
12. Pass **Rodriguez**
13. Unsuccessful pass **Lichtsteiner**
14. Clearance **Pazdan**
15. Goal **Shaqiri**

KEY

Ball movement	▬▬▬	Player with ball	••••••••••
Shot	▬▬⚽	Player without ball	••••••••••

HAL ROBSON-KANU – Wales vs Belgium

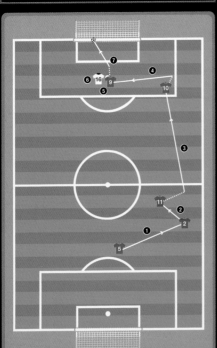

1. Pass **Chester**
2. Pass **Gunter**
3. Pass **Bale**
4. Pass **Ramsey**
5. Take on **Robson-Kanu**
6. Unsuccessful challenge **Meunier**
7. Goal **Robson-Kanu**

ANTOINE GRIEZMANN – France vs Iceland

1. Pass **Pogba**
2. Pass **Matuidi**
3. Lay-off **Payet**
4. Pass **Umtiti**
5. Pass **Koscielny**
6. Pass **Pogba**
7. Lay-off **Griezmann**
8. Pass **Pogba**
9. Pass **Sagna**
10. Pass **Koscielny**
11. Pass **Umtiti**
12. Pass **Pogba**
13. Pass **Giroud**
14. Goal **Griezmann**

CRISTIANO RONALDO – Portugal vs Hungary

1. Pass **Patricio**
2. Pass **Carvalho**
3. Pass **Ronaldo**
4. Pass **Eliseu**
5. Pass **Carvalho**
6. Pass **Pepe**
7. Pass **Carvalho**
8. Pass **Patricio**
9. Pass **Pepe**
10. Pass **Vierinha**
11. Pass **Mario**
12. Pass **Nani**
13. Pass **Mario**
14. Goal **Ronaldo**

ROMELU LUKAKU – Belgium vs Republic of Ireland

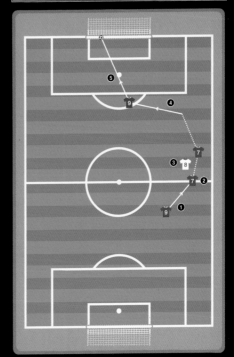

1. Pass **Lukaku**
2. Take on **De Bruyne**
3. Unsuccessful challenge **McCarthy**
4. Pass **De Bruyne**
5. Goal **Lukaku**

COPA AMÉRICA
RECORDS BY NATION

The South American Football Championship is the oldest international continental soccer competition. The first event took place in Argentina in 1916 and was held annually (if sporadically) until 1967. The Copa América itself began in 1975 and, from 2007, has continued in a four-year cycle. It was originally contested by 10 teams, enlarged to 12 in 1993 and 16 (including the rest of the Americas) for a special 2016 centenary tournament in the US. After the 2019 tournament takes place in Brazil, the US will host a 2020 Copa América to move the competition to even-numbered years.

The 2019 Copa América will feature 16 teams: among the guest teams to have been invited – for the first time – are Spain, France and Italy.

QUALIFICATION NOTES
Also competed: Mexico (10), Costa Rica (5), United States (4), Jamaica (2), Haiti (1), Honduras (1), Japan (1). No host (3).

Chile celebrate winning their second successive Copa América championship after beating Argentina on penalties at MetLife Stadium in East Rutherford, USA.

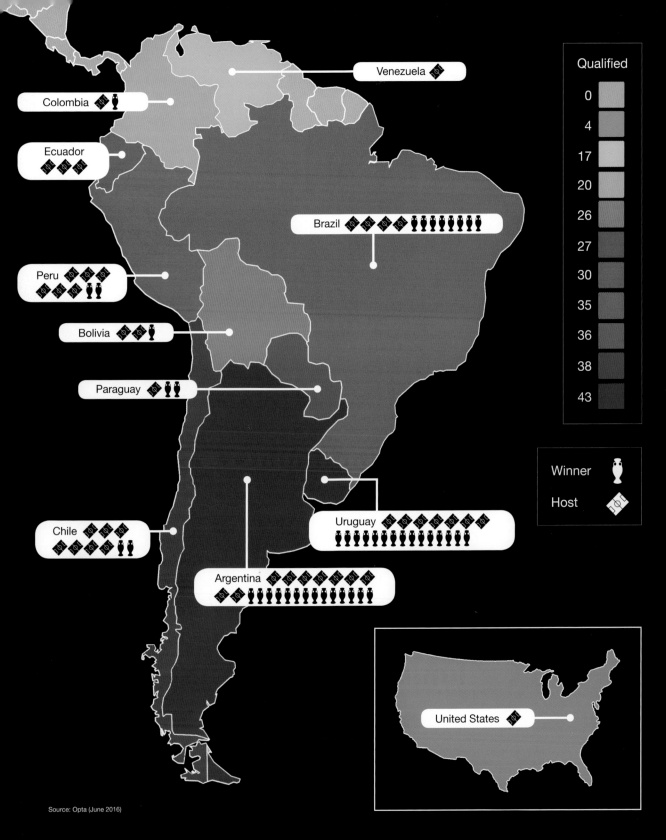

Qualified

0	
4	
17	
20	
26	
27	
30	
35	
36	
38	
43	

Winner

Host

Venezuela

Colombia

Ecuador

Brazil

Peru

Bolivia

Paraguay

Chile

Argentina

Uruguay

United States

Source: Opta (June 2016)

COPA AMÉRICA TROPHIES, WINS, AND GOALS

The South American international tournament, Copa América is one of the most intensely fought competitions in world football. There have been 45 (often intermittent) tournaments in the Copa América's 100 years, in which all but Ecuador and Venezuela have been victors. Bolivia's sole victory came on high-altitude home soil in 1963, while Chile contested the most tournaments without a win until 2015, then won again in the centenary competition in 2016. Interestingly, both Pelé and Maradona—and their World Cup-winning teams—failed to secure a Copa América triumph.

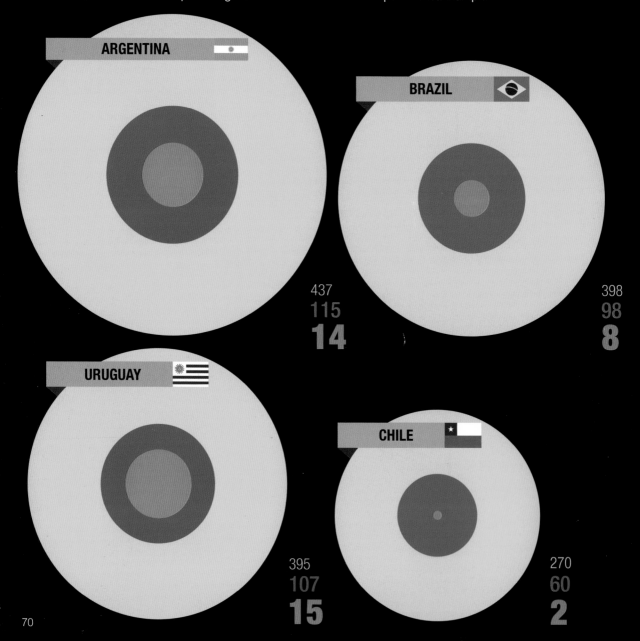

ARGENTINA

437
115
14

BRAZIL

398
98
8

URUGUAY

395
107
15

CHILE

270
60
2

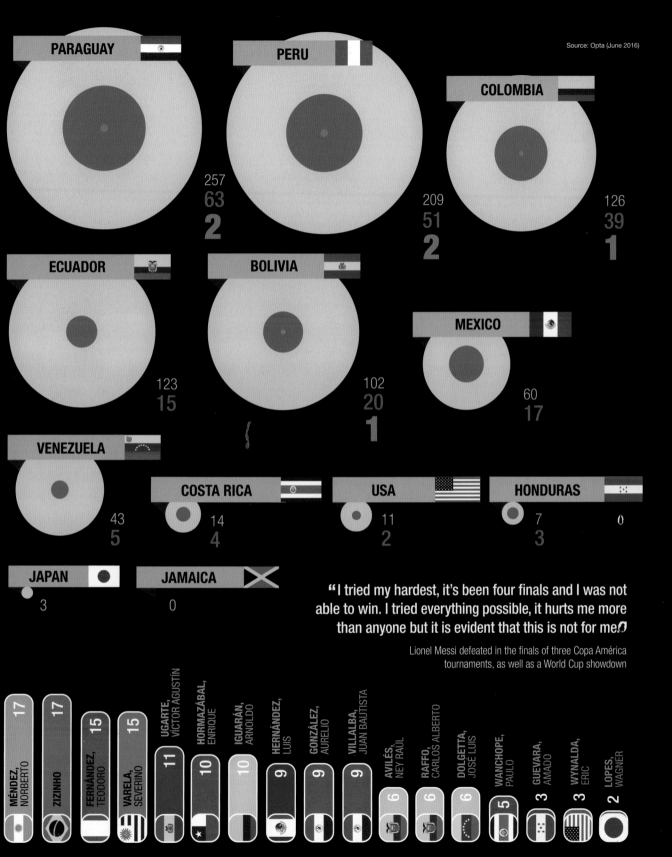

PARAGUAY

PERU

COLOMBIA

257
63
2

209
51
2

126
39
1

ECUADOR

BOLIVIA

MEXICO

123
15

102
20
1

60
17

VENEZUELA

COSTA RICA

USA

HONDURAS

43
5

14
4

11
2

7
3

0

JAPAN

JAMAICA

3

0

"I tried my hardest, it's been four finals and I was not able to win. I tried everything possible, it hurts me more than anyone but it is evident that this is not for me.

Lionel Messi defeated in the finals of three Copa América tournaments, as well as a World Cup showdown

17	17	15	15	11	10	10	9	9	9	6	6	6	5	3	3	2
MÉNDEZ, NORBERTO	ZIZINHO	FERNÁNDEZ, TEODORO	VARELA, SEVERINO	UGARTE, VÍCTOR AGUSTÍN	HORMAZÁBAL, ENRIQUE	IGUARÁN, ARNOLDO	HERNÁNDEZ, LUIS	GONZÁLEZ, AURELIO	VILLALBA, JUAN BAUTISTA	AVILÉS, NEY RAÚL	RAFFO, CARLOS ALBERTO	DOLGETTA, JOSÉ LUIS	WANCHOPE, PAULO	GUEVARA, AMADO	WYNALDA, ERIC	LOPES, WAGNER

AFRICA CUP OF NATIONS RECORDS BY NATION

The biennial Africa Cup of Nations tournament, contested by the nations of the Confederation of African Football, has been played since 1957. Just Egypt, Sudan, and Ethiopia played the first two tournaments before it was enlarged to include four (1962), six (1963), eight (1968), 12 (1992) and then 16 teams (1996). Because of its apartheid policy South Africa was excluded from the competition until 1996. The tournament moved to odd-numbered years from 2013 to avoid conflict with the World Cup; this meant there were tournaments in consecutive years.

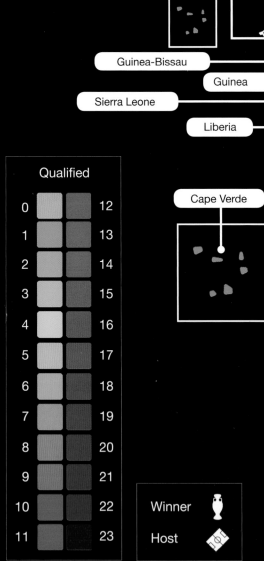

Senegal

Guinea-Bissau

Guinea

Sierra Leone

Liberia

Cape Verde

Qualified

0	12
1	13
2	14
3	15
4	16
5	17
6	18
7	19
8	20
9	21
10	22
11	23

Winner

Host

Cameroon celebrate winning the 2017 Africa Cup of Nations after the Indomitable Lions came from behind to beat Egypt 2–1 in Libreville, Gabon, to seal a fifth tournament victory.

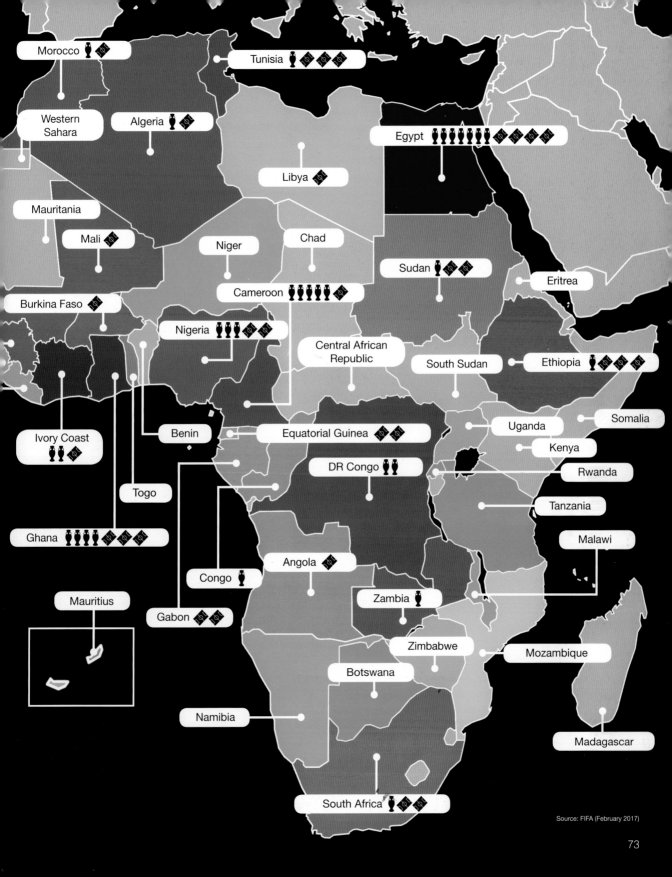

Source: FIFA (February 2017)

73

AFRICA CUP OF NATIONS TROPHIES, WINS, AND GOALS

What began in 1957 with a three-team competition has developed 31 tournaments later into a month-long, 16-team extravaganza. The tournament has witnessed many great moments, including Benni McCarthy hitting four goals in 13 minutes against Namibia in 1998; Ivory Coast's second-choice keeper Boubacar Barry saving two penalties before hitting the winner in the shootout in 2015 and Vincent Aboubakar's sensational 88th-minute strike to win the trophy for Cameroon in 2017.

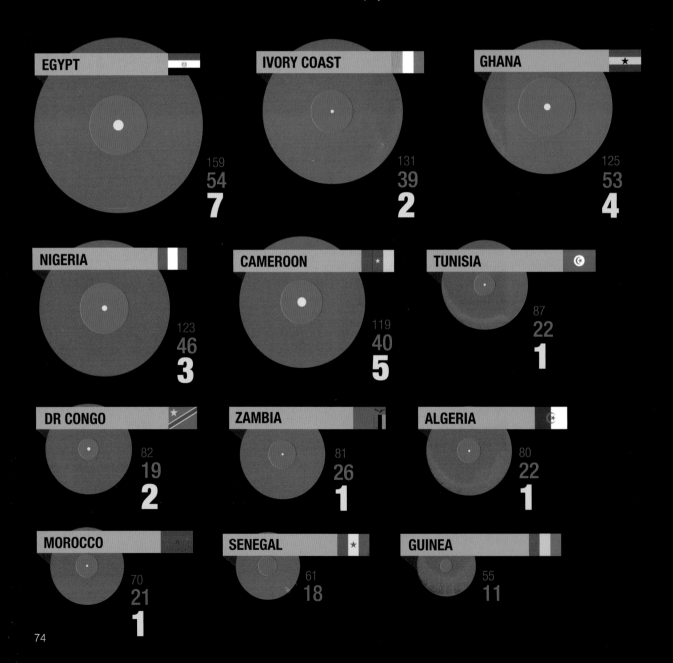

EGYPT 159 54 7

IVORY COAST 131 39 2

GHANA 125 53 4

NIGERIA 123 46 3

CAMEROON 119 40 5

TUNISIA 87 22 1

DR CONGO 82 19 2

ZAMBIA 81 26 1

ALGERIA 80 22 1

MOROCCO 70 21 1

SENEGAL 61 18

GUINEA 55 11

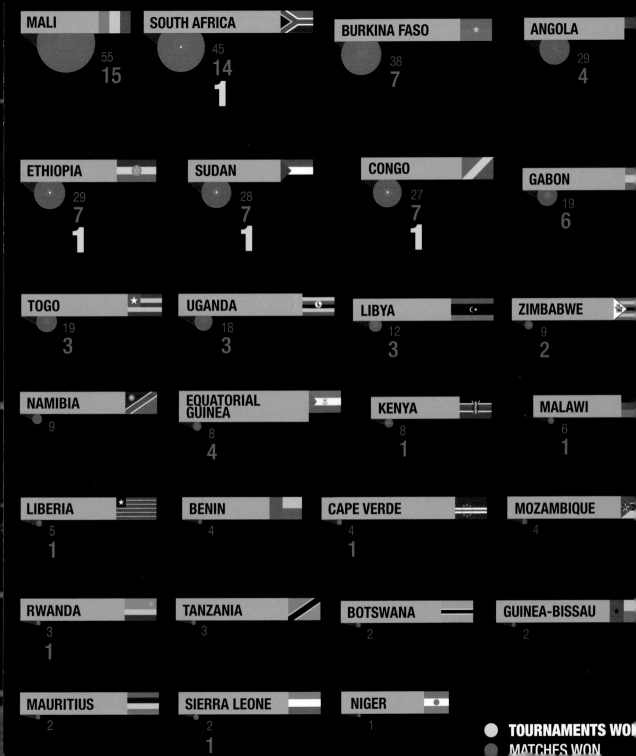

MALI
55
15

SOUTH AFRICA
45
14
1

BURKINA FASO
38
7

ANGOLA
29
4

ETHIOPIA
29
7
1

SUDAN
28
7
1

CONGO
27
7
1

GABON
19
6

TOGO
19
3

UGANDA
18
3

LIBYA
12
3

ZIMBABWE
9
2

NAMIBIA
9

EQUATORIAL GUINEA
8
4

KENYA
8
1

MALAWI
6
1

LIBERIA
5
1

BENIN
4

CAPE VERDE
4
1

MOZAMBIQUE
4

RWANDA
3
1

TANZANIA
3

BOTSWANA
2

GUINEA-BISSAU
2

MAURITIUS
2

SIERRA LEONE
2
1

NIGER
1

● **TOURNAMENTS WO[N]**
● **MATCHES WON**

ASIAN CUP RECORDS BY NATION AND REGION

The Asian Cup is contested by the nations and regions of the Asian Football Confederation, which stretches from the Middle East to Japan and Australia (who joined the AFC in 2006). It was held every four years from the inaugural 1956 tournament until 2004, then from 2007 (switching to avoid conflicting with the Olympics and European Championship). The number of nations competing in the finals increased from an original 4 to 12 in 1996, to 16 in 2004 and will increase to 24 in 2019.

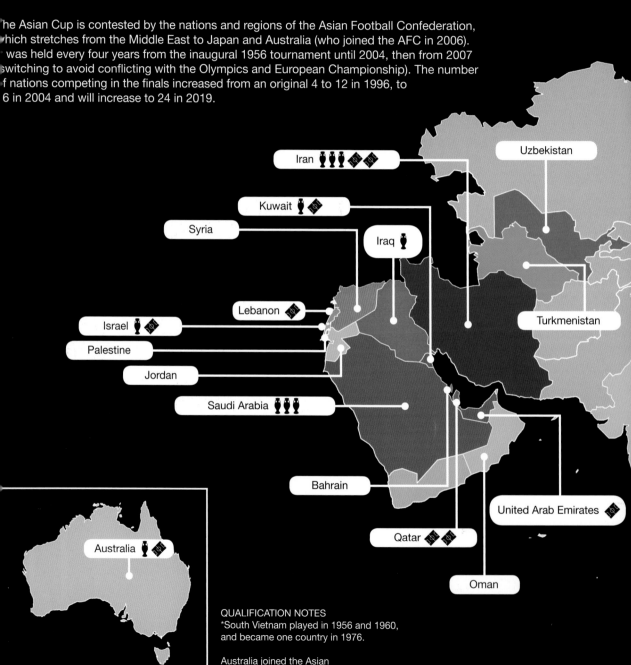

Uzbekistan

Iran

Kuwait

Syria

Iraq

Turkmenistan

Lebanon

Israel

Palestine

Jordan

Saudi Arabia

Bahrain

United Arab Emirates

Qatar

Oman

Australia

QUALIFICATION NOTES
*South Vietnam played in 1956 and 1960, and became one country in 1976.

Australia joined the Asian
Football Confederation in 2006

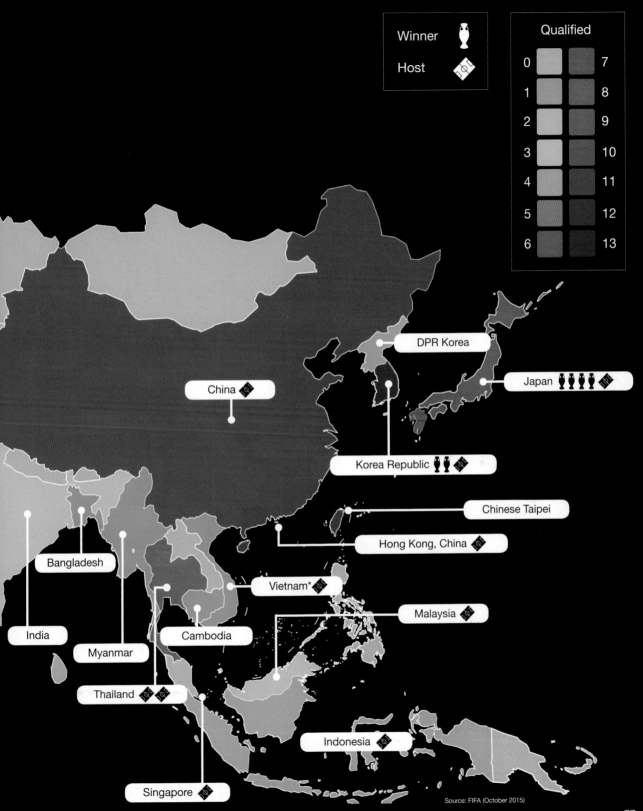

Winner

Host

Qualified

0	7
1	8
2	9
3	10
4	11
5	12
6	13

DPR Korea

China

Japan

Korea Republic

Chinese Taipei

Hong Kong, China

Bangladesh

Vietnam*

Malaysia

India

Myanmar

Cambodia

Thailand

Indonesia

Singapore

Source: FIFA (October 2015)

77

AFC ASIAN CUP TROPHIES, WINS, AND GOALS

The most recent AFC Asian Cup in 2015 crowned host nation Australia the Champions of Asia after defeating the Republic of Korea 2–1 after extra time. The next tournament in 2019, which is to be hosted by the United Arab Emirates, will see the possible number of national teams expand from 16 to 24. The Asian Cup is the world's second oldest continental soccer championship, after Copa América, and the cup's most consistent side to date is Japan, who have triumphantly held the trophy aloft in four out of seven tournaments since 1992.

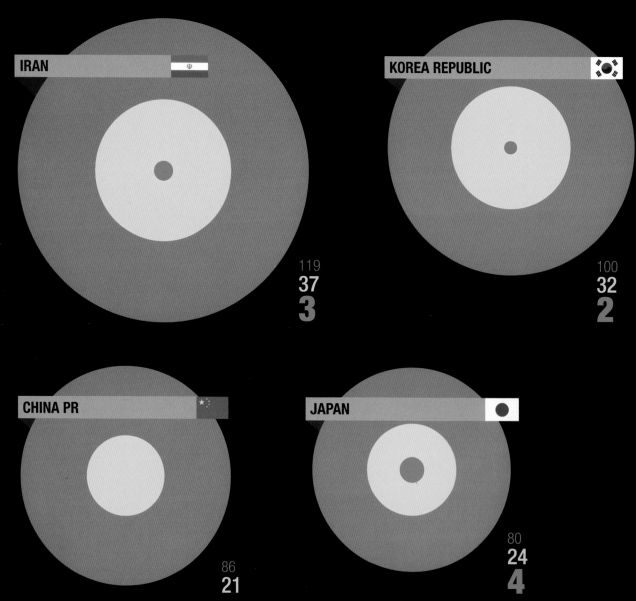

IRAN
119
37
3

KOREA REPUBLIC
100
32
2

CHINA PR
86
21

JAPAN
80
24
4

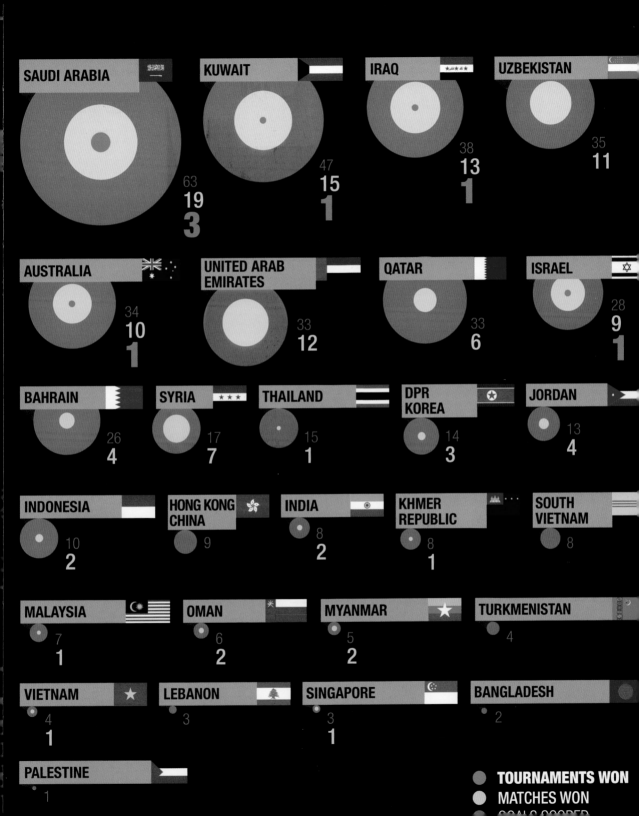

SAUDI ARABIA

63
19
3

KUWAIT

47
15
1

IRAQ

38
13
1

UZBEKISTAN

35
11

AUSTRALIA

34
10
1

UNITED ARAB EMIRATES

33
12

QATAR

33
6

ISRAEL

28
9
1

BAHRAIN

26
4

SYRIA

17
7

THAILAND

15
1

DPR KOREA

14
3

JORDAN

13
4

INDONESIA

10
2

HONG KONG CHINA

9

INDIA

8
2

KHMER REPUBLIC

8
1

SOUTH VIETNAM

8

MALAYSIA

7
1

OMAN

6
2

MYANMAR

5
2

TURKMENISTAN

4

VIETNAM

4
1

LEBANON

3

SINGAPORE

3
1

BANGLADESH

2

PALESTINE

1

TOURNAMENTS WON
MATCHES WON
GOALS SCORED

CONCACAF GOLD CUP RECORDS BY NATION

The CONCACAF Gold Cup is a biennial competition for nations from North and Central America and the Caribbean. The six-team tournament was first held in 1963 and then every two years. Between 1973 and 1989, the competition was held every four years and doubled as a World Cup qualifying process. In 1991 it was expanded to eight teams and reverted to a biennial format and in 2001 it was enlarged to 12 nations. Between 1997 and 2003 guest teams, including Brazil and Colombia, also competed in the tournament. The most recent CONCACAF Gold Cup was hosted—and won—by the US in 2017.

QUALIFICATION NOTES
The color coding and winners and hosts icons are based only on the Gold Cup since 1991.

Mexico have won the CONCACAF Gold Cup a record 10 times.

Lesser Antilles

Guadeloupe

Martinique

Saint Vincent

Grenada

Trinidad & Tobago

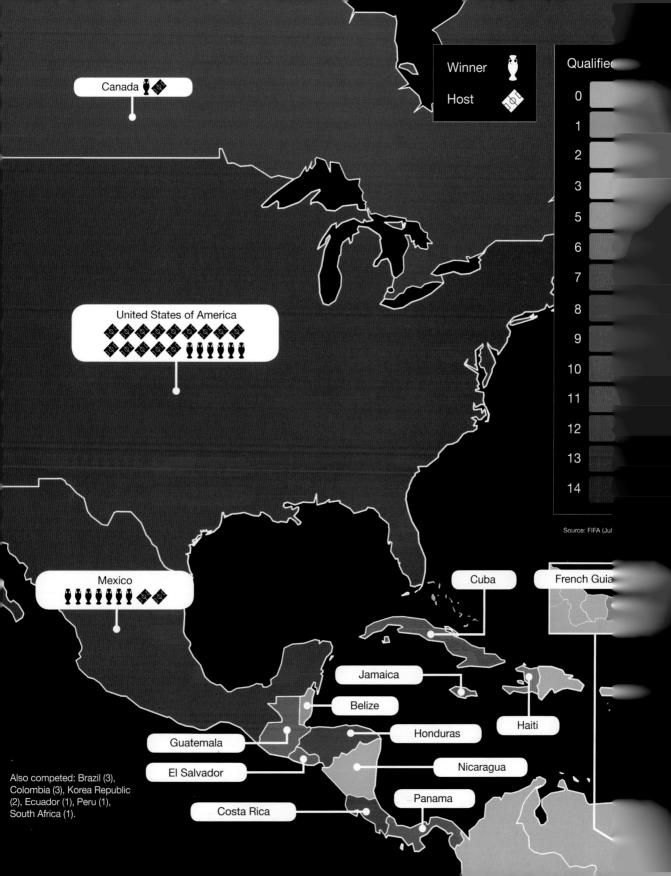

Canada

Winner

Host

Qualified

0
1
2
3
5
6
7
8
9
10
11
12
13
14

Source: FIFA (Jul

United States of America

Mexico

Cuba

French Guia

Jamaica

Belize

Honduras

Haiti

Guatemala

El Salvador

Nicaragua

Panama

Costa Rica

Also competed: Brazil (3),
Colombia (3), Korea Republic
(2), Ecuador (1), Peru (1),
South Africa (1).

100 INTERNATIONAL CAPS

At Wembley Stadium, on April 11, 1959, England captain Billy Wright became the first soccer player to make 100 appearances for his country, but since then this feat has been repeated by many players around the world. The modern game's proliferation of matches (major nations play more games a year than their pre-1990s counterparts) and multiple substitution rules give today's players a better chance of becoming Centurions and also accounts for the absence in the list of such greats as Pelé (92 appearances), Diego Maradona (91), Eusébio (64) and Johan Cruyff (48).

Player	Country	Caps
Ahmed Hassan	Egypt	184
Hossam Hassan	Egypt	178
Claudio Suárez	Mexico	177
Mohamed Al-Deayea	Saudi Arabia	172
Iván Hurtado	Ecuador	168
Gianlugli Buffon	Italy	168
Iker Casillas	Spain	167
Vitalijs Astafjevs	Latvia	165
Cobi Jones	United States	164
Mohammed Al-Khilaiwi	Saudi Arabia	163
Adnan Al-Talyani	United Arab Emirates	161
Bader Al-Mutawa	Kuwait	158
Landon Donovan	United States	157
Sami Al-Jaber	Saudi Arabia	156
Martin Reim	Estonia	156
Essam El-Hadary	Egypt	153
Yasuhito Endo	Japan	152
Lothar Matthäus	West Germany / Germany	150
Salman Isa	Bahrain	149
Ali Daei	Iran	149
Javad Nekounam	Iran	148
Younis Mahmoud	Iraq	148
Robbie Keane	Republic of Ireland	146
Mohammed Husain	Bahrain	145
Pável Pardo	Mexico	145
Paulo da Silva	Paraguay	144
Anatoliy Tymoshchuk	Ukraine	144
Javier Zanetti	Argentina	143
Gerado Torrado	Mexico	143
Fawzi Doorbeen	Oman	143
Thomas Ravelli	Sweden	143
Anders Svensson	Sweden	143
Cafu	Brazil	142
Marko Kristal	Estonia	142
Lilan Thuram	France	142
Sergio Ramos	Spain	142
Abdullah Zubromawi	Saudi Arabia	141
Ahmed Mubarek	Oman	140
Giorgos Karagounis	Greece	139
Cristiano Ronaldo	Portugal	138
Rigobert Song	Cameroon	137
Jari Litmanen	Finland	137
Miroslav Klose	Germany	137
Amado Guevara	Honduras	137
Hussein Saeed	Iraq	137
Rafael Márquez	Mexico	137
Javier Mascherano	Argentina	136
Maynor Figueroa	Honduras	136
Fabio Cannavaro	Italy	136
Hong Myung-Bo	South Korea	136
Walter Centeno	Costa Rica	135
Noel Valladares	Honduras	135
Amer Shafi	Jordan	135
Waleed Ali Jumah	Kuwait	135
Andrés Guardado	Mexico	135
Daniel Bennett	Singapore	135
Darijo Srna	Croatia	134
Shay Given	Republic of Ireland	134
Dorinel Munteanu	Romania	134
Hussein Sulaimani	Saudi Arabia	134
Shahril Bin Ishak	Singapore	134
Jeff Agoos	United States	134
Andres Oper	Estonia	133
Carlos Ruiz	Guatemala	133
Bashar Abdullah	Kuwait	133
Saud Kariri	Saudi Arabia	133
Xavi	Spain	133
Andreas Isaksson	Sweden	133
Clint Dempsey	United States	132
Gabriel Gómez	Panama	131
Kim Källström	Sweden	131
Lee Woon-Jae	South Korea	131
Kiatisuk Senamuang	Thailand	131
Sargis Hovseyan	Armenia	130
Lukas Podolski	Germany	130
Edwin van der Sar	Netherlands	130
Baihakki Bin Khaizan	Singapore	130
Michael Bradley	United States	130
Jorge Campos	Mexico	130
Roberto Palacios	Peru	129
Juan Arango	Venezuela	128
Dennis Rommedahl	Denmark	127
Ali Karimi	Iran	127
Linval Dixon	Jamaica	127
Luís Figo	Portugal	127
Lee Young-Pyo	South Korea	127
Marcelo Balboa	United States	127
Luís Marin	Costa Rica	126
Paolo Maldini	Italy	126
Wesley Sneijder	Netherlands	126
Ali Al-Habsi	Oman	126
Andoni Zubizarreta	Spain	126
Roberto Carlos	Brazil	125
Ibrahim Hassan	Egypt	125
Peter Shilton	England	125
Musaed Neda	Kuwait	125
Mario Fick	Liechtenstein	125
Peter Jehle	Liechtenstein	125
Petr Cech	Czech Republic	124
Hany Ramzy	Egypt	124
Ian Goodison	Jamaica	124
Jaime Penedo	Panama	124
Gheorghe Hagi	Romania	124
DaMarcus Beasley	United States	124
Thierry Henry	France	123
Didier Zokora	Ivory Coast	123
Michael Mifsud	Malta	123
Server Djeparov	Uzbekistan	123
Masami Ihara	Japan	122
Carlos Salcido	Mexico	122
Amad Al-Hosni	Oman	122
Ismail Matar	United Arab Emirates	122
Peter Schmeichel	Denmark	121
Walter Ayoví	Ecuador	121
Enar Jääger	Estonia	121
Bastian Schweinsteiger	Germany	121
Mohamed Abd Al-Jawad	Saudi Arabia	121
Osama Al-Hawsawi	Saudi Arabia	121
Aide Iskandar	Singapore	121
Ahmed Fathi	Egypt	120
Mart Poom	Estonia	120
Sergei Ignashevich	Russia	120
Yoo Sang-Chul	South Korea	120
Rüstü Reçber	Turkey	120
Subait Khater Al-Junaibi	United Arab Emirates	120
Wayne Rooney	England	119
Theodoros Zagorakis	Greece	119
Boniek García	Honduras	119
David Carabott	Malta	119
Gilbert Agius	Malta	119
Ramón Ramirez	Mexico	119
Cuauhtémoc Blanco	Mexico	119
Pat Jennings	Northern Ireland	119
Justo Villar	Paraguay	119
Cha-Bum-Kun	South Korea	119
Timur Kapadze	Uzbekistan	119
Heinz Hermann	Switzerland	118
Geremi	Cameroon	118
Samuel Eto'o	Cameroon	118
Karel Poborský	Czech Republic	118
Kolo Touré	Ivory Coast	118
Maxi Pereira	Uruguay	118
Lionel Messi	Argentina	117
Amer Khalil	Jordan	117
Sebastián Soria	Qatar	117
Mohammed Al-Shalhoub	Saudi Arabia	117
Olof Mellberg	Sweden	117
Ragnar Klavan	Estonia	116
Marcel Desailly	France	116
Kostas Katsouranis	Greece	116
Andrea Pirlo	Italy	116
Theodore Whitmore	Jamaica	116
Yoshikatsu Kawaguchi	Japan	116
John O'Shea	Republic of Ireland	116
Majed Abdullah	Saudi Arabia	116
Ahmed Madani	Saudi Arabia	116
Taisir Al-Jassim	Saudi Arabia	116
Andrés Iniesta	Spain	116
Roland Nilsson	Sweden	116
Zlatan Ibrahimovic	Sweden	116
Roberto Ayala	Argentina	115
David Beckham	England	115
Noureddine Naybet	Morocco	115
Gheorghe Popescu	Romania	115
Khairul Amri	Singapore	115
Shunmugham Subramani	Singapore	115
Abdulraheem Jumaa	United Arab Emirates	115
Stipe Pletikosa	Croatia	114
Steven Gerrard	England	114
Kristen Viikmäe	Estonia	114
Raio Piiroja	Estonia	114

Source: Google (June 2017)

Player	Country	Caps
Nawaf Al-Khaldi	Kuwait	114
Khaled Al-Muwallid	Saudi Arabia	114
Indra Sahdan Daud	Singapore	114
Björn Nordqvist	Sweden	114
Abdulla Al-Mazooqi	Bahrain	113
Viktor Onopko	CIS/Russia	113
Philipp Lahm	Germany	113
Ali Hussein Rehema	Iraq	113
Andrejs Rubins	Latvia	113
Martin Stocklasa	Liechtenstein	113
Ahmad Al-Dossari	Saudi Arabia	113
Xabi Alonso	Spain	113
Angus Eve	Trinidad & Tobago	113
Tim Howard	United States	113
Alain Geiger	Switzerland	113
Li Weifeng	PR China	112
Yénier Márquez	Cuba	112
Jon Dahl Tomasson	Denmark	112
Édison Méndez	Ecuador	
Abdel-Zaher El-Saqua	Egypt	112
Daniele De Rossi	Italy	112
Dino Zoff	Italy	112
Juris Laizans	Latvia	112
Frank de Boer	Netherlands	112
Roque Santa Cruz	Paraguay	112
Claudio Bravo	Spain	112
Wesam Abdulmajid	Qatar	112
Yasser Al-Qahtani	Saudi Arabia	
Hakan Sükür	Turkey	112
Zuhair Bakheet	United Arab Emirates	112
Diego Forlán	Uruguay	112
Carlos Valderrama	Colombia	112
Hussain Ali Baba	Bahrain	112
Rolando Fonseca	Costa Rica	111
Odelín Molina	Cuba	111
Wael Gomaa	Egypt	111
Nashat Akram	Iraq	111
Jarah Al-Ataiqi	Kuwait	111
Blas Pérez	Panama	111
Cesc Fàbregas	Spain	111
David Silva	Spain	111
Andriy Shevchenko	Ukraine	111
Abdulsalam Jumaa	United Arab Emirates	111
Claudio Reyna	United States	111
Kennedy Mweene	Zambia	111
Mehdi Mahdavikia	Iran	110
Yuli Nakazawa	Japan	110
Carmel Busuttil	Malta	110
John Arne Riise	Norway	110
Carlos Gamarra	Paraguay	110
Fernando Couto	Portugal	110
Kevin Kilbane	Republic of Ireland	110
Fernando Torres	Spain	110
Paul Caligiuri	United States	110
Mark Schwarzer	Australia	109
Sayed Mohammed Jaffer	Bahrain	109
Mauricio Solis	Costa Rica	109
Hawar Mulla Mohammed	Iraq	109
Rafael van der Vaart	Netherlands	109
Niclas Alexandersson	Sweden	109
Totchtawan Sripan	Thailand	109
José Rey	Venezuela	109
Alexis Sanchez	Chile	108
Álvaro Saborío	Costa Rica	108
Thomas Helveg	Denmark	108
Álex Aguinaga	Ecuador	108
Zinedine Zidane	France	108
Gábor Király	Hungary	108
Nohayr Al-Mutairi	Kuwait	108
Alberto García Aspe	Mexico	108
Bilal Mohammed	Qatar	108
Răzvan Raţ	Romania	108
Stern John	Trinidad & Tobago	108
Diego Godin	Uruguay	108
Carlos Bocanegra	United States	108
Jürgen Klinsmann	West Germany/Germany	108
Ahmed El-Kass	Egypt	107
Bobby Moore	England	107
Ashley Cole	England	107
Joel Lindpere	Estonia	107
Patrick Vieira	France	107
Jalal Hosseini	Iran	107
Jamal Mubarak	Kuwait	107
Miroslav Karhan	Slovakia	107
Aaron Mokoena	South Africa	107
Henrik Larsson	Sweden	107
Diego Simeone	Argentina	106
Rashad Sadygov	Azerbaijan	106
Ismail Abdul-Latif	Bahrain	106
Fan Zhiyi	PR China	106
Hao Haidong	PR China	106
Frank Lampard	England	106
Dmitri Kruglov	Estonia	106
Guillermo Ramirez	Guatemala	106
Shinji Okazaki	Japan	106
Francisco Javier Rodriguez	Mexico	106
Giovanni van Bronckhorst	Netherlands	106
Nani	Portugal	106
Muhsin Musabah	United Arab Emirates	106
Eric Wynalda	United States	106
Joseph Musonda	Zambia	106
Ildefons Lima	Andorra	105
Óscar Sonejee	Andorra	105
Lúcio	Brazil	105
Stiliyan Petrov	Bulgaria	105
Tomáš Rosický	Czech Republic	105
Bobby Charlton	England	105
Jonatan Johansson	Finland	105
Sami Hyypiä	Finland	105
Imants Bleidelis	Latvia	105
Franz Burgmeier	Liechtenstein	105
Khamis Al-Dosari	Saudi Arabia	105
Radhi Jaïdi	Tunisia	105
Jürgen Kohler	West Germany / Germany	105
Josip Šimunic	Croatia	105
Nader El-Sayed	Egypt	104
Billy Wright	England	104
Per Mertesacker	Germany	104
Gustavo Cabrera	Guatemala	104
Didier Drogba	Ivory Coast	104
Makoto Hasebe	Japan	104
Mihails Zemļinskis	Latvia	104
Dirk Kuyt	Netherlands	104
Aaron Hughes	Northern Ireland	104
Héctor Chumpitaz	Peru	104
Kim Tae-Young	South Korea	104
Stéphane Chapuisat	Switzerland	103
Andreas Herzog	Austria	103
Faouzi Aaish	Bahrain	103
Ioannis Okkas	Cyprus	103
Michael Laudrup	Denmark	103
Indrek Zelinski	Estonia	103
Didier Deschamps	France	103
Mahdi Kareem	Iraq	103
Máris Verpakovskis	Latvia	103
Mohammed Al-Jahani	Saudi Arabia	103
Hwang Sun-Hong	South Korea	103
Lee Dong-Gook	South Korea	103
Franz Beckenbauer	West Germany	103
Mario Yepes	Colombia	102
Ivica Olic	Croatia	102
Martin Jørgensen	Denmark	102
Aleksandr Dmitrijev	Estonia	102
Joseph Kamwendo	Malawi	102
Hani Al-Dhabit	Oman	102
Román Torres	Panama	102
Michal Żewłakow	Poland	102
Steve Staunton	Republic of Ireland	102
Kenny Dalglish	Scotland	102
Raúl	Spain	102
Bülent Korkmaz	Turkey	102
Mohamed Omar	United Arab Emirates	102
Jozy Altidore	USA	102
Savo Milošević	Fr Yugoslavia/Serbia & Montenegro/Serbia	102
Dejan Stankovic	Fr Yugoslavia/Serbia & Montenegro/Serbia	102
Christopher Katongo	Zambia	102
Husain Ahmed	Bahrain	101
Alyaksandr Kulchy	Belarus	101
Taffarel	Brazil	101
Gonzalo Jara	Chile	101
Leonel Álvarez	Colombia	101
Thomas Häßler	West Germany / Germany	101
Ulises De La Cruz	Ecuador	101
Ahmed Shobair	Egypt	101
József Bozsik	Hungary	101
Andranik Teymourian	Iran	101
Joe Brincat	Malta	101
Phillip Cocu	Netherlands	101
Robin van Persie	Netherlands	101
Vincent Enyeama	Nigeria	101
Joseph Yobo	Nigeria	101
Thorbjørn Svensson	Norway	101
Luis Tejada	Peru	101
László Bölöni	Romania	101
Vasiliy Berezutskiy	Russia	101
Oleg Blokhin	Soviet Union	101
Kasey Keller	United States	101
Thomas Sørenson	Denmark	101
Elijah Tana	Zambia	101
Lakhdar Belloumi	Algeria	100
Dani Alves	Brazil	100
Robinho	Brazil	100
Dario Šimic	Croatia	100
Hans-Jurgen Dörner	East Germany	100
Ulf Kirsten	East Germany / Germany	100
Luis Capurro	Ecuador	100
Mohamed Aboutrika	Egypt	100
Ari Hjelm	Finland	100
Didier Ovono	Gabon	100
Levan Kobiashvili	Georgia	100
Angelos Basinas	Greece	100
Carlos Pavón	Honduras	100
Rúnar Kristinsson	Iceland	100
Emad Mohammed	Iraq	100
Siaka Tiéné	Ivory Coast	100
Yaya Toure	Ivory Coast	100
Donovan Rcketts	Jamaica	100
Fahad Awadh	Kuwait	100
Igors Stepanovs	Latvia	100
Goce Sedloski	Macedonia	100
Henning Berg	Norway	100
Román Torres	Panama	100
Roberto Acuña	Paraguay	100
Denis Caniza	Paraguay	100
Jorge Soto	Peru	100
Grzegorz Lato	Poland	100
Damien Duff	Republic of Ireland	100
Nazri Bin Nasir	Singapore	100
Park Ji-Sung	South Korea	100
Carles Puyol	Spain	100
Piyapong Pue-on	Thailand	100
Joe-Max Moore	United States	100
Earnie Stewart	United States	100
Tony Meola	United States	100

EUROPEAN CUP WINS BY NATION

The recent Champions League successes of Barcelona and Real Madrid have secured Spain's claim to be the most successful European nation. Real Madrid's consecutive triumphs in the European Cup's first five competitions help Spain top the list, although England have had more successful clubs and Italy have had more finalists. In later years, the concentration of financial might in Europe's major leagues has increased the dominance of those nations. The era of the Champions League (beginning in 1992) has seen Spain register 10 wins, followed by Italy (five), England (four) and Germany (three).

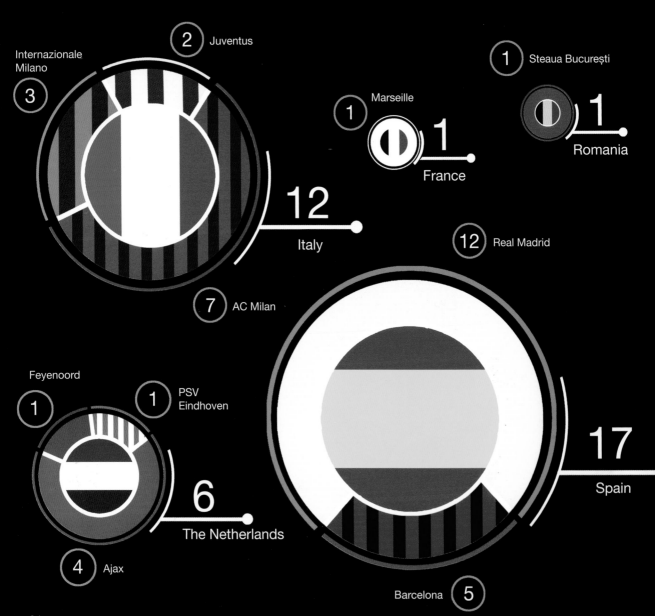

2 Juventus

Internazionale Milano

3

Marseille

1

1 Steaua București

1

1 Romania

12 Italy

12 Real Madrid

7 AC Milan

Feyenoord

1

1 PSV Eindhoven

6 The Netherlands

4 Ajax

17 Spain

Barcelona 5

1 Chelsea

1 Aston Viilla

Nottingham Forest

2

3

Manchester United

12 England

5 Liverpool

Hamburger SV

1 Borussia Dortmund

1

7 Germany

5 Bayern München

1 Celtic

1 Scotland

Porto 2

4 Portugal

1 Red Star Belgrade

2 Benfica

1 Yugoslavia

Source: Opta (June 2017)

UEFA CHAMPIONS LEAGUE DECADE-BY-DECADE PERFORMANCE

England remains the supplier of the biggest number of clubs to reach the semifinals of the European Cup and Champions League. Ten teams from the English league have made the final four—Manchester United (12 times), Liverpool (9), Chelsea (7), Leeds United (3), Arsenal (2), Nottingham Forest (2), Derby County (1), Manchester City (1), Tottenham Hotspur (1), and Aston Villa (1). France and Germany have provided eight different clubs, while seven Spanish clubs, six different Italian teams, and five Scottish have also made the final hurdle.

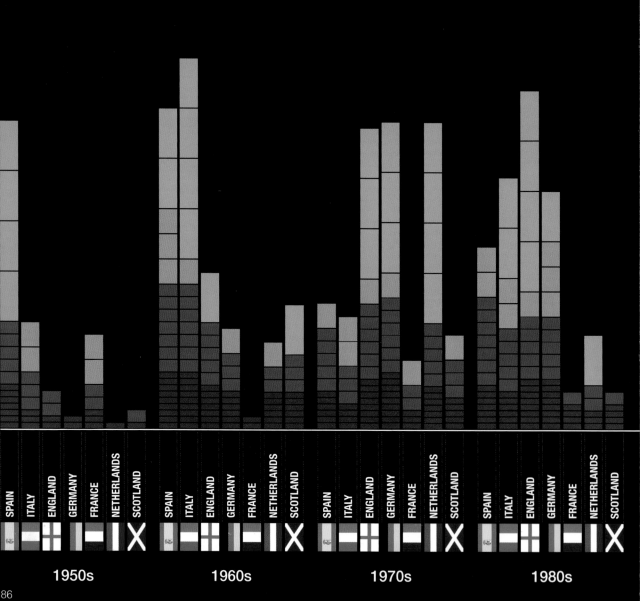

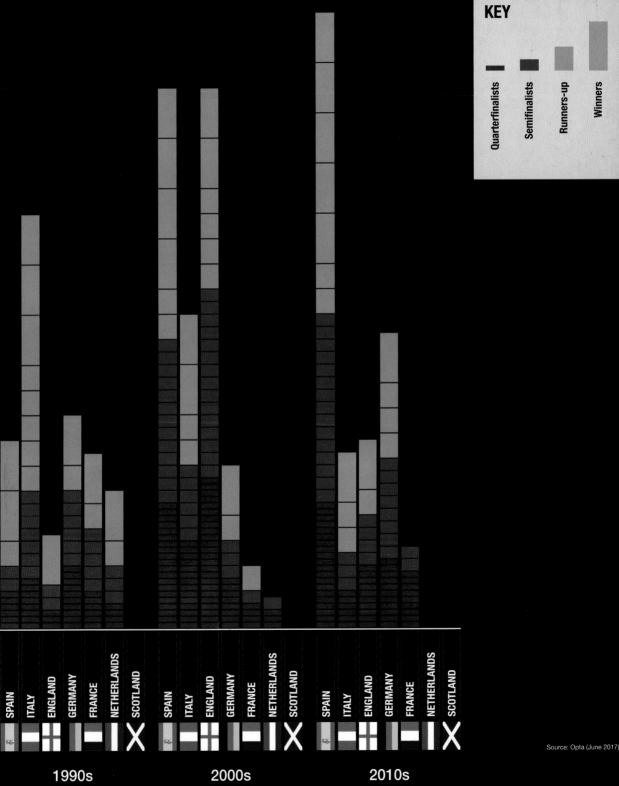

KEY

Quarterfinalists
Semifinalists
Runners-up
Winners

SPAIN ITALY ENGLAND GERMANY FRANCE NETHERLANDS SCOTLAND

SPAIN ITALY ENGLAND GERMANY FRANCE NETHERLANDS SCOTLAND

SPAIN ITALY ENGLAND GERMANY FRANCE NETHERLANDS SCOTLAND

1990s

2000s

2010s

Source: Opta (June 2017)

EUROPEAN CUP & CHAMPIONS LEAGUE RECORD GOALSCORERS

Real Madrid strikers have dominated the table of goalscorers in the Champions League and its forerunner, the European Cup. Legendary striker Alfredo di Stéfano led the table for many years before he was succeeded by Raúl in 2007. Barcelona's Lionel Messi managed to take the record in November 2014, only to be equaled by Cristiano Ronaldo a day later. The great rivals continue to spar for the crown, the Real striker scoring an astonishing nine goals in the 2017 knockout stages and notching his hundredth goal with a quarterfinal hat trick against Bayern München.

15 Manchester United
90 Real Madrid

1. Cristiano Ronaldo

105 Total goals scored

94 Barcelona

2. Lionel Messi

94 Total goals scored

5 Schalke
66 Real Madrid

3. Raúl

71 Total goals scored

13 Real Madrid   8 PSV
35 Manchester United

4. Ruud van Nistelrooy

56 Total goals scored

12 Lyon
39 Real Madrid

5. Karim Benzema

51 Total goals scored

8 Barcelona   7 Monaco
35 Arsenal

6. Thierry Henry

50 Total goals scored

49 Real Madrid

7. Alfredo Di Stéfano

49 Total goals scored

15 Dynamo Kiev   4 Chelsea
29 AC Milan

8. Andriy Shevchenko

48 Total goals scored

9 AC Milan   6 Inter
Paris Saint-
20 Germain

9. Zlatan Ibrahimović

48 Total goals scored

6 Ajax
4 Barcelona
3 Juventus

> **"I want to consistently play well and win titles...
> I'm only at the beginning."**

Cristiano Ronaldo

46 Benfica

10. Eusébio

46 Total goals scored

17 Juventus

29 AC Milan

10. Filippo Inzaghi

46 Total goals scored

5 Marseille   3 Galatasaray

36 Chelsea

12. Didier Drogba

44 Total goals scored

Source: Opta (June 2017)

EUROPEAN CUP & CHAMPIONS LEAGUE RECORD GOALSCORERS

42 Juventus

13. Alessandro Del Piero

42 Total goals scored

17 Borussia Dortmund

23 Bayern München

14. Robert Lewandowski

40 Total goals scored

39 Bayern München

15. Thomas Müller

39 Total goals scored

1 Honvéd

35 Real Madrid

16. Ferenc Puskás

36 Total goals scored

34 Bayern München

17. Gerd Müller

34 Total goals scored

9 Monaco

6 Valencia

17 Real Madrid

1 Liverpool

18. Fernando Morientes

33 Total goals scored

5 Real Madrid

25 AC Milan

19. Kaká

30 Total Goals Scored

30 Real Madrid

19. Paco Gento

30 Total Goals Scored

30 Manchester United

19. Wayne Rooney

30 Total Goals Scored

10 Inter

3 Chelsea

16 Barcelona

1 Mallorca

19. Samuel Eto'o

30 Total goals scored

3 PSV

2 Chelsea

23 Bayern München

1 Real Madrid

23. Arjen Robben

29 Total goals scored

4 Monaco

25 Juventus

23. David Trezeguet

29 Total goals scored

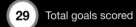

12 Deportivo de La Coruña

17 Bayern München

23. Roy Makaay

29 Total goals scored

9 Ajax

20 Barcelona

23. Patrick Kluivert

29 Total goals scored

28 Manchester United

27. Ryan Giggs

28 Total goals scored

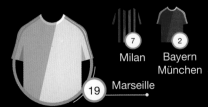

7 Milan

2 Bayern München

19 Marseille

27. Jean-Pierre Papin

28 Total goals scored

3 Olympiacos

2 AC Milan

22 Barcelona

29. Rivaldo

27 Total goals scored

5 Atlético de Madrid

22 Manchester City

29. Sergio Agüero

27 Total goals scored

" If he kicked the ball once, he scored two goals. "

Zoltán Czibor on his International teammate Ferenc Puskás, scorer of a first-half

hat trick for Real Madrid in the 1962 UEFA European Cup Final

Legendary Players

21 Liverpool

Steven Gerrard

18 Ajax

Johan Cruyff

17 Roma

Francesco Totti

17 Juventus

Michel Platini

9 Manchester United

George Best

UEFA CUP/EUROPA LEAGUE RECORDS BY NATION

The Europa League is UEFA's tournament for the continent's top teams who have failed to qualify for the Champions League, who have won their domestic cup or who have been eliminated in the early stages of the Champions League. It originated as the UEFA Cup in 1971–72 but, since 2009–10, the competition has been known as the UEFA Europa League. It now invites 177 different teams from 54 nations who enter the tournament at different stages. A team reaching the final from the first qualifying round would play a total of 23 matches. Atlético Madrid (2012) and Sevilla (2014) have both won the competition having began their journey in the third qualifying round.

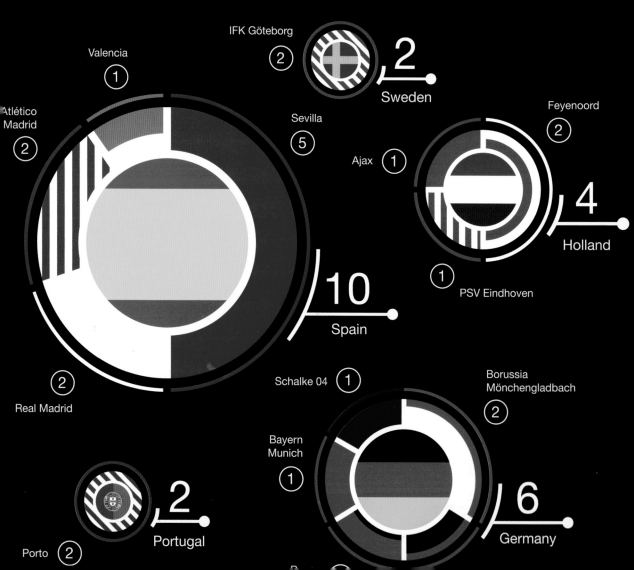

IFK Göteborg (2)

2 Sweden

Valencia (1)

Atlético Madrid (2)

Real Madrid (2)

Sevilla (5)

Ajax (1)

10 Spain

Feyenoord (2)

4 Holland

PSV Eindhoven (1)

Schalke 04 (1)

Borussia Mönchengladbach (2)

Bayern Munich (1)

6 Germany

Porto (2)

2 Portugal

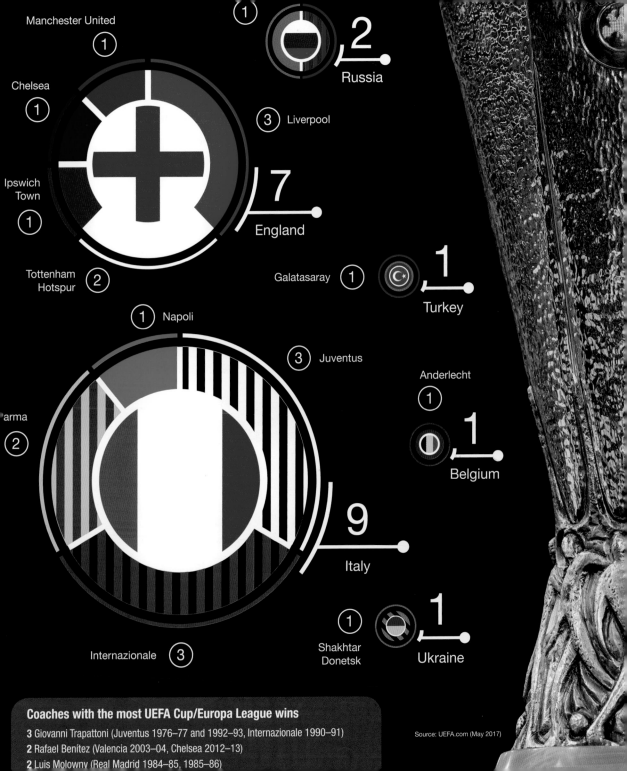

Manchester United ①

① ② Russia

Chelsea ①

③ Liverpool

Ipswich Town ①

7 England

Tottenham Hotspur ②

Galatasaray ① 1 Turkey

① Napoli

③ Juventus

Anderlecht ①

Parma ② 1 Belgium

9 Italy

Internazionale ③

① Shakhtar Donetsk 1 Ukraine

Coaches with the most UEFA Cup/Europa League wins

3 Giovanni Trapattoni (Juventus 1976–77 and 1992–93, Internazionale 1990–91)
2 Rafael Benítez (Valencia 2003–04, Chelsea 2012–13)
2 Luis Molowny (Real Madrid 1984–85, 1985–86)

Source: UEFA.com (May 2017)

MOST SUCCESSFUL EUROPEAN MANAGERS SINCE 1960

1	Bob Paisley
2	Carlo Ancelotti
3	Alex Ferguson
4	Helenio Herrera
5	José Mourinho
6	Nereo Rocco
7	José Villalonga
8	Luis Carniglia
9	Ottmar Hitzfeld
10	Miguel Muñoz

Source: Google (June 2017)

No matter how wealthy the club, it is a magnificent feat to guide a club to a league title. It is something else to take them to European success. Repeating the achievement takes a coach to legendary status. Separating the greatest from the great, however, is a tougher call. How do we rank Bob Paisley's European and League titles against Helenio Herrera's record? And, how much greater an achievement are the against-the-odds European triumphs of José Mourinho's Porto or Jock Stein's Celtic?

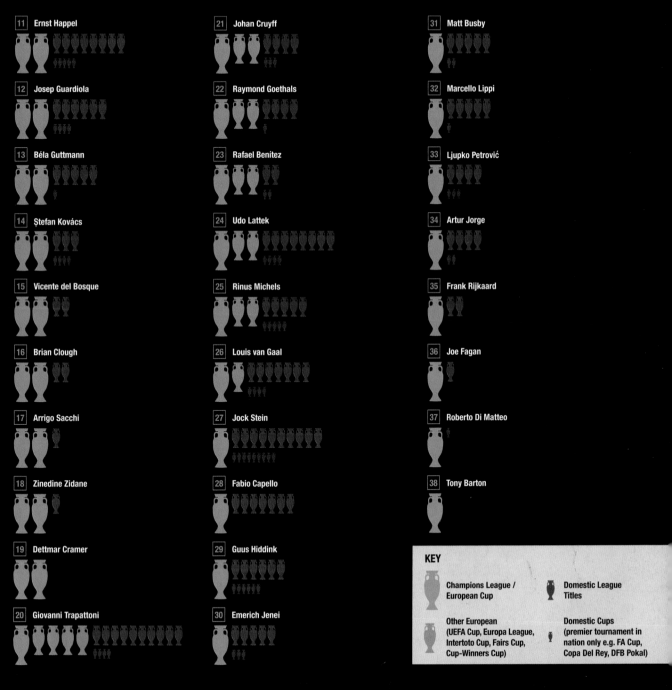

11 Ernst Happel

12 Josep Guardiola

13 Béla Guttmann

14 Ştefan Kovács

15 Vicente del Bosque

16 Brian Clough

17 Arrigo Sacchi

18 Zinedine Zidane

19 Dettmar Cramer

20 Giovanni Trapattoni

21 Johan Cruyff

22 Raymond Goethals

23 Rafael Benítez

24 Udo Lattek

25 Rinus Michels

26 Louis van Gaal

27 Jock Stein

28 Fabio Capello

29 Guus Hiddink

30 Emerich Jenei

31 Matt Busby

32 Marcello Lippi

33 Ljupko Petrović

34 Artur Jorge

35 Frank Rijkaard

36 Joe Fagan

37 Roberto Di Matteo

38 Tony Barton

KEY

Champions League / European Cup

Domestic League Titles

Other European (UEFA Cup, Europa League, Intertoto Cup, Fairs Cup, Cup-Winners Cup)

Domestic Cups (premier tournament in nation only e.g. FA Cup, Copa Del Rey, DFB Pokal)

COPA LIBERTADORES WINS BY NATION

Copa Libertadores de América is the most prestigious club tournament in South America. It is broadcast in over 130 countries and watched by more than a billion viewers. Played annually from February through qualifying, group stages and then a home and away knock-out stage, the tournament is now contested by 38 teams from 11 countries (including Mexican teams since 2000). At least three clubs from each country compete in the tournament with Argentina and Brazil each entitled to enter five teams.

The 2016 final between Colombia's Atletico Nacional and Independiente del Valle of Ecuador was the first between teams from countries on South America's Pacific coast and also the first in 25 years not to feature Argentinian or Brazilian sides.

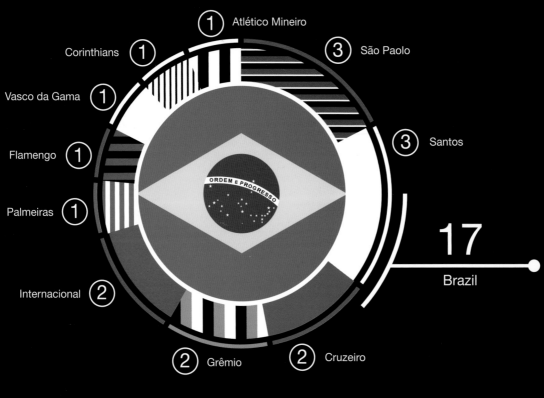

Atlético Mineiro ①
São Paolo ③
Corinthians ①
Santos ③
Vasco da Gama ①
Flamengo ①
17 Brazil
Palmeiras ①
Internacional ②
② Grêmio
② Cruzeiro

Colo-Colo ①
1 Chile

Peñarol ⑤
Nacional ③
8 Uruguay

96

1 Once Caldas

2 Atlético Nacional

3 Colombia

LDU Quito

1

1 Ecuador

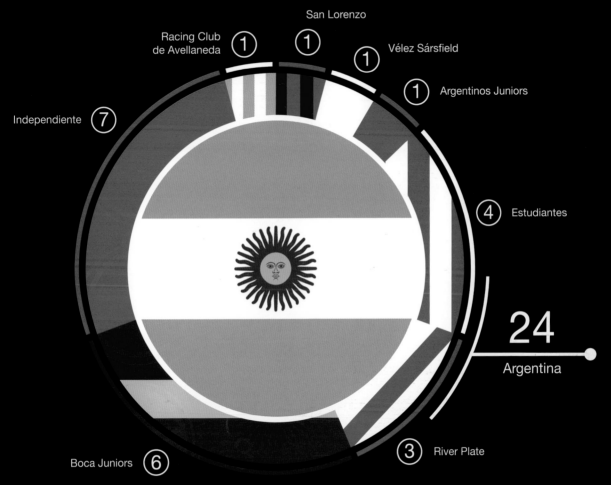

Racing Club de Avellaneda **1**

San Lorenzo **1**

Vélez Sársfield **1**

Argentinos Juniors **1**

Independiente **7**

Estudiantes **4**

24
Argentina

Boca Juniors **6**

River Plate **3**

Olimpia

3

3 Paraguay

Source: Opta (July 2016)

SOCCER RIVALRIES: PART 1

History, tradition, passion, and pride—these are the elements that come to the fore when great soccer rivals collide. Every nation has its rival teams. Some, such as Tottenham Hotspur and Arsenal, are born from geographical proximity—they're based four miles apart. France's Olympique de Marseille and Paris Saint-Germain may reside further apart, but the rivalry between the North and South, and the country's two biggest cities, makes the "Le Classique" derby just as bitterly fought.

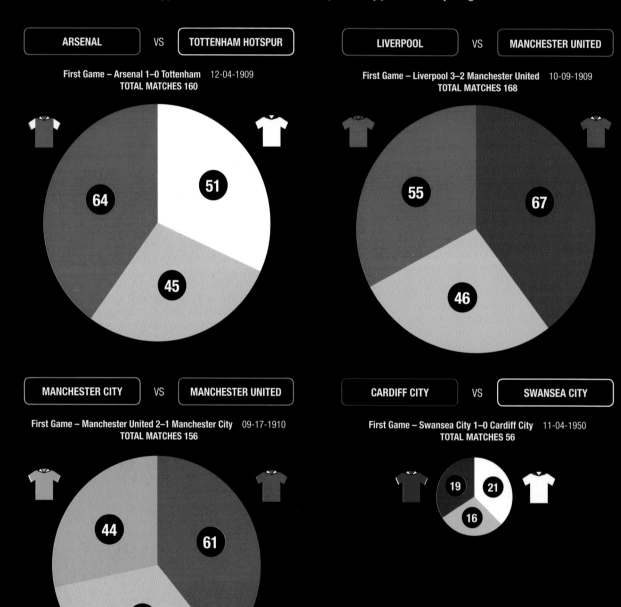

| ARSENAL | VS | TOTTENHAM HOTSPUR |

First Game – Arsenal 1–0 Tottenham   12-04-1909
TOTAL MATCHES 160

64   51   45

| LIVERPOOL | VS | MANCHESTER UNITED |

First Game – Liverpool 3–2 Manchester United   10-09-1909
TOTAL MATCHES 168

55   67   46

| MANCHESTER CITY | VS | MANCHESTER UNITED |

First Game – Manchester United 2–1 Manchester City   09-17-1910
TOTAL MATCHES 156

44   61   51

| CARDIFF CITY | VS | SWANSEA CITY |

First Game – Swansea City 1–0 Cardiff City   11-04-1950
TOTAL MATCHES 56

19   21   16

HAMBURGER SV   VS   BAYERN MÜNCHEN

First Game – Hamburger SV 0–4 Bayern München   10-20-1965
TOTAL MATCHES 104

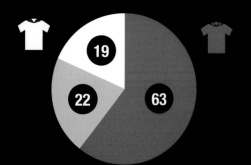

BAYERN MÜNCHEN   VS   BORUSSIA DORTMUND

First Game – Borussia Dortmund 2–0 Bayern München   10-16-1965
TOTAL MATCHES 96

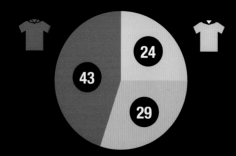

OLYMPIQUE DE MARSEILLE   VS   SAINT-ÉTIENNE

First Game – Saint-Étienne 1–0 Olympique de Marseille   11-06-1938
TOTAL MATCHES 104

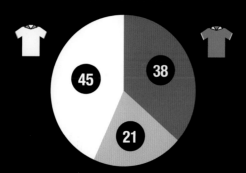

OLYMPIQUE LYONNAIS   VS   OLYMPIQUE DE MARSEILLE

First Game – Olympique Lyonnais 2–2 Olympique de Marseille   11-11-1951
TOTAL MATCHES 94

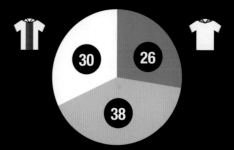

OLYMPIQUE DE MARSEILLE   VS   PARIS SAINT-GERMAIN

First Game – Olympique de Marseille 4–2 Paris Saint-Germain   12-12-1971
TOTAL MATCHES 76

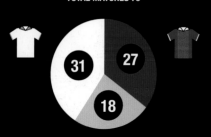

> **"**On derby day in Manchester the city is cut in two. The Blues and the Reds invade the street and if your team wins the city belongs to you.**"**

Eric Cantona, Manchester United

Source: Opta (May 2017)

SOCCER RIVALRIES: PART 2

"The Derby" is an unofficial competition recognized across the soccer world. It signifies a two-match battle between two rival teams each season, where the victorious side wins hometown pride and temporary bragging rights over the other. Italy plays host to some of the sport's more heated rivalries, the oldest being the *Derby della Lanterna* in which Genoa duel Sampdoria, while *Derby d'Italia* brings together Internazionale Milano and Juventus. Meanwhile, in Spain's La Liga, the dominance of powerhouses Barcelona and Real Madrid has fired *El Clásico*, a rivalry constantly simmering through decades of interconnected history, politics, and geography.

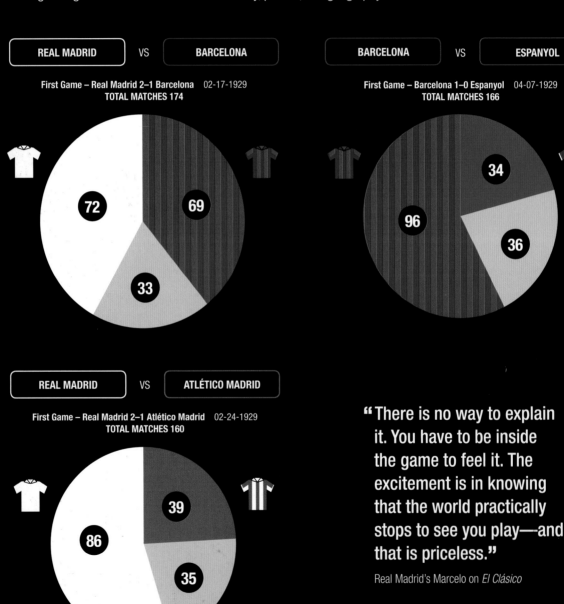

| REAL MADRID | VS | BARCELONA |

First Game – Real Madrid 2–1 Barcelona   02-17-1929
TOTAL MATCHES 174

72   69   33

| BARCELONA | VS | ESPANYOL |

First Game – Barcelona 1–0 Espanyol   04-07-1929
TOTAL MATCHES 166

34   96   36

| REAL MADRID | VS | ATLÉTICO MADRID |

First Game – Real Madrid 2–1 Atlético Madrid   02-24-1929
TOTAL MATCHES 160

39   86   35

" There is no way to explain it. You have to be inside the game to feel it. The excitement is in knowing that the world practically stops to see you play—and that is priceless."

Real Madrid's Marcelo on *El Clásico*

| INTERNAZIONALE MILANO | VS | **JUVENTUS** | | INTERNAZIONALE MILANO | VS | AC MILAN |

First Game – Internazionale Milano 2–1 Juventus   02-02-1930
TOTAL MATCHES 168

First Game – Internazionale Milano 2–1 AC Milan   11-10-1929
TOTAL MATCHES 166

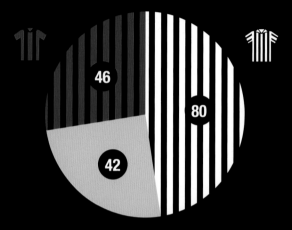

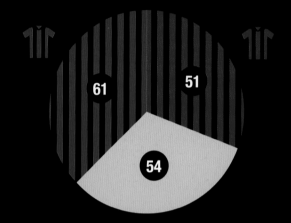

| SS LAZIO | VS | AS ROMA | | JUVENTUS | VS | TORINO FC |

First Game – AS Roma 1–0 SS Lazio   12-08-1929
TOTAL MATCHES 146

First Game – Juventus 0–0 Torino FC   11-24-1929
TOTAL MATCHES 144

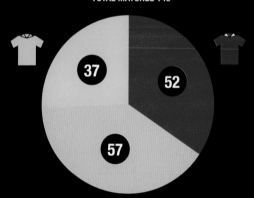

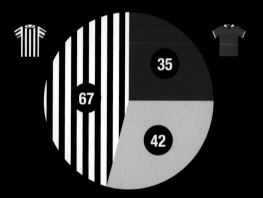

| GENOA | VS | UC SAMPDORIA |

First Game – Genoa 2–1 UC Sampdoria   10-06-1935
TOTAL MATCHES 68

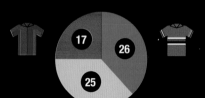

Source: Opta (May 2017)

SOCCER RIVALRIES: PART 3

Soccer fans know that it's the tough and tense matches between fierce rivals that really heighten their emotions during a season. AFC Ajax vs Feyenoord, for example, has become the most ferocious game in the Netherlands as the capital's city slickers do battle with the working-class port laborers. In Turkey's capital Istanbul, neighbors Fenerbahçe S.K. and Galatasaray S.K. continue a rivalry more than 100 years old. Across the Atlantic Ocean, it is New York City FC and the New York Red Bulls that have developed a more recent mutual antagonism after just a handful of matches.

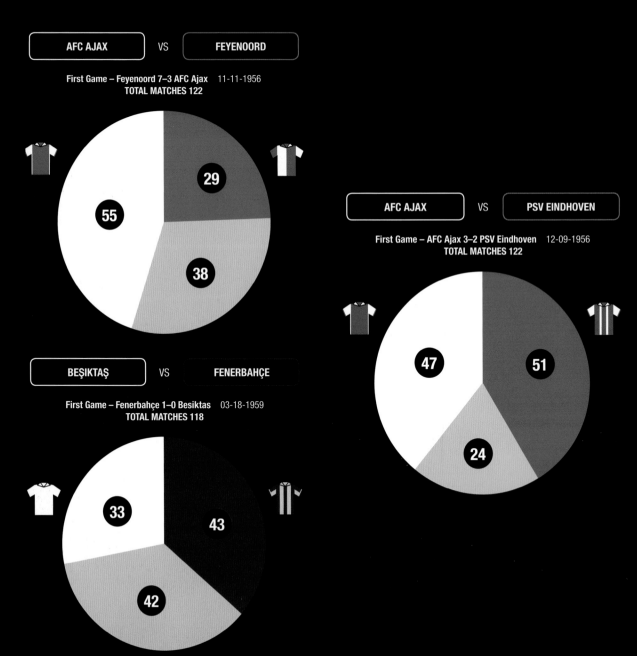

AFC AJAX VS **FEYENOORD**

First Game – Feyenoord 7–3 AFC Ajax   11-11-1956
TOTAL MATCHES 122

55   29   38

AFC AJAX VS **PSV EINDHOVEN**

First Game – AFC Ajax 3–2 PSV Eindhoven   12-09-1956
TOTAL MATCHES 122

47   51   24

BEŞİKTAŞ VS **FENERBAHÇE**

First Game – Fenerbahçe 1–0 Besiktas   03-18-1959
TOTAL MATCHES 118

33   43   42

It's nowhere near as steeped in history as El Clasico or the Old Firm Derby, but New York is growing its own bitterly fought rivalry. The Hudson River Derby pitches the New York Red Bulls, who play in NJ, against their neighbors NYCFC, who set up home in Yankee Stadium in the Bronx. New York Red Bulls had been established for nearly 20 years (with sworn enemies in Washington's DC United) before neighbors NYCFC arrived in 2015. They dealt out four beatings before the newcomers finally tasted victory.

FENERBAHÇE VS GALATASARAY

First Game – Fenerbahçe 1–0 Galatasaray   12-17-1959
TOTAL MATCHES 120

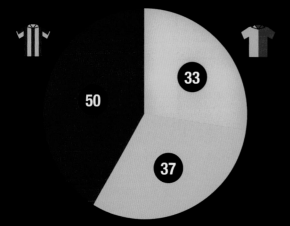

BEŞIKTAŞ VS GALATASARAY

First Game – Besiktas 1–0 Galatasaray   12-02-1959
TOTAL MATCHES 118

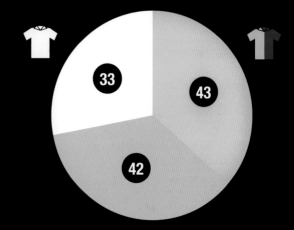

LA GALAXY VS SAN JOSE EARTHQUAKES

First Game – LA Galaxy 2–0 San Jose Earthquakes   04-03-2008
TOTAL MATCHES 27

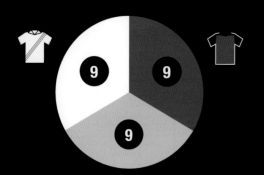

NEW YORK CITY FC VS NEW YORK RED BULLS

First Game – New York Red Bulls 2–1 New York City FC   05-10-2015
TOTAL MATCHES 7

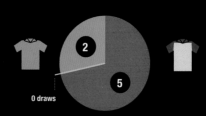

0 draws

Source: Opta (May 2017)

PREMIER LEAGUE TITLE WINNERS

The Premier League was formed in 1992. It is far and away the wealthiest league, most of the clubs featuring among the top-50 richest soccer brands in the world. Since its formation, the Premier League has been contested by 47 clubs, and games are broadcast in more than 200 countries. For many years the title was fought over by the "big four"—Manchester United, Arsenal, Chelsea, and Liverpool—but Manchester City and, more recently, Tottenham Hotspur have joined them. Even more surprising, then, was Leicester City's triumph against all odds in 2016.

Note: For the first three seasons of its existence, the Premier League comprised 22 teams rather than 20, as became the norm.

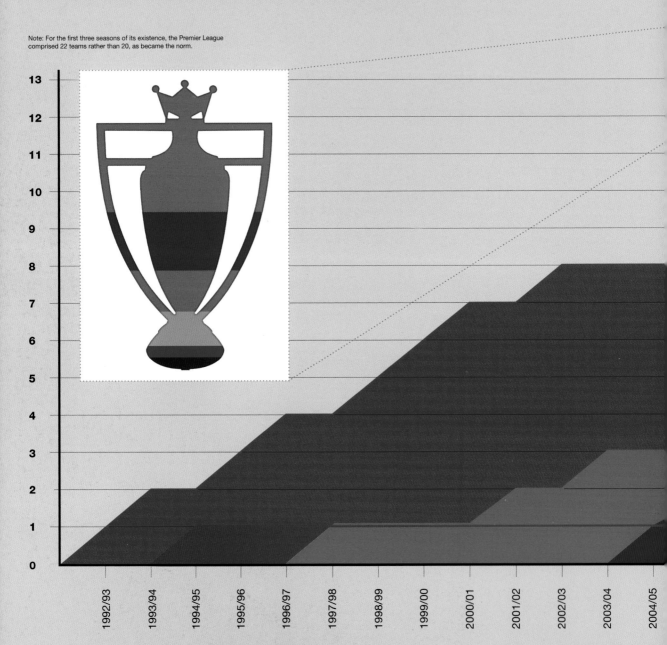

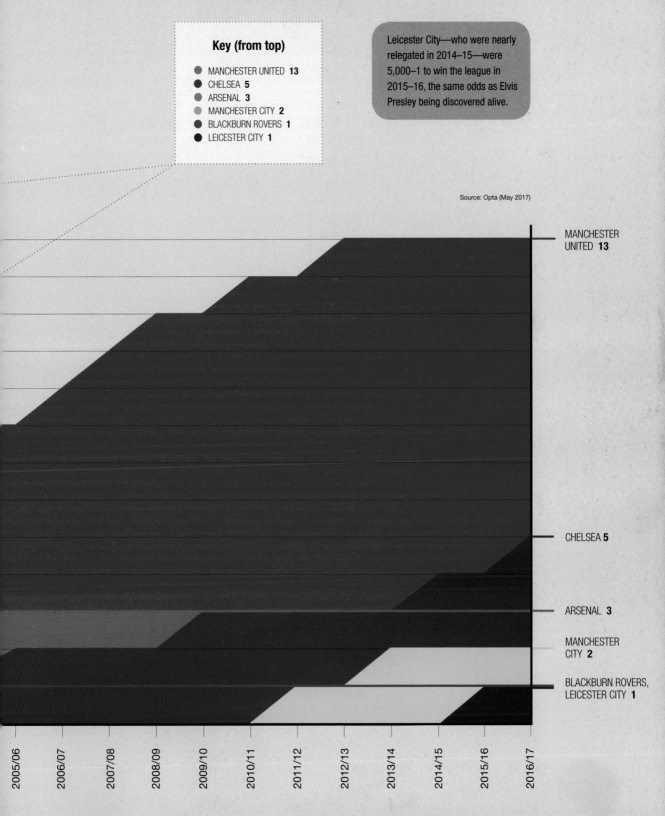

Key (from top)

● MANCHESTER UNITED **13**
● CHELSEA **5**
● ARSENAL **3**
● MANCHESTER CITY **2**
● BLACKBURN ROVERS **1**
● LEICESTER CITY **1**

Leicester City—who were nearly relegated in 2014–15—were 5,000–1 to win the league in 2015–16, the same odds as Elvis Presley being discovered alive.

Source: Opta (May 2017)

MANCHESTER UNITED **13**

CHELSEA **5**

ARSENAL **3**

MANCHESTER CITY **2**

BLACKBURN ROVERS, LEICESTER CITY **1**

2005/06 2006/07 2007/08 2008/09 2009/10 2010/11 2011/12 2012/13 2013/14 2014/15 2015/16 2016/17

PREMIER LEAGUE EVER-PRESENTS

The relegation of Aston Villa to the Championship in 2016 reduced the survivors from the founding season of the Premier League to six. Of the 47 teams that have played in the top league, all but these six have spent time in lower leagues—Coventry City, Swindon Town, Blackpool, Portsmouth, and Bradford City have all subsequently fallen as far as the fourth tier. Brighton & Hove Albion and Huddersfield Town's 2017 promotion to the top flight will make them the 48th and 49th clubs to play in the Premier League.

Source: Opta (May 2017)

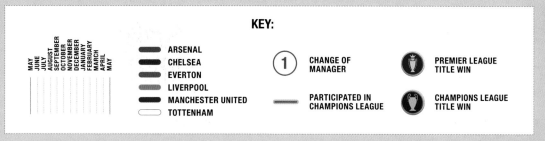

Source: Opta May 2017

Note: For the first three seasons of its existence, the Premier League comprised
22 teams rather than 20, as became the established contingent.

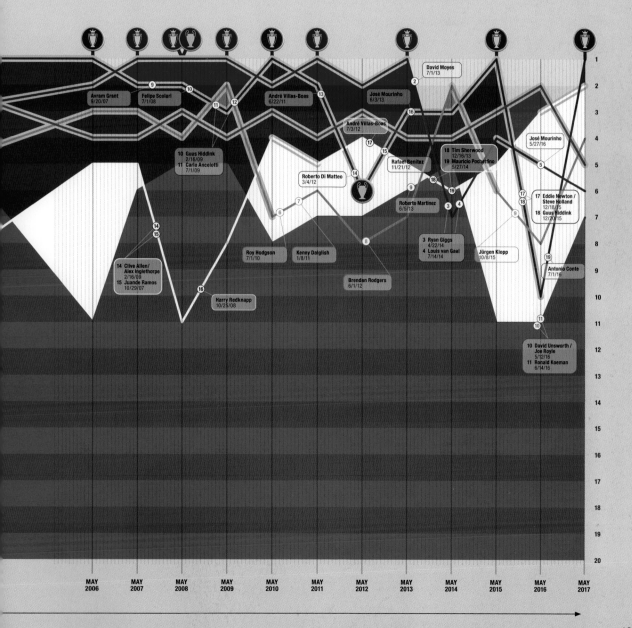

PREMIER LEAGUE GAME WINS PER CLUB

The Premier League thrives on the ability of any of its teams to beat another. Although the elite teams generally dominate the top of the table, they cannot be sure of winning every game. The league winners collect around 27 wins in a season, Chelsea holding the record with 30 wins (2016–17). Consecutive runs of eight or more victories are rare, Arsenal setting the bar at 14 in 2002.

Source: Opta (May 2017)

Club	Wins
IPSWICH TOWN	57
NOTTINGHAM FOREST	60
DERBY COUNTY	68
BIRMINGHAM CITY	73
SWANSEA CITY	74
PORTSMOUTH	79
QUEENS PARK RANGERS	81
WIGAN ATHLETIC	85
CRYSTAL PALACE	86
NORWICH CITY	89
CHARLTON ATHLETIC	93
WIMBLEDON	99
COVENTRY CITY	99
SHEFFIELD WEDNESDAY	101
WEST BROMWICH ALBION	106
STOKE CITY	109
LEICESTER CITY	130
BOLTON WANDERERS	149
FULHAM	150
SUNDERLAND	138
MIDDLESBROUGH	165
LEEDS UNITED	189
SOUTHAMPTON	222
BLACKBURN ROVERS	262
WEST HAM UNITED	265
ASTON VILLA	316

“Of course the Premier League is the most difficult league in the world because it’s so even. I think you can’t really compare other leagues with the Premier League. In the Premier League, every team can beat every team, and in football, that’s something where you can have surprises.”

Mesut Özil, Arsenal

Under 50 Wins

HULL CITY **41**
WATFORD **34**
WOLVERHAMPTON WANDERERS **32**
READING **32**
SHEFFIELD UNITED **32**
BURNLEY **26**
BOURNEMOUTH **23**
OLDHAM ATHLETIC **22**
BRADFORD CITY **14**
BLACKPOOL **10**
BARNSLEY **10**
CARDIFF CITY **7**
SWINDON TOWN **5**

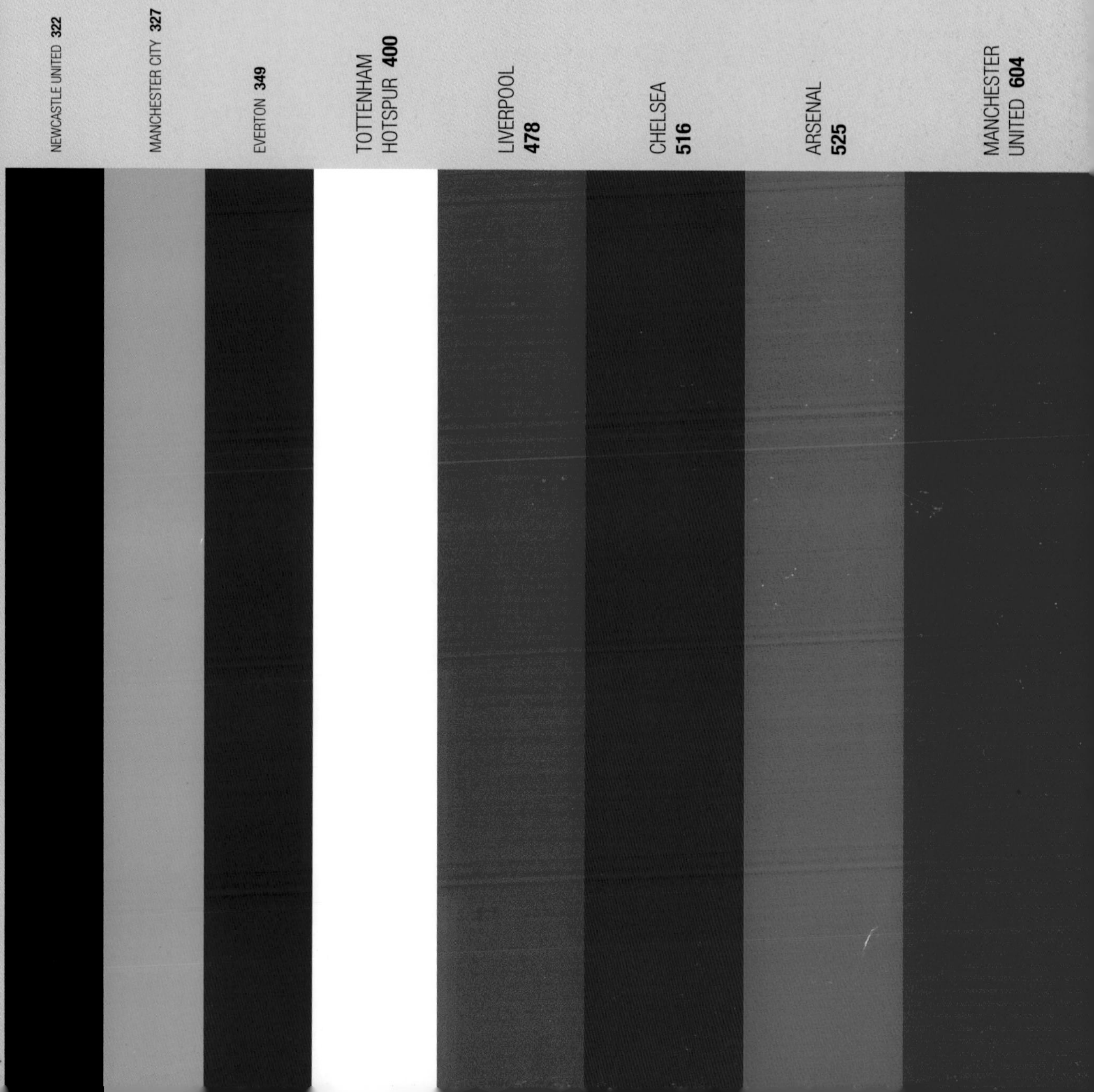
NEWCASTLE UNITED 322
MANCHESTER CITY 327
EVERTON 349
TOTTENHAM HOTSPUR 400
LIVERPOOL 478
CHELSEA 516
ARSENAL 525
MANCHESTER UNITED 604

PREMIER LEAGUE GOALS PER CLUB

The elite list of Premier League goalscorers changes very slowly—very few of the 100 goal club are still playing. But there are some exceptions. Jermain Defoe moved into the top 10 with his Indian summer at Sunderland, Peter Crouch hit his 100th goal in February 2017 and Sergio Agüero surged up the list with 44 goals in two seasons (2015–16 to 2016–17). Who might be next to join them? The smart money is on Romelu Lukaku (85), Harry Kane (78), or Christian Benteke (66).

" Alan Shearer is the greatest English center-forward there has ever been without a shadow of a doubt; he's a very, very special player. He makes average balls into great balls. He's the scorer of every type of goal going."

Graeme Souness

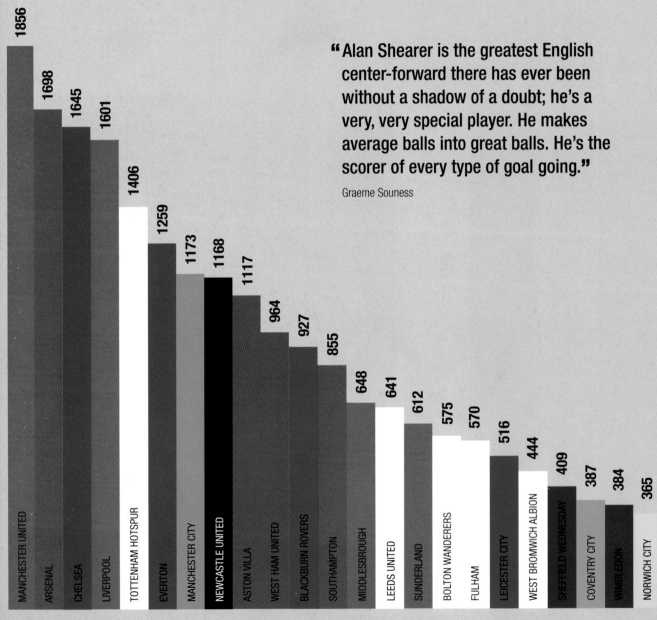

Club	Goals
MANCHESTER UNITED	1856
ARSENAL	1698
CHELSEA	1645
LIVERPOOL	1601
TOTTENHAM HOTSPUR	1406
EVERTON	1259
MANCHESTER CITY	1173
NEWCASTLE UNITED	1168
ASTON VILLA	1117
WEST HAM UNITED	964
BLACKBURN ROVERS	927
SOUTHAMPTON	855
MIDDLESBROUGH	648
LEEDS UNITED	641
SUNDERLAND	612
BOLTON WANDERERS	575
FULHAM	570
LEICESTER CITY	516
WEST BROMWICH ALBION	444
SHEFFIELD WEDNESDAY	409
COVENTRY CITY	387
WIMBLEDON	384
NORWICH CITY	365

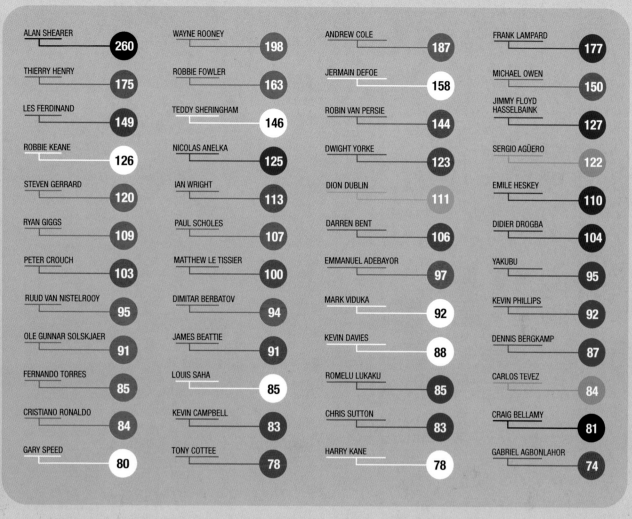

ALAN SHEARER **260**

THIERRY HENRY **175**

LES FERDINAND **149**

ROBBIE KEANE **126**

STEVEN GERRARD **120**

RYAN GIGGS **109**

PETER CROUCH **103**

RUUD VAN NISTELROOY **95**

OLE GUNNAR SOLSKJAER **91**

FERNANDO TORRES **85**

CRISTIANO RONALDO **84**

GARY SPEED **80**

WAYNE ROONEY **198**

ROBBIE FOWLER **163**

TEDDY SHERINGHAM **146**

NICOLAS ANELKA **125**

IAN WRIGHT **113**

PAUL SCHOLES **107**

MATTHEW LE TISSIER **100**

DIMITAR BERBATOV **94**

JAMES BEATTIE **91**

LOUIS SAHA **85**

KEVIN CAMPBELL **83**

TONY COTTEE **78**

ANDREW COLE **187**

JERMAIN DEFOE **158**

ROBIN VAN PERSIE **144**

DWIGHT YORKE **123**

DION DUBLIN **111**

DARREN BENT **106**

EMMANUEL ADEBAYOR **97**

MARK VIDUKA **92**

KEVIN DAVIES **88**

ROMELU LUKAKU **85**

CHRIS SUTTON **83**

HARRY KANE **78**

FRANK LAMPARD **177**

MICHAEL OWEN **150**

JIMMY FLOYD HASSELBAINK **127**

SERGIO AGÜERO **122**

EMILE HESKEY **110**

DIDIER DROGBA **104**

YAKUBU **95**

KEVIN PHILLIPS **92**

DENNIS BERGKAMP **87**

CARLOS TEVEZ **84**

CRAIG BELLAMY **81**

GABRIEL AGBONLAHOR **74**

Source: Opta (May 2017)
Color relates to the team the player scored the highest number of goals for.

STOKE CITY **363**

CHARLTON ATHLETIC **342**

QUEENS PARK RANGERS **339**

WIGAN ATHLETIC **316**

PORTSMOUTH **292**

BIRMINGHAM CITY **273**

DERBY COUNTY **271**

NOTTINGHAM FOREST **229**

IPSWICH TOWN **219**

HULL CITY **181**

WOLVERHAMPTON WANDERERS **156**

WATFORD **144**

READING **136**

SHEFFIELD UNITED **128**

BURNLEY **109**

OLDHAM ATHLETIC **105**

BOURNEMOUTH **100**

BRADFORD CITY **68**

BLACKPOOL **55**

SWINDON TOWN **47**

BARNSLEY **37**

CARDIFF CITY **32**

PREMIER LEAGUE PLAYER APPEARANCES

With only 38 Premier League games played a season, a player needs a long career at the highest level to get anywhere near this list. It helps, of course, to start young (you'll need at least 12 seasons in the first team), stay injury-free and play into your 30s. Even then, it's tough. The youngest to play was Fulham's Matthew Brigg, 16, and 65 days when he made his debut in 2007, he amassed a total of 30 appearances. No wonder only around 100 players have notched up over 300 appearances.

KEY:

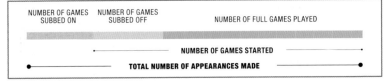

NUMBER OF GAMES SUBBED ON	NUMBER OF GAMES SUBBED OFF	NUMBER OF FULL GAMES PLAYED

NUMBER OF GAMES STARTED

TOTAL NUMBER OF APPEARANCES MADE

* Active up to and including season 2016–17

Source: Opta (May 2017)

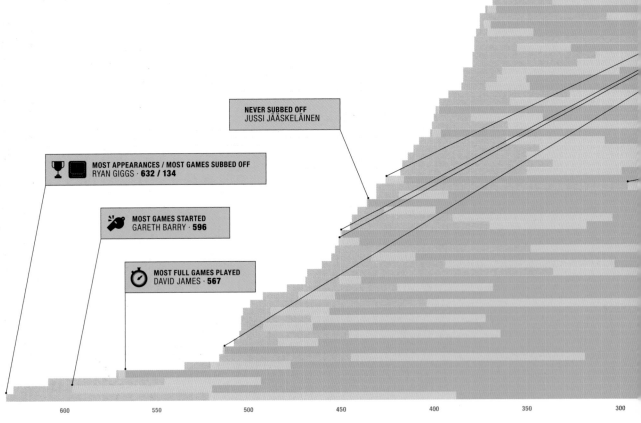

NEVER SUBBED OFF
JUSSI JÄÄSKELÄINEN

MOST APPEARANCES / MOST GAMES SUBBED OFF
RYAN GIGGS · **632 / 134**

MOST GAMES STARTED
GARETH BARRY · **596**

MOST FULL GAMES PLAYED
DAVID JAMES · **567**

600   550   500   450   400   350   300

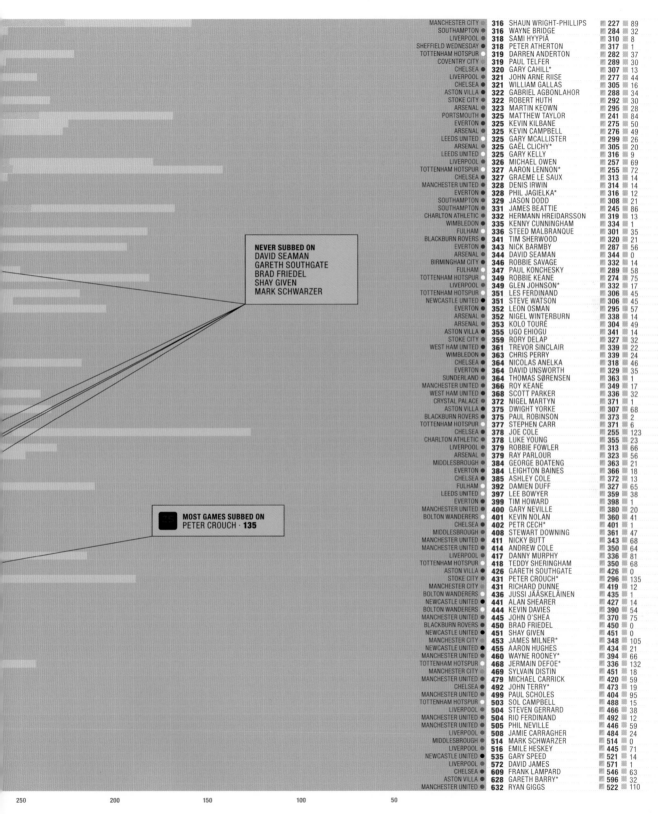

Team		Player		
MANCHESTER CITY	316	SHAUN WRIGHT-PHILLIPS	227	89
SOUTHAMPTON	316	WAYNE BRIDGE	284	32
LIVERPOOL	318	SAMI HYYPIÄ	310	8
SHEFFIELD WEDNESDAY	318	PETER ATHERTON	317	1
TOTTENHAM HOTSPUR	319	DARREN ANDERTON	282	37
COVENTRY CITY	319	PAUL TELFER	289	30
CHELSEA	320	GARY CAHILL*	307	13
LIVERPOOL	321	JOHN ARNE RIISE	277	44
CHELSEA	321	WILLIAM GALLAS	305	16
ASTON VILLA	322	GABRIEL AGBONLAHOR	288	34
STOKE CITY	322	ROBERT HUTH	292	30
ARSENAL	323	MARTIN KEOWN	295	28
PORTSMOUTH	325	MATTHEW TAYLOR	241	84
EVERTON	325	KEVIN KILBANE	275	50
ARSENAL	325	KEVIN CAMPBELL	276	49
LEEDS UNITED	325	GARY MCALLISTER	299	26
ARSENAL	325	GAËL CLICHY*	305	20
LEEDS UNITED	325	GARY KELLY	316	9
LIVERPOOL	326	MICHAEL OWEN	257	69
TOTTENHAM HOTSPUR	327	AARON LENNON*	255	72
CHELSEA	327	GRAEME LE SAUX	313	14
MANCHESTER UNITED	328	DENIS IRWIN	314	14
EVERTON	328	PHIL JAGIELKA*	316	12
SOUTHAMPTON	329	JASON DODD	308	21
SOUTHAMPTON	331	JAMES BEATTIE	245	86
CHARLTON ATHLETIC	332	HERMANN HREIDARSSON	319	13
WIMBLEDON	335	KENNY CUNNINGHAM	334	1
FULHAM	336	STEED MALBRANQUE	301	35
BLACKBURN ROVERS	341	TIM SHERWOOD	320	21
EVERTON	343	NICK BARMBY	287	56
ARSENAL	344	DAVID SEAMAN	344	0
BIRMINGHAM CITY	346	ROBBIE SAVAGE	332	14
FULHAM	347	PAUL KONCHESKY	289	58
TOTTENHAM HOTSPUR	349	ROBBIE KEANE	274	75
LIVERPOOL	349	GLEN JOHNSON*	332	17
TOTTENHAM HOTSPUR	351	LES FERDINAND	306	45
NEWCASTLE UNITED	351	STEVE WATSON	306	45
EVERTON	352	LEON OSMAN	295	57
ARSENAL	352	NIGEL WINTERBURN	338	14
ARSENAL	353	KOLO TOURÉ	304	49
ASTON VILLA	355	UGO EHIOGU	341	14
STOKE CITY	359	RORY DELAP	327	32
WEST HAM UNITED	361	TREVOR SINCLAIR	339	22
WIMBLEDON	363	CHRIS PERRY	339	24
CHELSEA	364	NICOLAS ANELKA	318	46
EVERTON	364	DAVID UNSWORTH	329	35
SUNDERLAND	364	THOMAS SØRENSEN	363	1
MANCHESTER UNITED	366	ROY KEANE	349	17
WEST HAM UNITED	368	SCOTT PARKER	336	32
CRYSTAL PALACE	372	NIGEL MARTYN	371	1
ASTON VILLA	375	DWIGHT YORKE	307	68
BLACKBURN ROVERS	375	PAUL ROBINSON	373	2
TOTTENHAM HOTSPUR	377	STEPHEN CARR	371	6
CHELSEA	378	JOE COLE	255	123
CHARLTON ATHLETIC	378	LUKE YOUNG	355	23
LIVERPOOL	379	ROBBIE FOWLER	313	66
ARSENAL	379	RAY PARLOUR	323	56
MIDDLESBROUGH	384	GEORGE BOATENG	363	21
EVERTON	384	LEIGHTON BAINES	366	18
CHELSEA	385	ASHLEY COLE	372	13
FULHAM	392	DAMIEN DUFF	327	65
LEEDS UNITED	397	LEE BOWYER	359	38
EVERTON	399	TIM HOWARD	398	1
MANCHESTER UNITED	400	GARY NEVILLE	380	20
BOLTON WANDERERS	401	KEVIN NOLAN	360	41
CHELSEA	402	PETR CECH*	401	1
MIDDLESBROUGH	408	STEWART DOWNING	361	47
MANCHESTER UNITED	411	NICKY BUTT	343	68
MANCHESTER UNITED	414	ANDREW COLE	350	64
LIVERPOOL	417	DANNY MURPHY	336	81
TOTTENHAM HOTSPUR	418	TEDDY SHERINGHAM	350	68
ASTON VILLA	426	GARETH SOUTHGATE	426	0
STOKE CITY	431	PETER CROUCH*	296	135
MANCHESTER CITY	431	RICHARD DUNNE	419	12
BOLTON WANDERERS	436	JUSSI JÄÄSKELÄINEN	435	1
NEWCASTLE UNITED	441	ALAN SHEARER	427	14
BOLTON WANDERERS	444	KEVIN DAVIES	390	54
MANCHESTER UNITED	445	JOHN O'SHEA	370	75
BLACKBURN ROVERS	450	BRAD FRIEDEL	450	0
NEWCASTLE UNITED	451	SHAY GIVEN	451	0
MANCHESTER CITY	453	JAMES MILNER*	348	105
NEWCASTLE UNITED	455	AARON HUGHES	434	21
MANCHESTER UNITED	460	WAYNE ROONEY*	394	66
TOTTENHAM HOTSPUR	468	JERMAIN DEFOE*	336	132
MANCHESTER CITY	469	SYLVAIN DISTIN	451	18
MANCHESTER UNITED	479	MICHAEL CARRICK	420	59
CHELSEA	492	JOHN TERRY*	473	19
MANCHESTER UNITED	499	PAUL SCHOLES	404	95
TOTTENHAM HOTSPUR	503	SOL CAMPBELL	488	15
LIVERPOOL	504	STEVEN GERRARD	466	38
MANCHESTER UNITED	504	RIO FERDINAND	492	12
MANCHESTER UNITED	505	PHIL NEVILLE	446	59
LIVERPOOL	508	JAMIE CARRAGHER	484	24
MIDDLESBROUGH	514	MARK SCHWARZER	514	0
LIVERPOOL	516	EMILE HESKEY	445	71
NEWCASTLE UNITED	535	GARY SPEED	521	14
LIVERPOOL	572	DAVID JAMES	571	1
CHELSEA	609	FRANK LAMPARD	546	63
ASTON VILLA	628	GARETH BARRY*	596	32
MANCHESTER UNITED	632	RYAN GIGGS	522	110

NEVER SUBBED ON
DAVID SEAMAN
GARETH SOUTHGATE
BRAD FRIEDEL
SHAY GIVEN
MARK SCHWARZER

MOST GAMES SUBBED ON
PETER CROUCH · 135

250   200   150   100   50

PREMIER LEAGUE FOULS AND CARDS

The number of bookings and dismissals has been gradually increasing since the Premier League began in 1992. Although referee clampdowns and new rules to protect players from reckless challenges have increased the tally, statistics reveal a large number of indiscretions are due to rash decisions and second offenses. It appears that as the game gets quicker, and more skillful, tackling becomes a much riskier business. So, hats off to Ryan Giggs. He managed 632 Premier League appearances without seeing red once.

CHELSEA 1,536   EVERTON 1,465   ARSENAL 1,417   TOTTENHAM HOTSPUR 1,397   ASTON VILLA 1,362

MANCHESTER UNITED 1,336   WEST HAM UNITED 1,321   LIVERPOOL 1,220   NEWCASTLE UNITED 1,220   MANCHESTER CITY 1,158

BLACKBURN ROVERS 1,111   SUNDERLAND 1,095   SOUTHAMPTON 996   MIDDLESBROUGH 973   BOLTON WANDERERS 845

LEEDS UNITED 790   FULHAM 708   WEST BROMWICH ALBION 645   LEICESTER CITY 619   STOKE CITY 617

DERBY COUNTY 538   WIGAN ATHLETIC 513   COVENTRY CITY 481   CRYSTAL PALACE 477   BIRMINGHAM CITY 428

CHARLTON ATHLETIC 408   WIMBLEDON 407   PORTSMOUTH 398   NORWICH CITY 394   QUEENS PARK RANGERS 364

SHEFFIELD WEDNESDAY 341   HULL CITY 328   SWANSEA CITY 318   NOTTINGHAM FOREST 287   WATFORD 272

WOLVERHAMPTON WANDERERS 255   BURNLEY 186   IPSWICH TOWN 183   SHEFFIELD UNITED 170   READING 142

BRADFORD CITY 113   BOURNEMOUTH 105   OLDHAM ATHLETIC 70   BARNSLEY 66   CARDIFF CITY 50

BLACKPOOL 47   SWINDON TOWN 39

EVERTON 86

ARSENAL 84

NEWCASTLE UNITED 78

BLACKBURN ROVERS 76

CHELSEA 74

WEST HAM UNITED 68

MANCHESTER CITY 62

SUNDERLAND 61

MANCHESTER UNITED 60

TOTTENHAM HOTSPUR 59

ASTON VILLA 56

LIVERPOOL 54

SOUTHAMPTON 49

MIDDLESBROUGH 45

BOLTON WANDERERS 43

FULHAM 36

LEICESTER CITY 36

STOKE CITY 30

WEST BROMWICH ALBION 30

LEEDS UNITED 28

WIGAN ATHLETIC 27

WIMBLEDON 26

QUEENS PARK RANGERS 26

BIRMINGHAM CITY 26

COVENTRY CITY 24

CHARLTON ATHLETIC 24

HULL CITY 24

PORTSMOUTH 20

SHEFFIELD WEDNESDAY 19

CRYSTAL PALACE 18

DERBY COUNTY 17

NORWICH CITY 15

WATFORD 14

SWANSEA CITY 13

WOLVERHAMPTON WANDERERS 11

NOTTINGHAM FOREST 10

SHEFFIELD UNITED 9

READING 9

IPSWICH TOWN 6

BURNLEY 6

BOURNEMOUTH 4

OLDHAM ATHLETIC 4

BARNSLEY 4

BRADFORD CITY 2

BLACKPOOL 2

CARDIFF CITY 1

SWINDON TOWN 1

Total Fouls since 2003

EVERTON 6,679	FULHAM 5,233	BIRMINGHAM CITY 3,085	BURNLEY 1,296
ASTON VILLA 6,576	SUNDERLAND 5,105	CRYSTAL PALACE 2,440	QUEENS PARK RANGERS 1,262
MANCHESTER CITY 6,536	BLACKBURN ROVERS 5,044	HULL CITY 2,398	BOURNEMOUTH 729
CHELSEA 6,274	BOLTON WANDERERS 4,871	SWANSEA CITY 2,295	LEEDS UNITED 583
MANCHESTER UNITED 6,270	WEST BROMWICH ALBION 4,521	NORWICH CITY 2,254	DERBY COUNTY 548
TOTTENHAM HOTSPUR 6,259	STOKE CITY 4,222	CHARLTON ATHLETIC 2,013	SHEFFIELD UNITED 510
LIVERPOOL 6,151	WIGAN ATHLETIC 4,042	WOLVERHAMPTON WANDERERS 1,901	BLACKPOOL 440
ARSENAL 5,988	PORTSMOUTH 3,728	LEICESTER CITY 1,883	CARDIFF CITY 345
NEWCASTLE UNITED 5,771	MIDDLESBROUGH 3,648	WATFORD 1,573	
WEST HAM UNITED 5,292	SOUTHAMPTON 3,214	READING 1,341	

Source: Opta (May 2017)

GAMES TO REACH 100 GOALS

It's true that you need more than star power in order to score goals consistently.
You need a little luck, talented teammates, and a crumbling opposition too.
But when it comes to scoring a century (and more) for their club, the Premier
League players below have shown they've got what it takes to become truly
magical and, as a result, have joined an elite squad of top-scoring centurions.
For all strikers, this is the benchmark worth getting out of bed for.

Source: Opta (May 2017)

The players' colors below represents the team
color for which the player scored their 100th goal

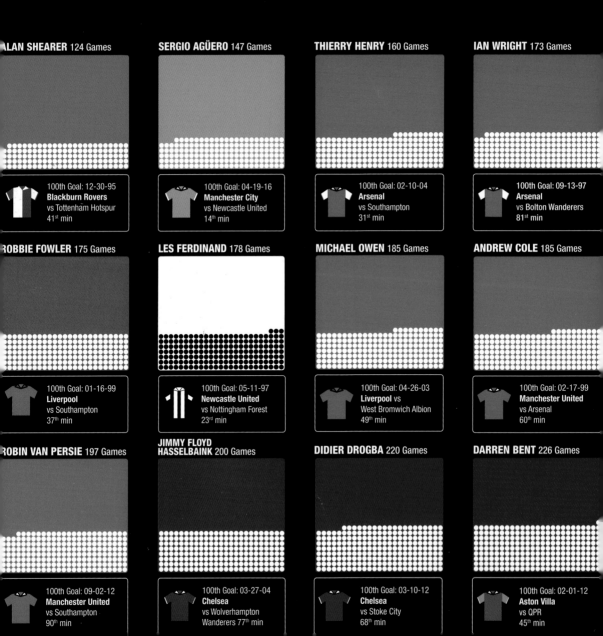

ALAN SHEARER 124 Games

100th Goal: 12-30-95
Blackburn Rovers
vs Tottenham Hotspur
41st min

SERGIO AGÜERO 147 Games

100th Goal: 04-19-16
Manchester City
vs Newcastle United
14th min

THIERRY HENRY 160 Games

100th Goal: 02-10-04
Arsenal
vs Southampton
31st min

IAN WRIGHT 173 Games

100th Goal: 09-13-97
Arsenal
vs Bolton Wanderers
81st min

ROBBIE FOWLER 175 Games

100th Goal: 01-16-99
Liverpool
vs Southampton
37th min

LES FERDINAND 178 Games

100th Goal: 05-11-97
Newcastle United
vs Nottingham Forest
23rd min

MICHAEL OWEN 185 Games

100th Goal: 04-26-03
Liverpool vs
West Bromwich Albion
49th min

ANDREW COLE 185 Games

100th Goal: 02-17-99
Manchester United
vs Arsenal
60th min

ROBIN VAN PERSIE 197 Games

100th Goal: 09-02-12
Manchester United
vs Southampton
90th min

JIMMY FLOYD HASSELBAINK 200 Games

100th Goal: 03-27-04
Chelsea
vs Wolverhampton
Wanderers 77th min

DIDIER DROGBA 220 Games

100th Goal: 03-10-12
Chelsea
vs Stoke City
68th min

DARREN BENT 226 Games

100th Goal: 02-01-12
Aston Villa
vs QPR
45th min

WAYNE ROONEY 247 Games

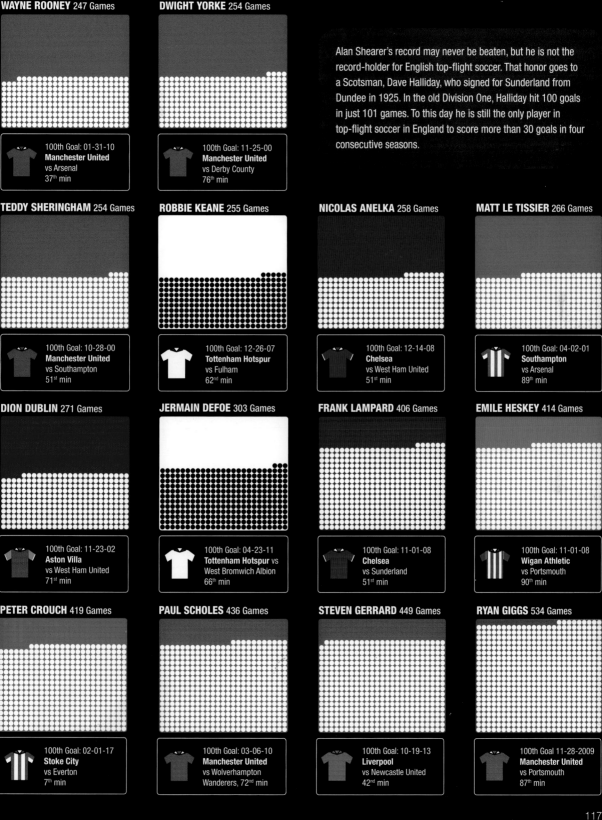

100th Goal: 01-31-10
Manchester United
vs Arsenal
37th min

DWIGHT YORKE 254 Games

100th Goal: 11-25-00
Manchester United
vs Derby County
76th min

Alan Shearer's record may never be beaten, but he is not the record-holder for English top-flight soccer. That honor goes to a Scotsman, Dave Halliday, who signed for Sunderland from Dundee in 1925. In the old Division One, Halliday hit 100 goals in just 101 games. To this day he is still the only player in top-flight soccer in England to score more than 30 goals in four consecutive seasons.

TEDDY SHERINGHAM 254 Games

100th Goal: 10-28-00
Manchester United
vs Southampton
51st min

ROBBIE KEANE 255 Games

100th Goal: 12-26-07
Tottenham Hotspur
vs Fulham
62nd min

NICOLAS ANELKA 258 Games

100th Goal: 12-14-08
Chelsea
vs West Ham United
51st min

MATT LE TISSIER 266 Games

100th Goal: 04-02-01
Southampton
vs Arsenal
89th min

DION DUBLIN 271 Games

100th Goal: 11-23-02
Aston Villa
vs West Ham United
71st min

JERMAIN DEFOE 303 Games

100th Goal: 04-23-11
Tottenham Hotspur vs
West Bromwich Albion
66th min

FRANK LAMPARD 406 Games

100th Goal: 11-01-08
Chelsea
vs Sunderland
51st min

EMILE HESKEY 414 Games

100th Goal: 11-01-08
Wigan Athletic
vs Portsmouth
90th min

PETER CROUCH 419 Games

100th Goal: 02-01-17
Stoke City
vs Everton
7th min

PAUL SCHOLES 436 Games

100th Goal: 03-06-10
Manchester United
vs Wolverhampton
Wanderers, 72nd min

STEVEN GERRARD 449 Games

100th Goal: 10-19-13
Liverpool
vs Newcastle United
42nd min

RYAN GIGGS 534 Games

100th Goal 11-28-2009
Manchester United
vs Portsmouth
87th min

117

FA CUP WINNERS AND RUNNERS-UP

Although overshadowed in recent times by the Premier League, the FA Cup remains the showpiece of English football. First played in the 1871–72 season, the English FA Cup is the oldest soccer competition in the world. Open to the top 10 levels of English football, the tournament includes hundreds of non-league teams (in 1901, Tottenham Hotspur became the only non-league team ever to win the trophy). Since 1923, the final has been played at Wembley (old and new) apart from the period between 2001 and 2006, when it was hosted at the Millennium Stadium in Cardiff.

Source: Opta (May 2017)

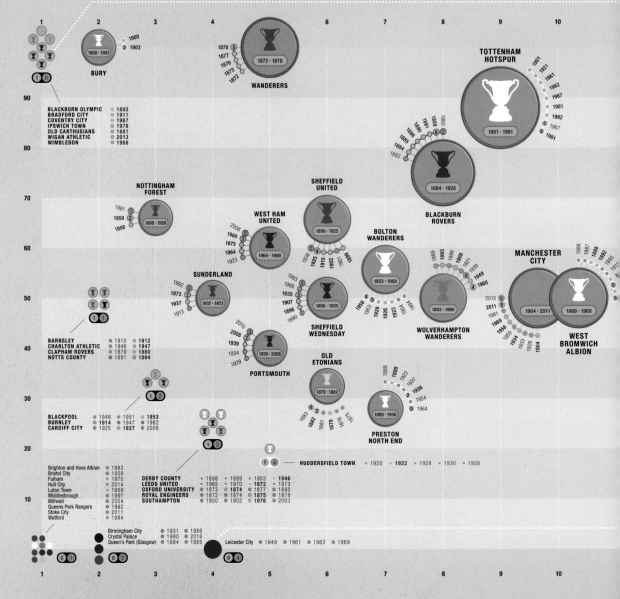

PERCENTAGE OF FINALS WON

NUMBER OF APPEARANCES IN THE FA CUP FINAL

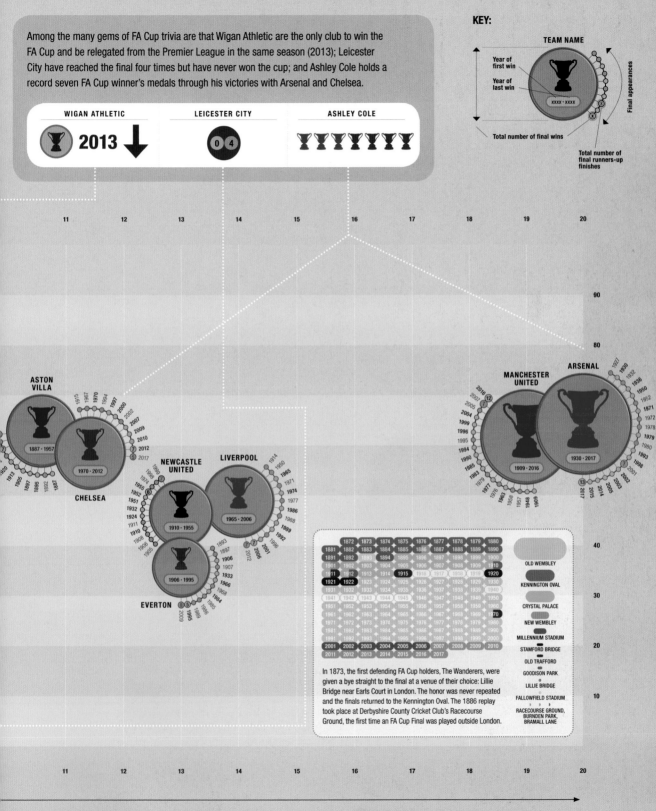

Among the many gems of FA Cup trivia are that Wigan Athletic are the only club to win the FA Cup and be relegated from the Premier League in the same season (2013); Leicester City have reached the final four times but have never won the cup; and Ashley Cole holds a record seven FA Cup winner's medals through his victories with Arsenal and Chelsea.

KEY:

TEAM NAME

Year of first win

Year of last win

XXXX · XXXX

Final appearances

Total number of final wins

Total number of final runners-up finishes

WIGAN ATHLETIC	LEICESTER CITY	ASHLEY COLE
2013 ↓	0 4	♔♔♔♔♔♔♔

ASTON VILLA
1887 · 1957

CHELSEA
1970 · 2012

NEWCASTLE UNITED
1910 · 1955

LIVERPOOL
1965 · 2006

EVERTON
1906 · 1995

MANCHESTER UNITED
1909 · 2016

ARSENAL
1930 · 2017

In 1873, the first defending FA Cup holders, The Wanderers, were given a bye straight to the final at a venue of their choice: Lillie Bridge near Earls Court in London. The honor was never repeated and the finals returned to the Kennington Oval. The 1886 replay took place at Derbyshire County Cricket Club's Racecourse Ground, the first time an FA Cup Final was played outside London.

OLD WEMBLEY
KENNINGTON OVAL
CRYSTAL PALACE
NEW WEMBLEY
MILLENNIUM STADIUM
STAMFORD BRIDGE
OLD TRAFFORD
GOODISON PARK
LILLIE BRIDGE
FALLOWFIELD STADIUM
RACECOURSE GROUND, BURNDEN PARK, BRAMALL LANE

LA LIGA TITLE WINNERS

La Liga, the elite league of Spanish soccer, was born in 1929 from a core group of teams playing for the national knockout competition, the Copa del Rey. Sixty different teams have since competed in the league and nine different teams have lifted the trophy. The league has been dominated by Barcelona and Real Madrid, the giants of Spanish football, while Athletic Bilbao, Atlético Madrid, and Valencia deserve honorable mentions too. With its teams faring well in European competition, La Liga is currently rated the best league in Europe.

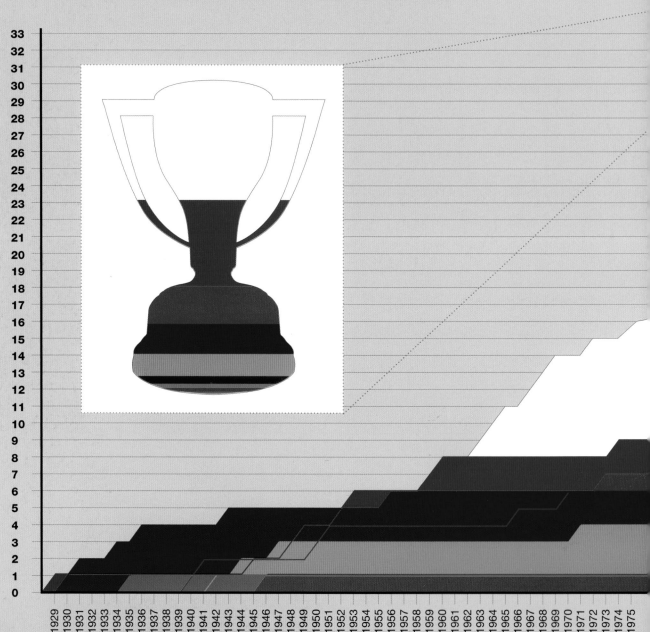

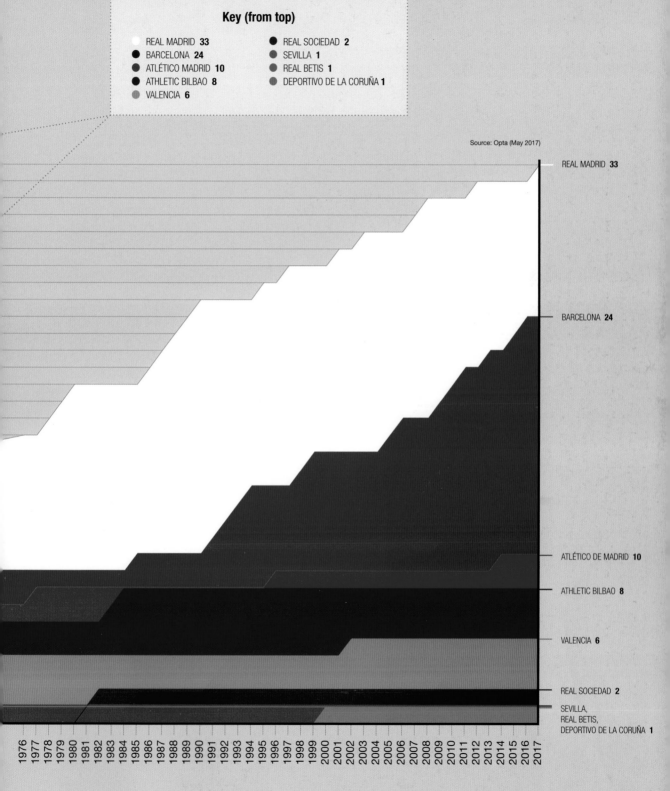

Key (from top)

- REAL MADRID **33**
- BARCELONA **24**
- ATLÉTICO MADRID **10**
- ATHLETIC BILBAO **8**
- VALENCIA **6**
- REAL SOCIEDAD **2**
- SEVILLA **1**
- REAL BETIS **1**
- DEPORTIVO DE LA CORUÑA **1**

Source: Opta (May 2017)

REAL MADRID **33**

BARCELONA **24**

ATLÉTICO DE MADRID **10**

ATHLETIC BILBAO **8**

VALENCIA **6**

REAL SOCIEDAD **2**

SEVILLA,
REAL BETIS,
DEPORTIVO DE LA CORUÑA **1**

1976 1977 1978 1979 1980 1981 1982 1983 1984 1985 1986 1987 1988 1989 1990 1991 1992 1993 1994 1995 1996 1997 1998 1999 2000 2001 2002 2003 2004 2005 2006 2007 2008 2009 2010 2011 2012 2013 2014 2015 2016 2017

LA LIGA GAME WINS PER CLUB

According to UEFA, La Liga has been the top league in Europe since 2012, and it has produced the continent's top-rated club twice as often as any other league. Few will be surprised to find the La Liga giants Real Madrid and Barcelona dominating this most-wins chart, but may be astounded by just how evenly matched they are. Even Real Madrid's 2011–12 record of 32 wins in a season was matched by Barcelona the following season and, although it took them until 2016, Real Madrid eventually equalled Barcelona's 2010–11 record of 16 consecutive victories.

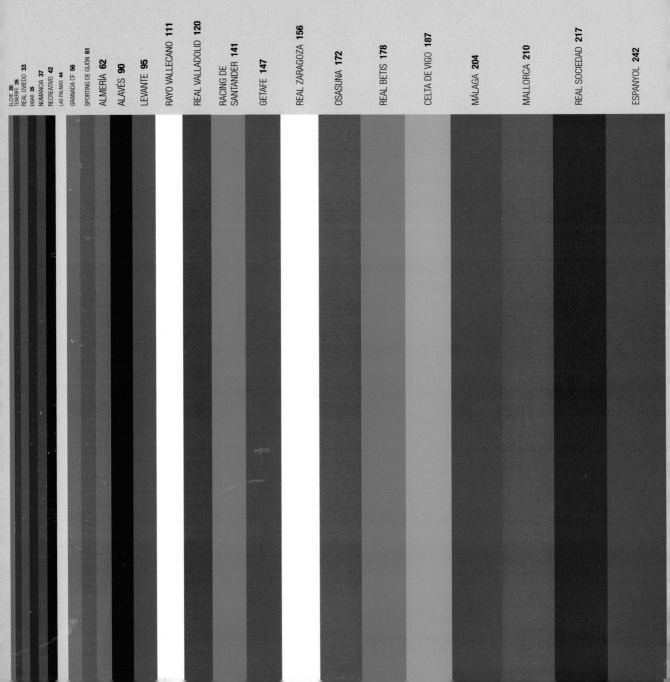

ELCHE 20
TENERIFE 26
REAL OVIEDO 33
EIBAR 35
NUMANCIA 37
RECREATIVO 42
LAS PALMAS 44
GRANADA CF 56
SPORTING DE GIJON 61
ALMERÍA 62
ALAVÉS 90
LEVANTE 95
RAYO VALLECANO 111
REAL VALLADOLID 120
RACING DE SANTANDER 141
GETAFE 147
REAL ZARAGOZA 156
OSASUNA 172
REAL BETIS 178
CELTA DE VIGO 187
MÁLAGA 204
MALLORCA 210
REAL SOCIEDAD 217
ESPANYOL 242

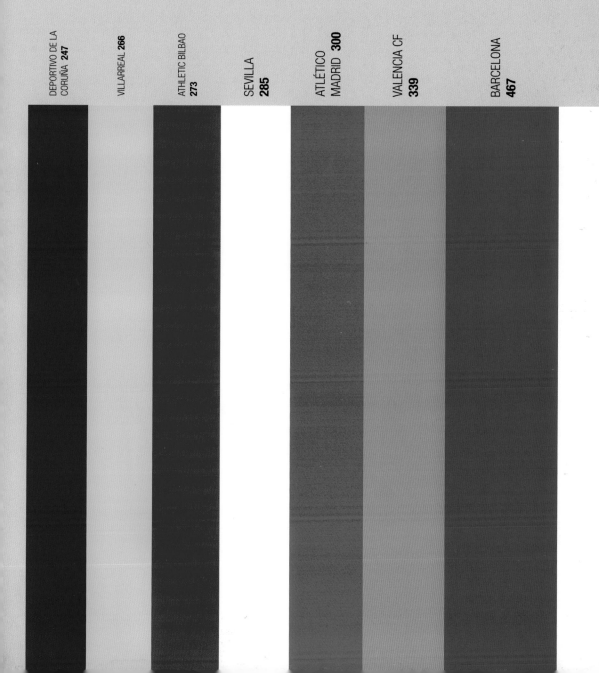

"You want to win games, break records, but I don't do it just for the records. I do it because I want to improve and see my players improve."

Zinedine Zidane, Real Madrid coach

Source: Opta (May 2017)

Under 20 Wins

ALBACETE	19	LEGANÉS	8
REAL MURCIA	12	XEREZ	8
HÉRCULES	9	SALAMANCA	7
CF EXTREMADURA	9	GIMNÀSTIC DE TARRAGON	7
CÁDIZ	8	CÓRDOBA	3

DEPORTIVO DE LA CORUÑA **247**

VILLARREAL **266**

ATHLETIC BILBAO **273**

SEVILLA **285**

ATLÉTICO MADRID **300**

VALENCIA CF **339**

BARCELONA **467**

REAL MADRID **475**

LA LIGA GOALS PER CLUB

The history of La Liga is filled with great coaches whose dynamic team engineering has helped squads amass huge goalscoring tallies—from the bowler-hatted Englishman Fred Pentland, whose 1930s' Athletic Bilbao conquered any team that stood before them, to the star-studded era of Miguel Muñoz at Real Madrid in the 1960s and 1970s. Johan Cruyff, and his successor Louis van Gaal, brought success back to Barcelona in the '90s. Leo Beenhakker, Vicente del Bosque, and Carlo Ancelotti have brought glory to Real Madrid in recent years, while Frank Rijkaard and Pep Guardiola made Barcelona the most feared team in Europe—though judging by the goal totals between those two teams now, there's still everything to play for...

In the 2011–12 season, *La Liga de los Récords* (The League of the Records), a rampant Real Madrid ripped up the record books. Among their notable achievements was the most league goals in a season, as they racked up an astonishing 121. Real boasted 13 different scorers, with Cristiano Ronaldo leading the list on 46, not so closely followed by Gonzalo Higuaín (22) and Karim Benzema (21).

After scoring in 64 consecutive matches, a 0-0 draw at Osasuna on October 19, 2013, brought to an end Real Madrid's record. Then, in February 2016, Barcelona began a run of their own; at the end of the 2016–17 season they had netted in 50 consecutive games … and counting.

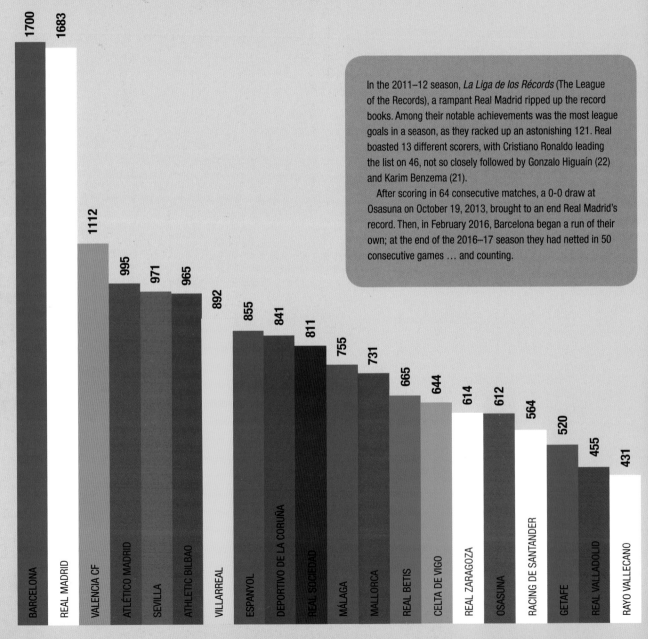

Club	Goals
BARCELONA	1700
REAL MADRID	1683
VALENCIA CF	1112
ATLÉTICO MADRID	995
SEVILLA	971
ATHLETIC BILBAO	965
VILLARREAL	892
ESPANYOL	855
DEPORTIVO DE LA CORUÑA	841
REAL SOCIEDAD	811
MÁLAGA	755
MALLORCA	731
REAL BETIS	665
CELTA DE VIGO	644
REAL ZARAGOZA	614
OSASUNA	612
RACING DE SANTANDER	564
GETAFE	520
REAL VALLADOLID	455
RAYO VALLECANO	431

"MSN", the fearsome Barcelona forward line of Messi, Suárez, and Neymar (before Neymar left for Paris Saint-Germain in summer 2017), amassed 79 goals between them in the 2016–17 season.

Source: Opta (May 2017)

LEVANTE **350**
ALAVÉS **290**
ALMERÍA **244**
SPORTING DE GIJÓN **242**
GRANADA CF **209**
LAS PALMAS **180**
RECREATIVO **163**
NUMANCIA **155**
EIBAR **139**
REAL OVIEDO **136**
TENERIFE **113**
ALBACETE **73**
REAL MURCIA **65**
ELCHE **65**
XEREZ **38**
CÁDIZ **36**
HÉRCULES **36**
LEGANÉS **36**
GIMNÀSTIC DE TARRAGONA **34**
SALAMANCA **29**
CF EXTREMADURA **27**
CÓRDOBA **22**

RONALDO vs MESSI

Future generations might well consider us blessed to have seen the two greatest players in the history of the game. Between them they have been named as FIFA's best two players in the world every year since 2008 (except 2010 when Iniesta was runner-up to Messi). Both players have scored in two UEFA Champions League finals, have regularly scored more than 50 goals in a single season, and struck their 500th goals for their club in 2017. But who wouldn't doubt the Argentinian would trade a fair few of them to match the South American equivalent of the European Championship winner's medal, won by Ronaldo in 2016?

CRISTIANO RONALDO

Club Record

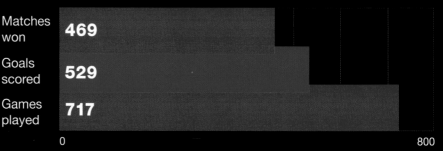

Matches won	**469**
Goals scored	**529**
Games played	**717**

0 — 800

International Record

Matches won	**84**
Goals scored	**75**
Games played	**142**

0 — 800

League Championships	🏆🏆🏆🏆🏆
National Cups	🏆🏆🏆
National League Cups	🏆🏆
Comm Shield/Super Cup	🏆🏆🏆
Champions League	🏆🏆🏆🏆
UEFA Super Cup	🏆
Club World Cup	🏆🏆🏆
European Championship	🏆
Total	**21**

> " Messi is outstanding in certain attributes but Ronaldo is such an all-round player."
>
> England international Michael Owen

" Messi or Ronaldo best player in the world? In the world,
I would say Ronaldo. Messi is from another planet. **"**

Turkey international Arda Turan

Source: Opta (June 2017)

LIONEL MESSI

Club Record

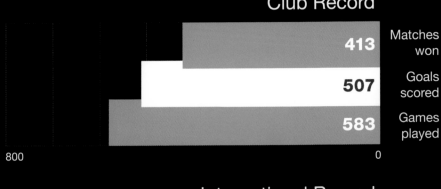

413	Matches won
507	Goals scored
583	Games played

800   0

International Record

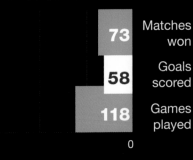

73	Matches won
58	Goals scored
118	Games played

800   0

 League Championships
National Cups
National League Cups
Comm Shield/Super Cup

Champions League
UEFA Super Cup
Club World Cup

Olympic Gold Medal

30   **Total**

LA LIGA TOP GOALSCORERS 1998–2017

ROBERTO SOLDADO **110**
GONZALO HIGUAÍN **107**
ANTOINE GRIEZMANN **100**
FERNANDO TORRES **97**
DIEGO TRISTÁN **95**
ROY MAKAAY **93**
RUBÉN CASTRO **92**
ISMAEL URZAIZ **91**
SAVO MILOŠEVIĆ **91**
PATRICK KLUIVERT **90**
FRÉDÉRIC KANOUTÉ **89**
LUIS SUÁREZ **85**
RONALDO **83**
WALTER PANDIANI **82**
FERNANDO MORIENTES **79**
NIHAT KAHVECI **76**
SALVA BALLESTA **75**
SERGIO AGÜERO **74**
LUIS GARCÍA **73**
LUÍS FABIANO **72**
VICTOR **71**
SERGIO GARCÍA **71**
JAVIER SAVIOLA **70**
RONALDINHO **69**
CARLOS VELA **68**
DELY VALDÉS **68**
NEYMAR **68**
DARKO KOVAČEVIĆ **67**
RIVALDO **67**
GUISEPPE ROSSI **64**
ETXEBERRIA **63**

Lionel Messi, all-time top goalscorer. In November 2012, the prodigious striker began a run of scoring in 21 consecutive games, including a goal against every other La Liga team.

Lionel Messi and Cristiano Ronaldo tower over La Liga goalscoring records. Their lead is considerable, but they also score around a goal a game—almost twice the rate of others in the chart. The only player in the league's history whose record stands the equal of these modern superstars is the great Telma Zarra. He played at Athletic Bilbao for 15 seasons, scoring at nearly a goal a game and helping Bilbao to a league title in 1943. His name now lives on in the award given to La Liga's top goalscorer each season.

In the 2010–11 season Cristiano Ronaldo became the first La Liga player in 20 years to score at a ratio of over a goal per game. Since then the feat has been achieved every season, Lionel Messi achieving the best ratio of 1.44 in 2012–13.

Source: Opta (May 2017)
Stats from La Liga 1998–99 to 2016–17

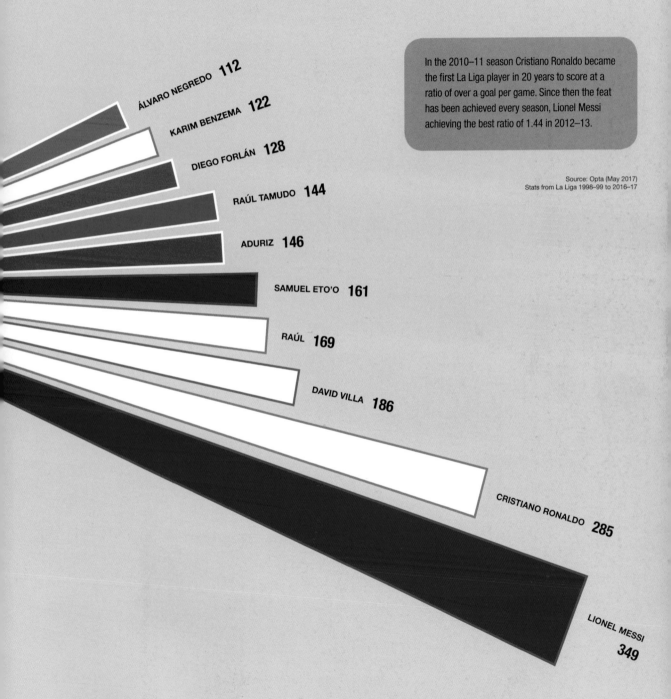

ÁLVARO NEGREDO **112**

KARIM BENZEMA **122**

DIEGO FORLÁN **128**

RAÚL TAMUDO **144**

ADURIZ **146**

SAMUEL ETO'O **161**

RAÚL **169**

DAVID VILLA **186**

CRISTIANO RONALDO **285**

LIONEL MESSI **349**

SERIE A TITLE WINNERS

Serie A has been the top-flight tournament in Italian soccer since the 1929–30 season. Rated as one of the most entertaining and thrilling leagues in the world, Serie A has a reputation for highly tactical performances and players with virtuoso and prodigious technical ability. However, the league has also been rocked by controversy and scandal, including the 2006 *Calciopoli*, as it became known, where some top teams were accused of rigging games by selecting biased referees. The winner of the league is awarded the *Scudetto*, a badge with the colors of the Italian flag, to be worn on the champions' shirts the following season.

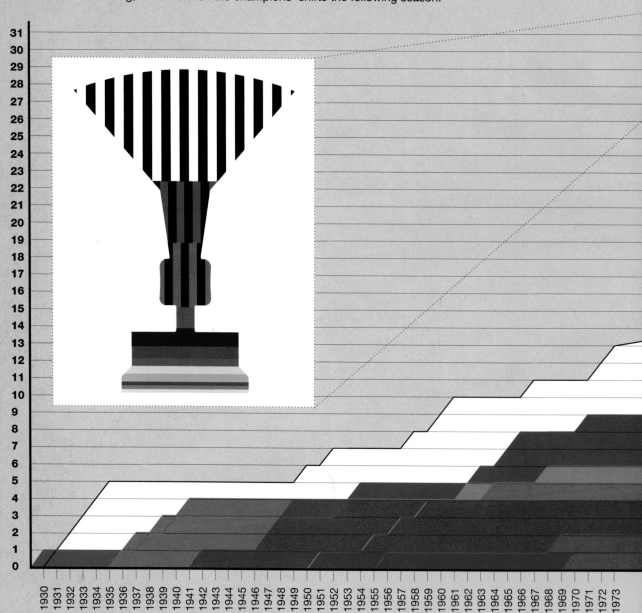

31
30
29
28
27
26
25
24
23
22
21
20
19
18
17
16
15
14
13
12
11
10
9
8
7
6
5
4
3
2
1
0

1930 1931 1932 1933 1934 1935 1936 1937 1938 1939 1940 1941 1942 1943 1944 1945 1946 1947 1948 1949 1950 1951 1952 1953 1954 1955 1956 1957 1958 1959 1960 1961 1962 1963 1964 1965 1966 1967 1968 1969 1970 1971 1972 1973

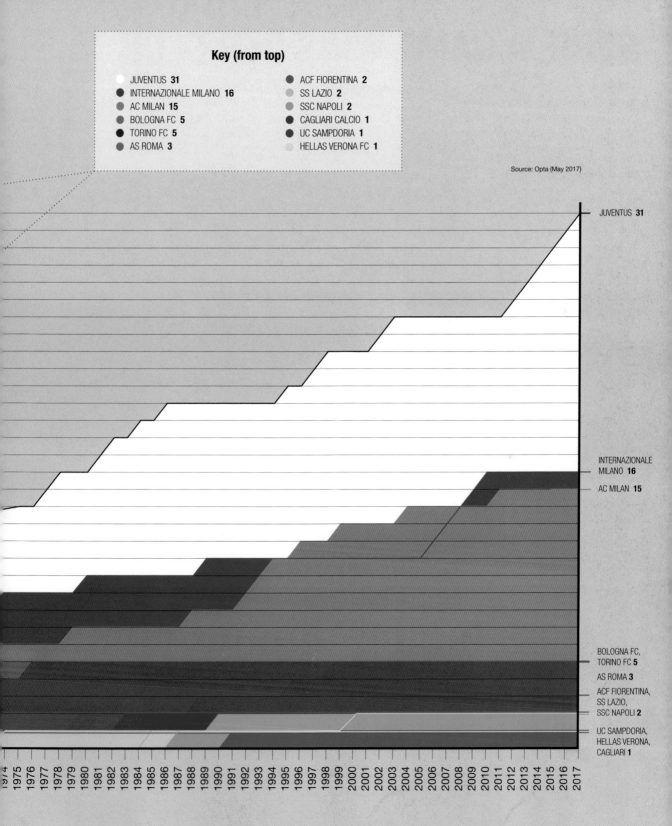

Key (from top)

- JUVENTUS **31**
- INTERNAZIONALE MILANO **16**
- AC MILAN **15**
- BOLOGNA FC **5**
- TORINO FC **5**
- AS ROMA **3**
- ACF FIORENTINA **2**
- SS LAZIO **2**
- SSC NAPOLI **2**
- CAGLIARI CALCIO **1**
- UC SAMPDORIA **1**
- HELLAS VERONA FC **1**

Source: Opta (May 2017)

JUVENTUS **31**

INTERNAZIONALE MILANO **16**

AC MILAN **15**

BOLOGNA FC, TORINO FC **5**

AS ROMA **3**

ACF FIORENTINA, SS LAZIO, SSC NAPOLI **2**

UC SAMPDORIA, HELLAS VERONA, CAGLIARI **1**

1974 1975 1976 1977 1978 1979 1980 1981 1982 1983 1984 1985 1986 1987 1988 1989 1990 1991 1992 1993 1994 1995 1996 1997 1998 1999 2000 2001 2002 2003 2004 2005 2006 2007 2008 2009 2010 2011 2012 2013 2014 2015 2016 2017

SERIE A GAME WINS PER CLUB

There are 65 teams who have participated in the 84 Serie A championships to have taken place to date, with only Internazionale having competed in every season. Apart from the largely pre-war success of Torino and Bologna, Serie A has been dominated by *Le Sette Sorelle* (The Seven Sisters): Juventus, Roma, Milan, Inter, Fiorentina, Lazio—and Parma, who have more recently been replaced by Napoli. The Italian league is usually secured by a team amassing a total of around 25 victories in the season, although Juventus won 33 and 29 out of 38, respectively, in their title-winning seasons of 2013–14 and 2015–16.

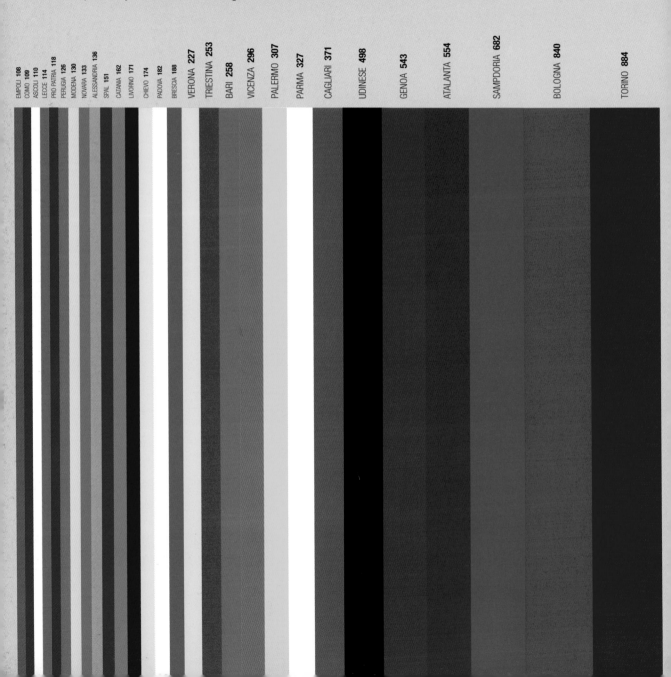

EMPOLI 108
COMO 109
ASCOLI 110
LECCE 114
PERUGIA 126
MODENA 130
NOVARA 133
ALESSANDRIA 136
SPAL 151
CATANIA 162
LIVORNO 171
CHIEVO 174
PADOVA 182
BRESCIA 188
VERONA 227
TRIESTINA 253
BARI 258
VICENZA 296
PALERMO 307
PARMA 327
CAGLIARI 371
UDINESE 498
GENOA 543
ATALANTA 554
SAMPDORIA 682
BOLOGNA 840
TORINO 884

Under 100 Wins

FOGGIA **95**	PRO VERCELLI **65**	PESCARA **36**	CARPI **9**
VENEZIA **94**	SASSUOLO **50**	VARESE **36**	CROTONE **9**
REGGINA **83**	MANTOVA **48**	CASALE **33**	ANCONA **8**
SIENA **83**	LIGURIA **44**	SAMPIERDARENESE **24**	FROSINONE **8**
CESENA **80**	CREMONESE **43**	SALERNITANA **23**	TERNANA **7**
LUCCHESE **80**	PISA **42**	LECCO **19**	PISTOIESE **6**
AVELLINO **79**	MESSINA **39**	LEGNANO **16**	TREVISO **3**
PIACENZA **65**	CATANZARO **38**	REGGIANA **16**	

NAPOLI **911**

LAZIO **935**

FIORENTINA **1054**

ROMA **1170**

AC MILAN **1340**

INTERNAZIONALE MILANO **1404**

SERIE A GOALS PER CLUB

Goals are said to be hard to come by in an often defensively minded Serie A, but if you are good enough… It certainly wasn't a problem for 1930s star Silvio Piola, whose record of 274 goals in 537 games—set with Novarro, Lazio, Juventus, and others—looks unassailable. Even the great Francesco Totti had eventually to concede that the target was out of sight. Among the young guns in the league, only Inter's Mauro Icardi (82 goals), Torino's Andrea Belotti (67), and Lazio's Keita (25) look capable of inclusion in future charts.

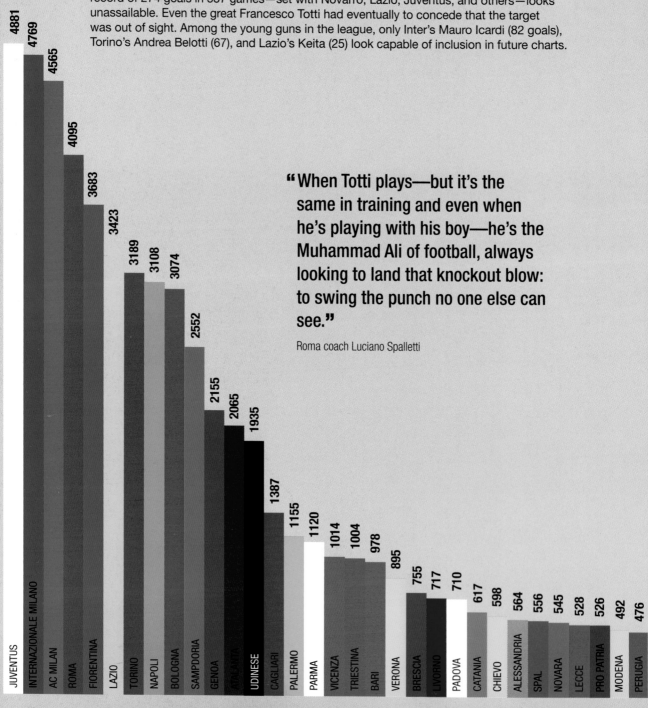

> "When Totti plays—but it's the same in training and even when he's playing with his boy—he's the Muhammad Ali of football, always looking to land that knockout blow: to swing the punch no one else can see."
>
> Roma coach Luciano Spalletti

Club	Goals
JUVENTUS	4881
INTERNAZIONALE MILANO	4769
AC MILAN	4565
ROMA	4095
FIORENTINA	3683
LAZIO	3423
TORINO	3189
NAPOLI	3108
BOLOGNA	3074
SAMPDORIA	2552
GENOA	2155
ATALANTA	2065
UDINESE	1935
CAGLIARI	1387
PALERMO	1155
PARMA	1120
VICENZA	1014
TRIESTINA	1004
BARI	978
VERONA	895
BRESCIA	755
LIVORNO	717
PADOVA	710
CATANIA	617
CHIEVO	598
ALESSANDRIA	564
SPAL	556
NOVARA	545
LECCE	528
PRO PATRIA	526
MODENA	492
PERUGIA	476

FRANCESCO TOTTI **250**	ANTONIO DI NATALE **209**	ALBERTO GILARDINO **188**	ALESSANDRO DEL PIERO **183**
LUCA TONI **157**	FILIPPO INZAGHI **156**	GABRIEL BATISTUTA **155**	HERNÁN CRESPO **153**
MARCO DI VAIO **143**	CHRISTIAN VIERI **141**	VINCENZO MONTELLA **141**	ENRICO CHIESA **137**
GIUSEPPE SIGNORI **128**	ANDRIY SHEVCHENKO **127**	DAVID TREZEGUET **123**	ZLATAN IBRAHIMOVIĆ **122**
CRISTIANO LUCARELLI **120**	ANTONIO CASSANO **113**	EDINSON CAVANI **112**	NICOLA AMORUSO **110**
FABIO QUAGLIARELLA **108**	GIAMPAOLO PAZZINI **107**	SERGIO PELLISSIER **107**	FABRIZIO MICCOLI **103**
ADRIAN MUTU **103**	TOMMASO ROCCHI **102**	OLIVER BIERHOFF **100**	ROBERTO BAGGIO **96**
MIRKO VUČINIĆ **96**	GONZALO HIGUAÍN **95**	MARCO BORRIELLO **95**	MAREK HAMŠÍK **93**
VINCENZO IAQUINTA **89**	ALESSANDRO MATRI **87**	DIEGO MILITO **86**	ROBERTO MUZZI **86**
AMAURI **85**			

Source: Opta (May 2017)
Player data: 1994–95 to 2016–17
Color relates to the team for which the player scored the highest number of goals.

Il Re di Roma (The King of Rome), Francesco Totti retired from his beloved club, Roma, at the end of the 2016–17 season. The five-time Italian footballer of the year, European Golden Boot holder (2007), and World Cup winner (2006) scored his first goal for the Giallorossi on the opening day of the 1994–95 season. His 250th and final league goal came in September 2016 at the age of 40. His loyalty to Roma has meant he has never achieved Champions League success, but there is no doubt of his status in the game. When Roma met Barcelona in a pre-season friendly, Lionel Messi uploaded a shot of him in Totti's shirt with the caption: "A great! What a phenomenon!!" It got 1.8 million likes.

ASCOLI 425 · VENEZIA 413 · COMO 411 · EMPOLI 404 · CESENA 364 · FOGGIA 360 · SIENA 356 · LUCCHESE 347 · REGGINA 324 · PIACENZA 281 · AVELLINO 268 · PRO VERCELLI 251 · CREMONESE 222 · PESCARA 205 · SASSUOLO 199 · MANTOVA 182 · PISA 174 · LIGURIA 168 · MESSINA 165 · VARESE 164 · CATANZARO 156 · CASALE 149 · LEGNANO 111 · SAMPIERDARENESE 93 · LECCO 84 · SALERNITANA 83 · REGGIANA 81 · ANCONA 60 · CARPI 37 · FROSINONE 35 · CROTONE 34 · TERNANA 33 · TREVISO 24 · PISTOIESE 19

BUNDESLIGA TITLE WINNERS

The Bundesliga was formed in 1963 to bring professionalism to the German game. The early years saw five different champions in five seasons before two promoted teams, Bayern München and Borussia Mönchengladbach, went on to dominate the league, both winning three successive titles. Bayern would continue to lead even after the league was revolutionized after 1989 at the unification of Germany. Various clubs—the latest being Borussia Dortmund— have risen to challenge Bayern's supremacy, but "FC Hollywood", as other teams' fans have continued to call them, remain the undisputed giants of the Bundesliga.

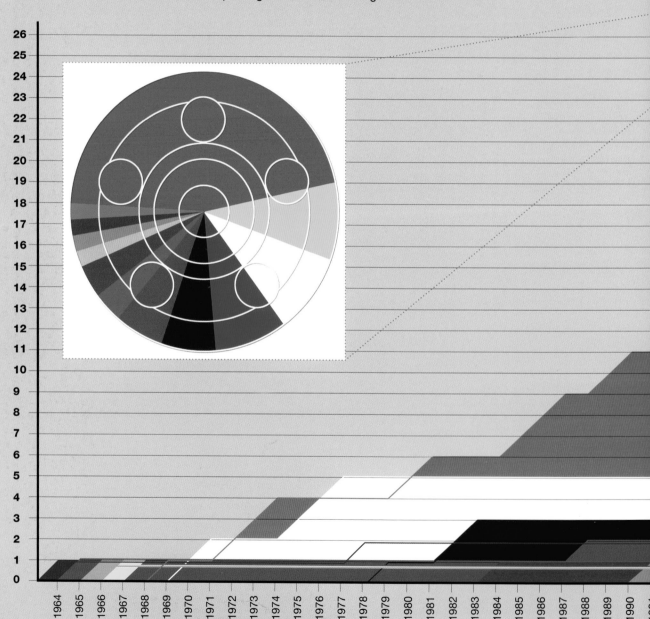

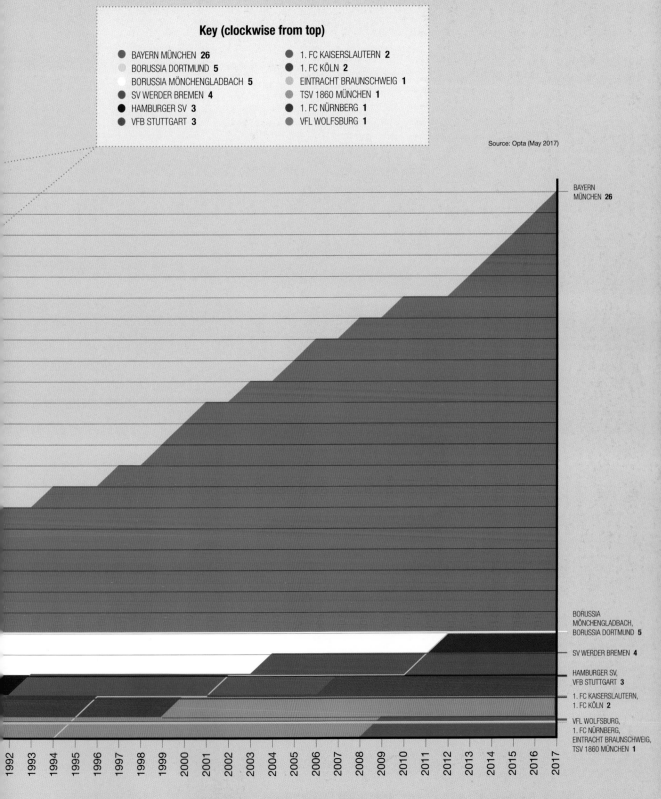

Key (clockwise from top)

- BAYERN MÜNCHEN **26**
- BORUSSIA DORTMUND **5**
- BORUSSIA MÖNCHENGLADBACH **5**
- SV WERDER BREMEN **4**
- HAMBURGER SV **3**
- VFB STUTTGART **3**
- 1. FC KAISERSLAUTERN **2**
- 1. FC KÖLN **2**
- EINTRACHT BRAUNSCHWEIG **1**
- TSV 1860 MÜNCHEN **1**
- 1. FC NÜRNBERG **1**
- VFL WOLFSBURG **1**

Source: Opta (May 2017)

BAYERN MÜNCHEN **26**

BORUSSIA MÖNCHENGLADBACH, BORUSSIA DORTMUND **5**

SV WERDER BREMEN **4**

HAMBURGER SV, VFB STUTTGART **3**

1. FC KAISERSLAUTERN, 1. FC KÖLN **2**

VFL WOLFSBURG, 1. FC NÜRNBERG, EINTRACHT BRAUNSCHWEIG, TSV 1860 MÜNCHEN **1**

1992 1993 1994 1995 1996 1997 1998 1999 2000 2001 2002 2003 2004 2005 2006 2007 2008 2009 2010 2011 2012 2013 2014 2015 2016 2017

BUNDESLIGA GAME WINS PER CLUB

Although there is no doubting the dominance of Bayern München over their Bundesliga rivals, this infographic illustrates the competitive nature of the league. A total of 53 clubs have competed in the Bundesliga over the 30 plus years, with more than 10 teams earning a win ratio of over 40%. Bayern hold the record for the most wins in a season, reaching 29 in both 2012–13 and 2013–14, clocking up a run of 19 games in the latter season. The last two seasons have seen Bayern extend their lead in this category with two emphatic Bundesliga titles, while only Borussia Dortmund, Lokomotive Leipzig, and Bayer Leverkusen have recorded better than a 50% win ratio.

ROT-WEISS ESSEN **61**
FC AUGSBURG **64**
SV WALDHOF MANNHEIM **71**
OFC KICKERS 1901 **77**
TSG 1899 HOFFENHEIM **103**
FC HANSA ROSTOCK **124**
1. FSV MAINZ 05 **127**
KFC UERDINGEN 05 **138**
DSC ARMINIA BIELEFELD **159**
SC FREIBURG **180**
TSV 1860 MÜNCHEN **238**
KARLSRUHER SC **241**
EINTRACHT BRAUNSCHWEIG **242**
FORTUNA DÜSSELDORF **245**
VFL WOLFSBURG **261**
HANNOVER 96 **293**
MSV DUISBERG **296**
1. FC NÜRNBERG **341**
VFL BOCHUM 1848 **356**
HERTHA BSC **421**
BAYER 04 LEVERKUSEN **550**
1. FC KAISERSLAUTERN **575**
EINTRACHT FRANKFURT **592**

Under 60 Wins

FC ST PAULI **58**
FC ENERGIE COTTBUS **56**
ALEMANNIA AACHEN **43**
ROT-WEISS OBERHAUSEN **36**
SG WATTENSCHEID 09 **34**
SG DYNAMO DRESDEN **33**

1. FC SAARBRÜCKEN **32**
SV DARMSTADT 98 **28**
SC BORUSSIA NEUNKIRCHEN **25**
WUPPERTALER SV **25**
FC 08 HOMBURG **21**
SPVGG UNTERHACHING **20**

STUTTGARTER KICKERS **20**
RB LEIPZIG **20**
FC INGOLSTADT **18**
TENNIS BORUSSIA BERLIN **11**
SSV ULM 1846 **9**
SC FORTUNA KÖLN **8**

SC PADERBORN 07 **7**
SC PREUSSEN MÜNSTER **7**
SPVGG GREUTHER FÜRTH **4**
BLAU-WEISS 1890 BERLIN **3**
VFB LEIPZIG **3**
TASMANIA 1900 BERLIN **2**

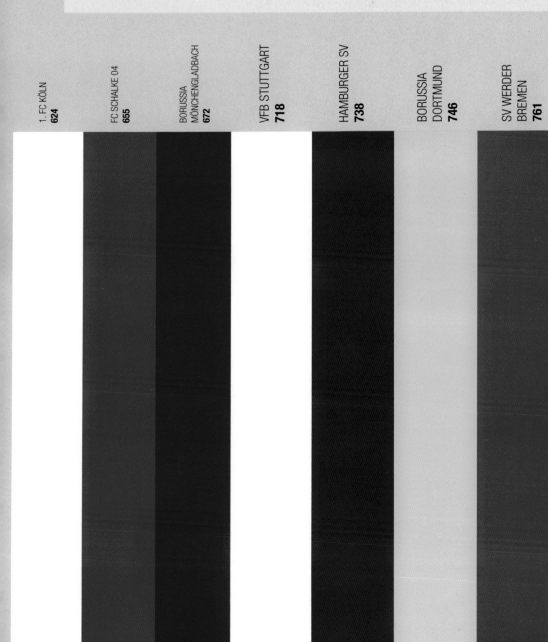

1. FC KÖLN
624

FC SCHALKE 04
655

BORUSSIA MÖNCHENGLADBACH
672

VFB STUTTGART
718

HAMBURGER SV
738

BORUSSIA DORTMUND
746

SV WERDER BREMEN
761

BAYERN MÜNCHEN
1043

BUNDESLIGA GOALS PER CLUB

The German Bundesliga is the go-to league for goals with the highest goals per game ratio in Europe at 2.94 a game. As in all Bundesliga records, it's hard to ignore Bayern München. They are the only team to net 100 goals in a season (101 in 1971–72) and in Gerd Müller, seven-time leading goalscorer, they have arguably the game's greatest ever goal poacher. Among recent heroes stand Robert Lewandowski with his incredible five goals in nine minutes against VfL Wolfsburg in September 2015, and Borussia Dortmund's Pierre-Emerick Aubameyang whose 31 strikes in 2016–17 made him the first player to score over 30 goals in a season for 40 years.

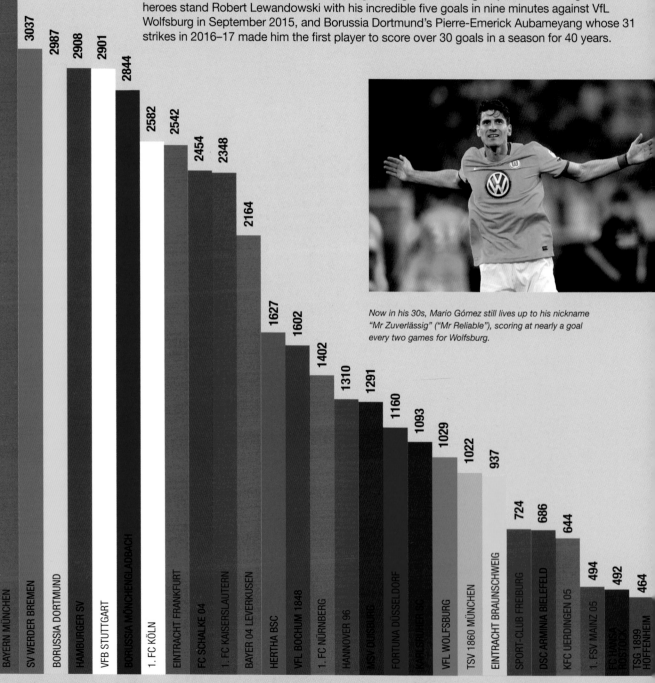

Now in his 30s, Mario Gómez still lives up to his nickname "Mr Zuverlässig" ("Mr Reliable"), scoring at nearly a goal every two games for Wolfsburg.

Club	Goals
BAYERN MÜNCHEN	3853
SV WERDER BREMEN	3037
BORUSSIA DORTMUND	2987
HAMBURGER SV	2908
VFB STUTTGART	2901
BORUSSIA MÖNCHENGLADBACH	2844
1. FC KÖLN	2582
EINTRACHT FRANKFURT	2542
FC SCHALKE 04	2454
1. FC KAISERSLAUTERN	2348
BAYER 04 LEVERKUSEN	2164
HERTHA BSC	1627
VFL BOCHUM 1848	1602
1. FC NÜRNBERG	1402
HANNOVER 96	1310
MSV DUISBURG	1291
FORTUNA DÜSSELDORF	1160
KARLSRUHER SC	1093
VFL WOLFSBURG	1029
TSV 1860 MÜNCHEN	1022
EINTRACHT BRAUNSCHWEIG	937
SPORT-CLUB FREIBURG	724
DSC ARMINIA BIELEFELD	686
KFC UERDINGEN 05	644
1. FSV MAINZ 05	494
FC HANSA ROSTOCK	492
TSG 1899 HOFFENHEIM	464

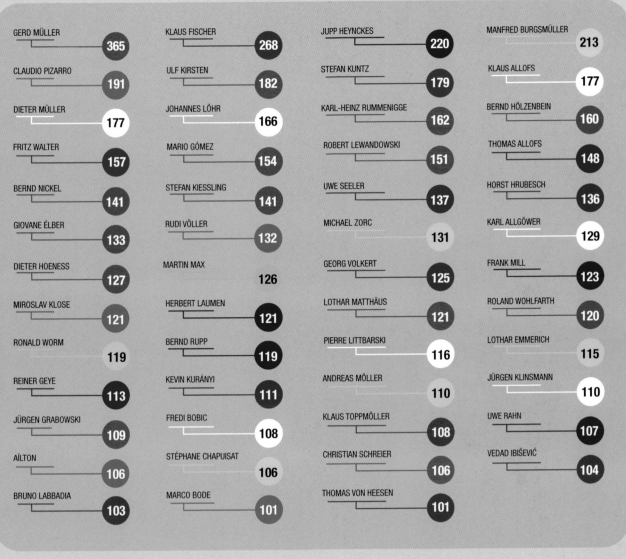

Player	Goals
GERD MÜLLER	365
CLAUDIO PIZARRO	191
DIETER MÜLLER	177
FRITZ WALTER	157
BERND NICKEL	141
GIOVANE ÉLBER	133
DIETER HOENESS	127
MIROSLAV KLOSE	121
RONALD WORM	119
REINER GEYE	113
JÜRGEN GRABOWSKI	109
AÍLTON	106
BRUNO LABBADIA	103
KLAUS FISCHER	268
ULF KIRSTEN	182
JOHANNES LÖHR	166
MARIO GÓMEZ	154
STEFAN KIESSLING	141
RUDI VÖLLER	132
MARTIN MAX	126
HERBERT LAUMEN	121
BERND RUPP	119
KEVIN KURÁNYI	111
FREDI BOBIC	108
STÉPHANE CHAPUISAT	106
MARCO BODE	101
JUPP HEYNCKES	220
STEFAN KUNTZ	179
KARL-HEINZ RUMMENIGGE	162
ROBERT LEWANDOWSKI	151
UWE SEELER	137
MICHAEL ZORC	131
GEORG VOLKERT	125
LOTHAR MATTHÄUS	121
PIERRE LITTBARSKI	116
ANDREAS MÖLLER	110
KLAUS TOPPMÖLLER	108
CHRISTIAN SCHREIER	106
THOMAS VON HEESEN	101
MANFRED BURGSMÜLLER	213
KLAUS ALLOFS	177
BERND HÖLZENBEIN	160
THOMAS ALLOFS	148
HORST HRUBESCH	136
KARL ALLGÖWER	129
FRANK MILL	123
ROLAND WOHLFARTH	120
LOTHAR EMMERICH	115
JÜRGEN KLINSMANN	110
UWE RAHN	107
VEDAD IBIŠEVIĆ	104

Source: Opta (May 2017)
Color relates to the team for which the player scored the highest number of goals.

Team	Goals
OFC KICKERS 1901	368
ROT-WEISS ESSEN	346
SV WALDHOF MANNHEIM	299
FC ST. PAULI	296
FC AUGSBURG	236
FC ENERGIE COTTBUS	211
1. FC SAARBRÜCKEN	202
ALEMANNIA AACHEN	186
SG WATTENSCHEID 09	186
ROT-WEISS OBERHAUSEN	182
SV DARMSTADT 98	152
WUPPERTALER SV	136
SG DYNAMO DRESDEN	132
BORUSSIA NEUNKIRCHEN	109
FC 08 HOMBURG	103
STUTTGARTER KICKERS	94
TENNIS BORUSSIA BERLIN	85
SPVGG UNTERHACHING	75
FC INGOLSTADT 04	69
RB LEIPZIG	66
FORTUNA KÖLN	46
BLAU-WEISS 90 BERLIN	36
SSV ULM 1846	36
SC PREUSSEN MÜNSTER	34
VFB LEIPZIG	32
SC PADERBORN 07	31
SPVGG GREUTHER FÜRTH	26
TASMANIA 1900 BERLIN	15

LIGUE 1 TITLE WINNERS

Ligue 1 has been graced by 69 teams in its history, with a third of them making a serious impression on league records. The sixth-ranked league in Europe, it has seen one of the most evident shifts between traditional clubs and those benefitting from wealthy benefactors and investors. Those familiar with the recent success of PSG might find it surprising to view their win record still lagging some way behind the league's long-standing clubs, including Sochaux, now a Ligue 2 side and still living off their glories of the 1930s and 1960s.

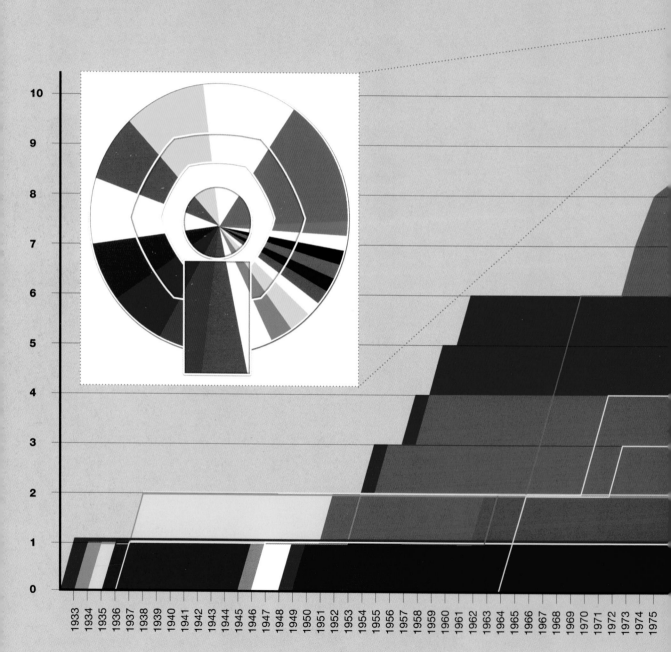

Key (anticlockwise from top-right)

- AS SAINT-ÉTIENNE **10**
- OLYMPIQUE DE MARSEILLE **9**
- FC NANTES **8**
- AS MONACO FC **8**
- OLYMPIQUE LYONNAIS **7**
- GIRONDINS DE BORDEAUX **6**
- STADE DE REIMS **6**

- PARIS SAINT-GERMAIN **6**
- OGC NICE **4**
- LILLE LOSC **3**
- FC SÈTE 34 **2**
- FC SOCHAUX-MONTBÉLIARD **2**
- AJ AUXERRE **1**

- OLYMPIQUE LILLOIS **1**
- MONTPELLIER HÉRRAULT SC **1**
- RC LENS **1**
- RCF PARIS **1**
- CO ROUBAIX-TOURCOING **1**
- RC STRASBOURG ALSACE **1**

Source: Opta (May 2017)

AS SAINT-ÉTIENNE **10**

OLYMPIQUE DE MARSEILLE **9**

FC NANTES, AS MONACO FC **8**

OLYMPIQUE LYONNAIS **7**

STADE DE REIMS, G/D BORDEAUX PARIS SAINT-GERMAIN **6**

OGC NICE **4**

LILLE LOSC **3**

SOCHAUX-M/B, FC SÈTE **2**

OLYMPIQUE LILLOIS, RCF PARIS, ROUBAIX-TOURCOING, STRASBOURG, AJ AUXERRE, RC LENS, MONTPELLIER **1**

1976 1977 1978 1979 1980 1981 1982 1983 1984 1985 1986 1987 1988 1989 1990 1991 1992 1993 1994 1995 1996 1997 1998 1999 2000 2001 2002 2003 2004 2005 2006 2007 2008 2009 2010 2011 2012 2013 2014 2015 2016 2017

LIGUE 1 GAME WINS PER CLUB

Ligue 1 began in 1932, switching to its current name in 2002. Although many view it as one of the weaker of the major European leagues, it is one of the most evenly contested. Until Monaco's 2017 triumph, PSG have recently held sway, but in modern times AS Saint-Etienne (League 1's most successful club), Olympique Lyon (winner of a record seven consecutive titles between 2002 and 2008), and Olympique de Marseille (most seasons and wins in top flight) have all dominated the league.

Club	Wins
SO MONTPELLIER	104
CO ROUBAIX	130
AJACCIO	131
GUINGAMP	133
TOULON	134
BREST	140
STADE FRANÇAIS	143
LORIENT	146
TROYES	151
LAVAL	157
RED STAR	168
FC NANCY	181
CAEN	183
SETE	198
ROUEN	233
CANNES	246
LE HAVRE	257
TOULOUSE FC	269
SEDAN	291
ANGERS	310
MONTPELLIER	315
TOULOUSE	345
NANCY	375
VALENCIENNES	375
RC PARIS	426
BASTIA	434
NIMES	482
AUXERRE	483
REIMS	523
STRASBOURG	690
METZ	709
RENNES	738

Under 100 Wins

OLYMPIQUE LILLOIS **98**	ALÈS **42**	CA PARIS **13**	AVIGNON **7**
FIVES **77**	LIMOGES **37**	COLMAR **12**	BOULOGNE-SUR-MER **7**
EXCELSIOR **75**	PARIS FC **31**	LYON OU **11**	AIX **6**
ANTIBES **65**	ANGOULÊME **30**	NIORT **11**	ISTRES **6**
LE MANS **65**	GRENOBLE **30**	BÉZIERS **9**	CLUB FRANCAIS **5**
MULHOUSE **51**	MARTIGUES **27**	CHÂTEAUROUX **8**	HYÈRES **4**
ÉVIAN TG **45**	RC ROUBAIX **26**	GUEUGNON **8**	ARLES-AVIGNON **3**
TOURS **44**	DIJON **17**	GFC AJACCIO **8**	

PARIS SAINT-GERMAIN **747**
RC LENS **770**
NICE **780**
NANTES **788**
LILLE **794**
SOCHAUX **859**
OLYMPIQUE LYONNAIS **908**
MONACO **955**
SAINT-ÉTIENNE **1001**
BORDEAUX **1021**
MARSEILLE **1058**

LIGUE 1 GOALS PER CLUB

Seen by many of the world's richest clubs as a nursery for emerging young players, Ligue 1 has given renowned forwards such as Thierry Henry, Didier Drogba, Karim Benzema, and Eden Hazard their first team breaks. Zlatan Ibrahimović, a rare star import to the league, hit 113 goals in just 122 Ligue 1 games, but left France long before catching record holder Delio Onnis (an Argentinian nicknamed "The Italian"!) who netted 299 goals in 449 appearances between 1972 and 1986.

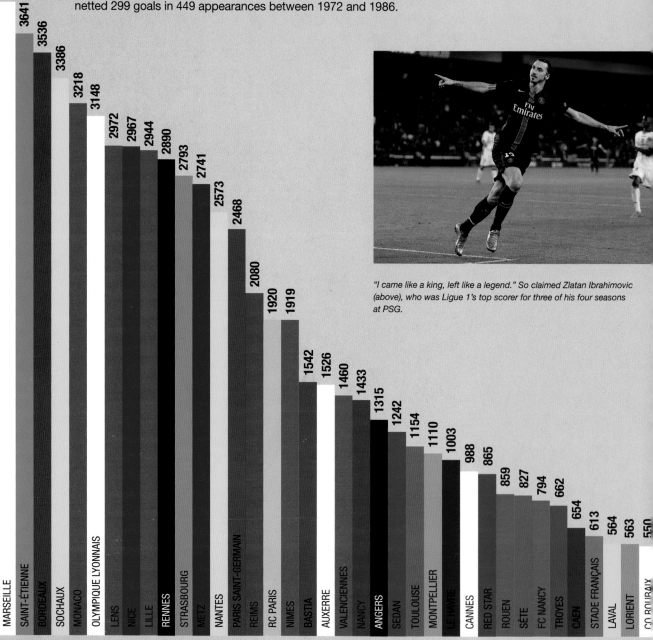

"I came like a king, left like a legend." So claimed Zlatan Ibrahimovic (above), who was Ligue 1's top scorer for three of his four seasons at PSG.

Club	Goals
MARSEILLE	3845
SAINT-ÉTIENNE	3641
BORDEAUX	3536
SOCHAUX	3386
MONACO	3218
OLYMPIQUE LYONNAIS	3148
LENS	2972
NICE	2967
LILLE	2944
RENNES	2890
STRASBOURG	2793
METZ	2741
NANTES	2573
PARIS SAINT-GERMAIN	2468
REIMS	2080
RC PARIS	1920
NIMES	1919
BASTIA	1542
AUXERRE	1526
VALENCIENNES	1460
NANCY	1433
ANGERS	1315
SEDAN	1242
TOULOUSE	1154
MONTPELLIER	1110
LE HAVRE	1003
CANNES	988
RED STAR	865
ROUEN	859
SÈTE	827
FC NANCY	794
TROYES	662
CAEN	654
STADE FRANÇAIS	613
LAVAL	564
LORIENT	563
CO ROUBAIX	550

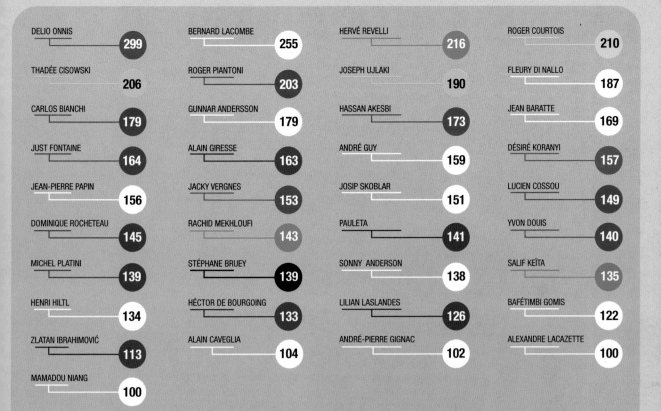

DELIO ONNIS **299**	BERNARD LACOMBE **255**	HERVÉ REVELLI **216**	ROGER COURTOIS **210**
THADÉE CISOWSKI **206**	ROGER PIANTONI **203**	JOSEPH UJLAKI **190**	FLEURY DI NALLO **187**
CARLOS BIANCHI **179**	GUNNAR ANDERSSON **179**	HASSAN AKESBI **173**	JEAN BARATTE **169**
JUST FONTAINE **164**	ALAIN GIRESSE **163**	ANDRÉ GUY **159**	DÉSIRÉ KORANYI **157**
JEAN-PIERRE PAPIN **156**	JACKY VERGNES **153**	JOSIP SKOBLAR **151**	LUCIEN COSSOU **149**
DOMINIQUE ROCHETEAU **145**	RACHID MEKHLOUFI **143**	PAULETA **141**	YVON DOUIS **140**
MICHEL PLATINI **139**	STÉPHANE BRUEY **139**	SONNY ANDERSON **138**	SALIF KEÏTA **135**
HENRI HILTL **134**	HÉCTOR DE BOURGOING **133**	LILIAN LASLANDES **126**	BAFÉTIMBI GOMIS **122**
ZLATAN IBRAHIMOVIĆ **113**	ALAIN CAVEGLIA **104**	ANDRÉ-PIERRE GIGNAC **102**	ALEXANDRE LACAZETTE **100**
MAMADOU NIANG **100**			

"I think that goalscoring is something that is born in a person—it's in the blood."

Jean-Pierre Papin

If ever there was a born goalscorer it was Papin. As Marseille's striker he was Ligue 1's top scorer in five consecutive seasons between 1988 and 1992. On returning to France from sojourns at Milan and Bayern, he carried on scoring at Bordeaux, taking his league tally to 156 goals in 270 appearances—the greatest goalscorer in modern French soccer.

Source: Opta (May 2017)
Seasons 1992–93 to 2016–17
Color relates to the team for which the player scored the highest number of goals.

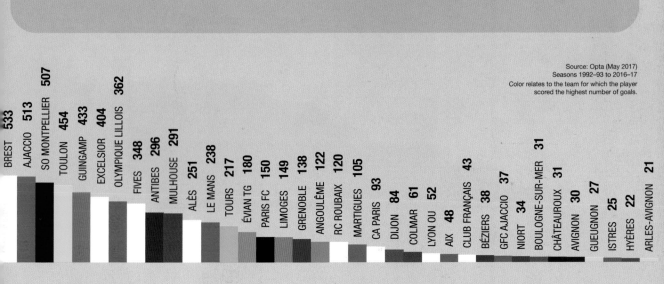

BREST **533** · AJACCIO **513** · SO MONTPELLIER **507** · TOULON **454** · GUINGAMP **433** · EXCELSIOR **404** · OLYMPIQUE LILLOIS **362** · FIVES **348** · ANTIBES **296** · MULHOUSE **291** · ALÈS **251** · LE MANS **238** · TOURS **217** · ÉVIAN TG **180** · PARIS FC **150** · LIMOGES **149** · GRENOBLE **138** · ANGOULÊME **122** · RC ROUBAIX **120** · MARTIGUES **105** · CA PARIS **93** · DIJON **84** · COLMAR **61** · LYON OU **52** · AIX **48** · CLUB FRANÇAIS **43** · BÉZIERS **38** · GFC AJACCIO **37** · NIORT **34** · BOULOGNE-SUR-MER **31** · CHÂTEAUROUX **31** · AVIGNON **30** · GUEUGNON **27** · ISTRES **25** · HYÈRES **22** · ARLES-AVIGNON **21**

EREDIVISIE TITLE WINNERS

The Eredivisie, the top league of the Netherlands, was founded in 1956, two years after the start of professional soccer in the country. It is placed 13th in UEFA's ranking of European leagues. The Dutch league has been dominated by three teams, all ever-presents in the league: Ajax (24 titles), PSV Eindhoven (18), and Feyenoord (10), whose 2017 success was their first for 18 years. Only AZ Alkmaar and FC Twente have managed to break the grip of the "Big Three" this century.

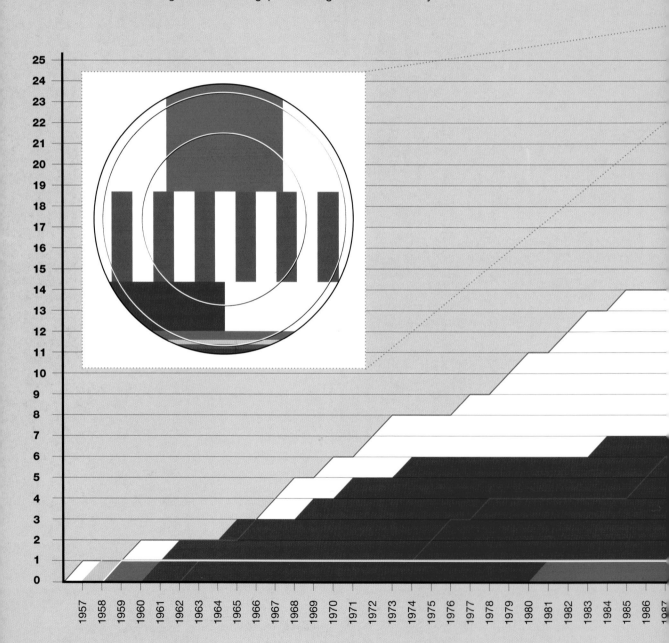

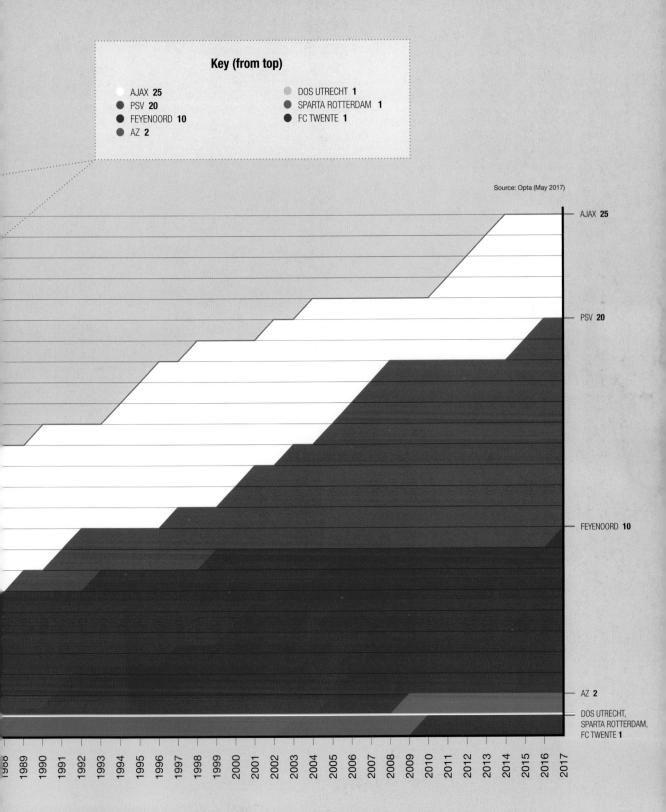

Key (from top)

- AJAX **25**
- PSV **20**
- FEYENOORD **10**
- AZ **2**
- DOS UTRECHT **1**
- SPARTA ROTTERDAM **1**
- FC TWENTE **1**

Source: Opta (May 2017)

AJAX **25**

PSV **20**

FEYENOORD **10**

AZ **2**

DOS UTRECHT,
SPARTA ROTTERDAM,
FC TWENTE **1**

1988 1989 1990 1991 1992 1993 1994 1995 1996 1997 1998 1999 2000 2001 2002 2003 2004 2005 2006 2007 2008 2009 2010 2011 2012 2013 2014 2015 2016 2017

EREDIVISIE GAME WINS PER CLUB

Ajax, Feyenoord, and PSV have been the dominant Eredivisie clubs, with all three having many successful spells—often sharing the limelight with the others. PSV had the Romario-inspired team around 1990 and Gus Hiddink's all-conquering side in the early 2000s. Feyenoord's 1971 European Cup side boasted the talents of Willem van Hanegem and winger Coen Moulijn, and Ajax have consistently competed for the title, reaching almost unsurpassable heights with the 1970s team of Johan Neeskens and Johan Cruyff and the '90s line-ups including Dennis Bergkamp, Patrick Kluivert, Edgar Davids, and Clarence Seedorf.

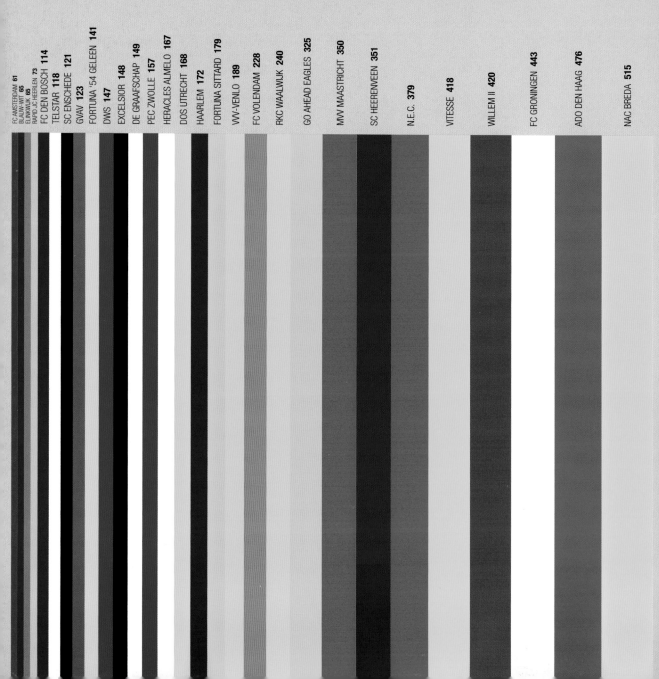

FC AMSTERDAM 61
BLAUW-WIT 65
ELINKWIJK
RAPID JC-HEERLEN 73
FC DEN BOSCH 114
TELSTAR 118
SC ENSCHEDE 121
GVAV 123
FORTUNA '54 GELEEN 141
DWS 147
EXCELSIOR 148
DE GRAAFSCHAP 149
PEC ZWOLLE 157
HERACLES ALMELO 167
DOS UTRECHT 168
HAARLEM 172
FORTUNA SITTARD 179
VVV-VENLO 189
FC VOLENDAM 228
RKC WAALWIJK 240
GO AHEAD EAGLES 325
MVV MAASTRICHT 350
SC HEERENVEEN 351
N.E.C. 379
VITESSE 418
WILLEM II 420
FC GRONINGEN 443
ADO DEN HAAG 476
NAC BREDA 515

Under 50 Wins

SC CAMBUUR **49**	XERXESDZB **26**	WAGENINGEN **13**
SHS **37**	FC EINDHOVEN **23**	HELMOND SPORT **12**
RBC ROOSENDAAL **35**	BVC AMSTERDAM **20**	VEENDAM **12**
NOAD **33**	BVV **18**	ALKMAAR **6**
SITTARDIA **32**	DE VOLEWIJCKERS **15**	
FC DORDRECHT **31**	SVV **13**	

RODA JC KERKRADE **555**

AZ **559**

FC UTRECHT **589**

SPARTA ROTTERDAM **612**

FC TWENTE **766**

FEYENOORD **1168**

PSV **1246**

AJAX **1360**

EREDIVISIE GOALS PER CLUB

Of course, the "big three" Netherlands teams dominate the goalscoring tables—Ajax even managed 122 in one season in 1966–67 and PSV's Coen Dillen, nicknamed "Het Kanon", struck 43 times in 1956–57. The modern Dutch goal masters—Cruyff, van Basten, Bergkamp, Van Nistelrooy—all figure as season's top scorers, but the lesser known Ruud Geels was the leading striker on five occasions (four times for Ajax, once for Sparta) between 1974 and 1981. More recently the minor teams strikers have topped the charts on several occasions, including Wilfrid Bony for Vitesse (2012–13), Alfreð Finnbogason of Heerenveen (2013–14), and AZ's Vincent Janssen (2015–16).

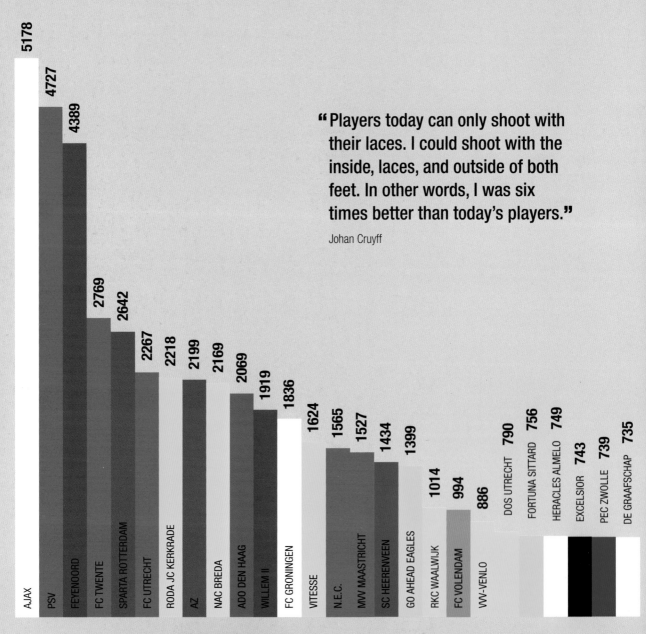

"Players today can only shoot with their laces. I could shoot with the inside, laces, and outside of both feet. In other words, I was six times better than today's players."

Johan Cruyff

Club	Goals
AJAX	5178
PSV	4727
FEYENOORD	4389
FC TWENTE	2769
SPARTA ROTTERDAM	2642
FC UTRECHT	2267
RODA JC KERKRADE	2218
AZ	2199
NAC BREDA	2169
ADO DEN HAAG	2069
WILLEM II	1919
FC GRONINGEN	1836
VITESSE	1624
N.E.C.	1565
MVV MAASTRICHT	1527
SC HEERENVEEN	1434
GO AHEAD EAGLES	1399
RKC WAALWIJK	1014
FC VOLENDAM	994
VVV-VENLO	886
DOS UTRECHT	790
FORTUNA SITTARD	756
HERACLES ALMELO	749
EXCELSIOR	743
PEC ZWOLLE	739
DE GRAAFSCHAP	735

WILLY VAN DER KUIJLEN 311	RUUD GEELS 265	JOHAN CRUYFF 215	KEES KIST 212
TONNY VAN DER LINDEN 206	HENK GROOT 195	PETER HOUTMAN 180	SJAAK SWART 175
LEO VAN VEEN 174	COR VAN DER GIJP 162	WIM KIEFT 158	DIRK KUYT 153
HALLVAR THORESEN 152	HENK "CHARLY" BOSVELD 152	JOHN BOSMAN 146	PIET KEIZER 146
LEX SCHOENMAKER 145	WILLY BROKAMP 145	JAN VENNEGOOR OF HESSELINK 134	CEES VAN KOOTEN 134
PIET KRUIVER 133	OVE KINDVALL 129	MARTIN VAN GEEL 127	MARCO VAN BASTEN 127
RONALD KOEMAN 126	PIET KEUR 126	THEO DE JONG 126	WILLEM VAN HANEGEM 126
PIERRE VAN HOOIJDONK 125	GERALD VANENBURG 124	COEN DILLEN 120	KLAAS NUNINGA 120
DICK NANNINGA 118	RENÉ VAN DE KERKHOF 118	MATTHEW AMOAH 116	BLAISE NKUFO 114
LEO CANJELS 114	HENK WERY 113	JON DAHL TOMASSON 112	HENNIE MEIJER 111
LUC NILIS 110	KLAAS-JAN HUNTELAAR 109	JACQUES VISSCHERS 109	DICK VAN DIJK 109
ANDRÉ HOEKSTRA 106	MATEJA KEŽMAN 105	CHRIS COENEN 105	KENNETH PEREZ 105
JOHN VAN LOEN 104	CAROL SCHUURMAN 104		

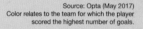

Source: Opta (May 2017)
Color relates to the team for which the player
scored the highest number of goals.

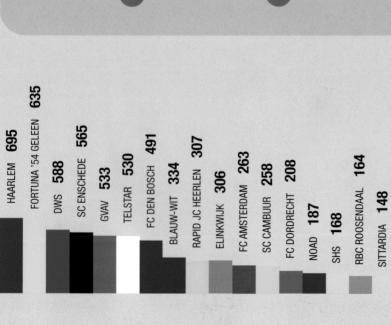

Team	Goals
HAARLEM	695
FORTUNA '54 GELEEN	635
DWS	588
SC ENSCHEDE	565
GVAV	533
TELSTAR	530
FC DEN BOSCH	491
BLAUW-WIT	334
RAPID JC HEERLEN	307
ELINKWIJK	306
FC AMSTERDAM	263
SC CAMBUUR	258
FC DORDRECHT	208
NOAD	187
SHS	168
RBC ROOSENDAAL	164
SITTARDIA	148
BVV	126
FC EINDHOVEN	107
BVC AMSTERDAM	103
DE VOLEWIJCKERS	99
HELMOND SPORT	93
XERXESDZB	92
VEENDAM	74
WAGENINGEN	72
SVV	62
ALKMAAR	39

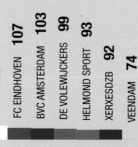

MLS TROPHY WINS PER CLUB

Major League Soccer (MLS), the top tier of soccer in the USA and Canada, was inspired by the success of the 1994 World Cup in the US. The league's first season took place in 1996 and consisted of 10 teams. In the following 20 years the number of teams has expanded to 22—including three teams from Canada—with further expansion planned for 2020. Organized into an Eastern and Western conference, clubs compete for a place in the national playoffs to represent their conference in a final to win the MLS—also known as the Philip F. Anschutz Trophy.

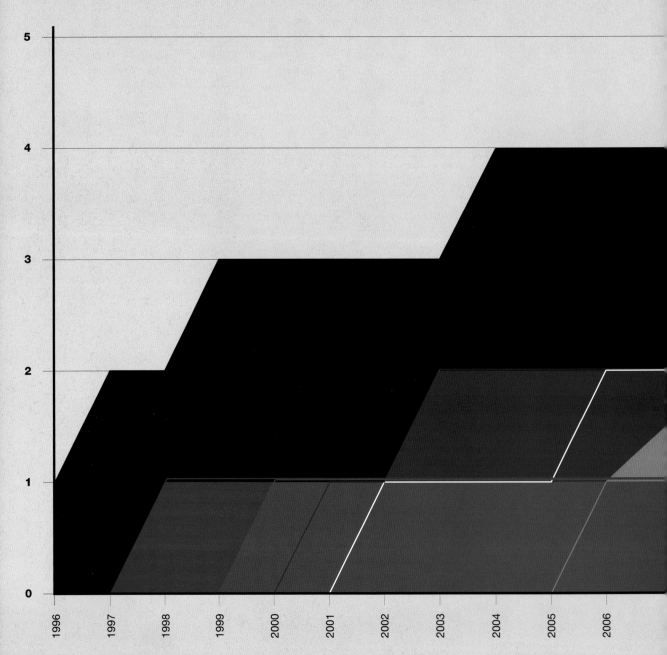

Key (from top)

- LA GALAXY **5**
- D.C. UNITED **4**
- SAN JOSE EARTHQUAKES **2**
- HOUSTON DYNAMO **2**
- SPORTING KANSAS CITY **2**
- CHICAGO FIRE **1**

- COLUMBUS CREW **1**
- REAL SALT LAKE **1**
- COLORADO RAPIDS **1**
- PORTLAND TIMBERS **1**
- SEATTLE SOUNDERS **1**

LA GALAXY **5**

D.C. UNITED **4**

SAN JOSE EARTHQUAKES,
HOUSTON DYNAMO,
SPORTING KANSAS CITY **2**

CHICAGO FIRE,
COLUMBUS CREW,
REAL SALT LAKE,
COLORADO RAPIDS,
PORTLAND TIMBERS,
SEATTLE SOUNDERS **1**

2007 2008 2009 2010 2011 2012 2013 2014 2015 2016

MLS GAME WINS PER CLUB

The forerunner to the MLS was the ill-fated North American Soccer League (NASL), a division that relied too heavily on imported celebrity players such as Pelé and Franz Beckenbauer to have home success. The MLS too once enlisted the assistance of foreign stars to boost its appeal, including David Beckham, Cuauhtémoc Blanco, Andrea Pirlo, and David Villa, but in recent years it has established itself as a sustainable league, attracting an average of 18,600 fans a game and global TV interest, and is dedicated to nurturing home-grown talent. Today, the MLS is the world's fastest-growing sport.

Source: Opta (October 2016)

- ORLANDO CITY SC **21**
- NEW YORK CITY FC **25**
- MIAMI FUSION **49**
- MONTREAL IMPACT **64**
- VANCOUVER WHITECAPS **68**
- PHILADELPHIA UNION **72**
- TAMPA BAY MUTINY **75**
- PORTLAND TIMBERS **77**
- CHIVAS USA **93**
- SPORTING KANSAS CITY **94**
- TORONTO FC **95**
- SAN JOSE EARTHQUAKES **98**
- SAN JOSE **122**
- SEATTLE SOUNDERS FC **134**
- HOUSTON DYNAMO **142**
- REAL SALT LAKE **150**
- KANSAS CITY WIZARDS **175**
- COLORADO RAPIDS **248**

As the most recent major league in world soccer, the MLS is still developing. This table needs to be read in relation to the number of seasons the team has been playing in the MLS. Although some clubs have changed their name, no teams have been relegated from the league.

1996: The original 10 teams comprise: Colorado Rapids, Columbus Crew, D.C. United, Dallas Burn (later FC Dallas), Kansas City Wizards, LA Galaxy, New England Revolution, NY/NJ Metro Stars (later New York Red Bulls), San Jose Clash (later Earthquakes) and Tampa Bay Mutiny.
1998: Chicago Fire, Miami Fusion

2005: Real Salt Lake, Chivas USA
2006: Houston Dynamo
2007: Toronto FC
2009: Seattle Sounders
2010: Philadelphia Union
2011: Portland Timbers, Vancouver Whitecaps
2012: Montreal Impact
2015: New York City FC, Orlando City
2017: Minnesota United, Atlanta United

NEW ENGLAND REVOLUTION **250**

CHICAGO FIRE **251**

NEW YORK RED BULLS **268**

COLUMBUS CREW SC **273**

FC DALLAS **275**

D.C. UNITED **279**

LA GALAXY **330**

MLS GOALS PER CLUB

Thierry Henry, Robbie Keane, and Didier Drogba have all scored freely in the States, but the record books are topped by home-grown heroes like Landon Donovan, Jeff Cunningham, and Chris Wondolowski. The goals recorded here include such gems as the 50-yard run by Metrostars' Clint Mathis to score the 2001 MLS Goal of the Year, the magnificent flick and volley from the Vancouver Whitecaps' Eric Hassli in 2011 and David Villa's exquisite chip from the halfway line for New York City FC in 2017.

Source: mlssoccer.com (October 2016)
Player data: Color relates to the team for which the player scored the highest number of goals.

Landon Donovan stands alone in MLS history. He is not only the clear all-time leading scorer but is also at the head of the all-time assists list. In 2009 he won the league's MVP award and in 2015 they named the award after him. Outside of short periods with Bayer Leverkusen, Bayern München, and Everton, Donovan has spent his whole career in the MLS; four seasons with San Jose Earthquakes (32 goals) and 11 seasons with LA Galaxy (113 goals). Donovan has won the MLS Cup a record six times—twice with the Earthquakes and four times with the Galaxy.

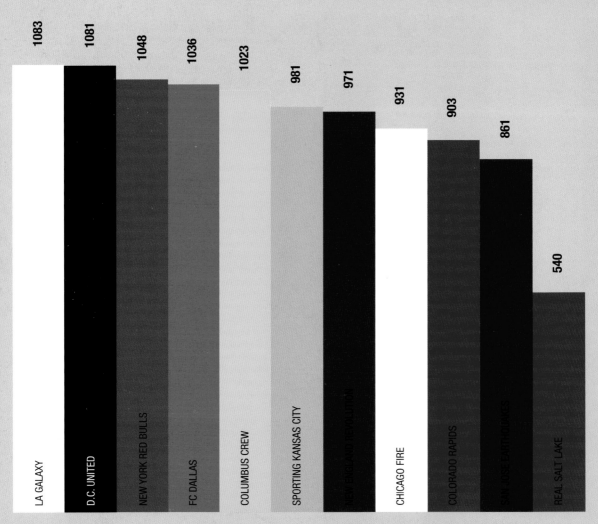

Club	Goals
LA GALAXY	1083
D.C. UNITED	1081
NEW YORK RED BULLS	1048
FC DALLAS	1036
COLUMBUS CREW	1023
SPORTING KANSAS CITY	981
NEW ENGLAND REVOLUTION	971
CHICAGO FIRE	931
COLORADO RAPIDS	903
SAN JOSE EARTHQUAKES	861
REAL SALT LAKE	540

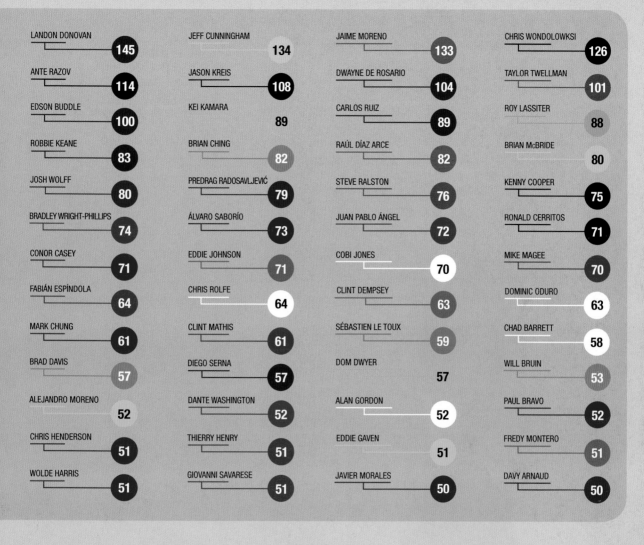

LANDON DONOVAN **145**	JEFF CUNNINGHAM **134**	JAIME MORENO **133**	CHRIS WONDOLOWKSI **126**
ANTE RAZOV **114**	JASON KREIS **108**	DWAYNE DE ROSARIO **104**	TAYLOR TWELLMAN **101**
EDSON BUDDLE **100**	KEI KAMARA **89**	CARLOS RUIZ **89**	ROY LASSITER **88**
ROBBIE KEANE **83**	BRIAN CHING **82**	RAÚL DÍAZ ARCE **82**	BRIAN McBRIDE **80**
JOSH WOLFF **80**	PREDRAG RADOSAVLJEVIĆ **79**	STEVE RALSTON **76**	KENNY COOPER **75**
BRADLEY WRIGHT-PHILLIPS **74**	ÁLVARO SABORÍO **73**	JUAN PABLO ÁNGEL **72**	RONALD CERRITOS **71**
CONOR CASEY **71**	EDDIE JOHNSON **71**	COBI JONES **70**	MIKE MAGEE **70**
FABIÁN ESPÍNDOLA **64**	CHRIS ROLFE **64**	CLINT DEMPSEY **63**	DOMINIC ODURO **63**
MARK CHUNG **61**	CLINT MATHIS **61**	SÉBASTIEN LE TOUX **59**	CHAD BARRETT **58**
BRAD DAVIS **57**	DIEGO SERNA **57**	DOM DWYER **57**	WILL BRUIN **53**
ALEJANDRO MORENO **52**	DANTE WASHINGTON **52**	ALAN GORDON **52**	PAUL BRAVO **52**
CHRIS HENDERSON **51**	THIERRY HENRY **51**	EDDIE GAVEN **51**	FREDY MONTERO **51**
WOLDE HARRIS **51**	GIOVANNI SAVARESE **51**	JAVIER MORALES **50**	DAVY ARNAUD **50**

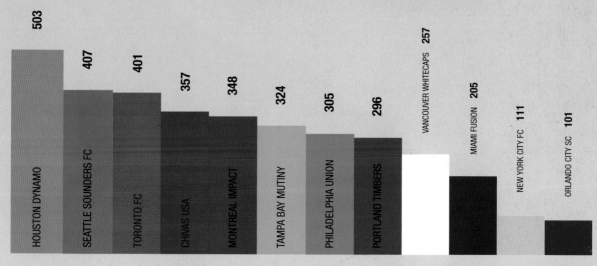

Team	Value
HOUSTON DYNAMO	503
SEATTLE SOUNDERS FC	407
TORONTO FC	401
CHIVAS USA	357
MONTREAL IMPACT	348
TAMPA BAY MUTINY	324
PHILADELPHIA UNION	305
PORTLAND TIMBERS	296
VANCOUVER WHITECAPS	257
MIAMI FUSION	205
NEW YORK CITY FC	111
ORLANDO CITY SC	101

SCOTTISH LEAGUE TITLE WINNERS

The Scottish Football League was established in 1890 just two years after its English counterpart. Dumbarton captured the first two titles, but the domination of Glasgow's Old Firm—Celtic and Rangers—soon took hold. The top flight was reorganized into the Scottish Premier League (1998–2013) and the Scottish Premiership (since 2013)—comprising 12 clubs since the 2000–01 season. All clubs play each other three times before the league is split in half, with teams playing a further single match against each of their section.

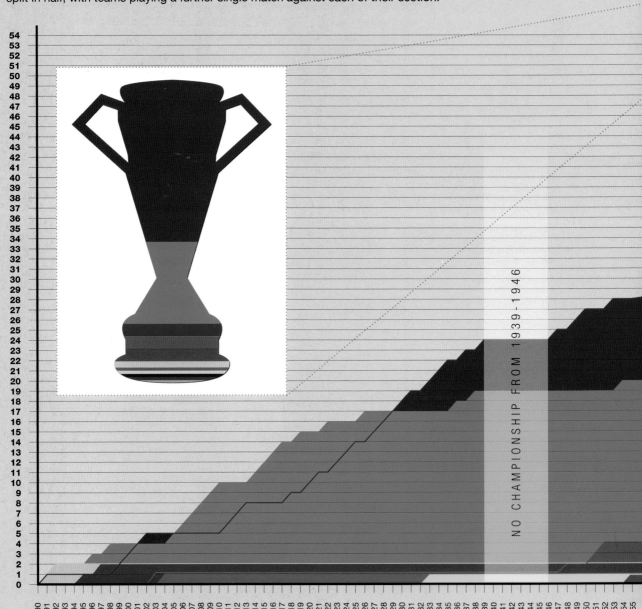

NO CHAMPIONSHIP FROM 1939-1946

Key (from top)

- RANGERS **54**
- CELTIC **48**
- HEART OF MIDLOTHIAN **4**
- HIBERNIAN **4**
- ABERDEEN **4**
- DUMBARTON **2**
- THIRD LANARK **1**
- MOTHERWELL **1**
- DUNDEE **1**
- KILMARNOCK **1**
- DUNDEE UNITED **1**

Source: Opta (May 2017)

RANGERS **54**

CELTIC **48**

HEART OF MIDLOTHIAN, HIBERNIAN, ABERDEEN **4**

DUMBARTON **2**

THIRD LANARK, MOTHERWELL, DUNDEE, KILMARNOCK, DUNDEE UNITED **1**

1956 1957 1958 1959 1960 1961 1962 1963 1964 1965 1966 1967 1968 1969 1970 1971 1972 1973 1974 1975 1976 1977 1978 1979 1980 1981 1982 1983 1984 1985 1986 1987 1988 1989 1990 1991 1992 1993 1994 1995 1996 1997 1998 1999 2000 2001 2002 2003 2004 2005 2006 2007 2008 2009 2010 2011 2012 2013 2014 2015 2016 2017

EUROPEAN ATTENDANCES

Attendances in the top tiers of European soccer average around 30,000 per game, with the Bundesliga and the Premier League attracting the highest average crowds. Despite rising ticket prices and more televised games, the gates in England, Germany, and Spain continue to rise, while those in Italy and France remain static. Over the next few years major new stadia and expansions by clubs who already sell out many games, including Tottenham Hotspur, Atlético Madrid, Barcelona, Valencia, and Liverpool, could see further sharp rises in attendance.

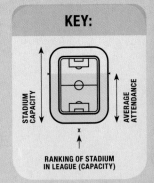

KEY:

STADIUM CAPACITY

AVERAGE ATTENDANCE

x

RANKING OF STADIUM IN LEAGUE (CAPACITY)

Source: Opta (May 2017)

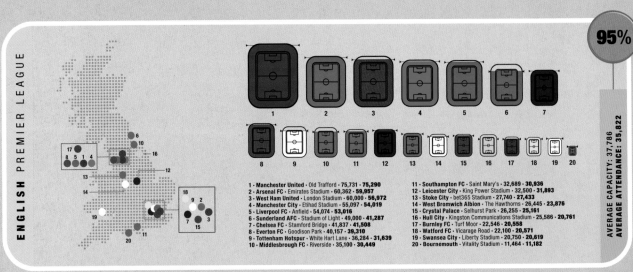

ENGLISH PREMIER LEAGUE

95%

AVERAGE CAPACITY: 37,786
AVERAGE ATTENDANCE: 35,822

1 · **Manchester United** · Old Trafford · 75,731 · **75,290**
2 · **Arsenal FC** · Emirates Stadium · 60,362 · **59,957**
3 · **West Ham United** · London Stadium · 60,000 · **56,972**
4 · **Manchester City** · Etihad Stadium · 55,097 · **54,019**
5 · **Liverpool FC** · Anfield · 54,074 · **53,016**
6 · **Sunderland AFC** · Stadium of Light · 49,000 · **41,287**
7 · **Chelsea FC** · Stamford Bridge · 41,837 · **41,508**
8 · **Everton FC** · Goodison Park · 40,157 · **39,310**
9 · **Tottenham Hotspur** · White Hart Lane · 36,284 · **31,639**
10 · **Middlesbrough FC** · Riverside · 35,100 · **30,449**

11 · **Southampton FC** · Saint Mary's · 32,689 · **30,936**
12 · **Leicester City** · King Power Stadium · 32,500 · **31,893**
13 · **Stoke City** · bet365 Stadium · 27,740 · **27,433**
14 · **West Bromwich Albion** · The Hawthorns · 26,445 · **23,876**
15 · **Crystal Palace** · Selhurst Park · 26,255 · **25,161**
16 · **Hull City** · Kingston Communications Stadium · 25,586 · **20,761**
17 · **Burnley FC** · Turf Moor · 22,546 · **20,558**
18 · **Watford FC** · Vicarage Road · 22,100 · **20,571**
19 · **Swansea City** · Liberty Stadium · 20,750 · **20,619**
20 · **Bournemouth** · Vitality Stadium · 11,464 · **11,182**

GERMAN BUNDESLIGA

93%

AVERAGE CAPACITY: 40,260
AVERAGE ATTENDANCE: 37,367

1 · **Borussia Dortmund** · Signal Iduna Park · 81,359 · **79,653**
2 · **Bayern München** · Allianz Arena · 75,000 · **75,000**
3 · **Hertha BSC** · Olympiastadion · 74,400 · **50,267**
4 · **FC Schalke 04** · Veltins-Arena · 62,271 · **60,703**
5 · **Hamburger SV** · Volksparkstadion · 57,000 · **52,341**
6 · **Bor. Mönchengladbach** · Borussia-Park · 54,067 · **51,494**
7 · **Eintracht Frankfurt** · Commerzbank-Arena · 51,500 · **49,176**
8 · **1. FC Köln** · RheinEnergieStadion · 50,997 · **49,571**
9 · **RB Leipzig** · Red Bull Arena · 44,279 · **41,454**

10 · **Werder Bremen** · Weser-Stadion · 42,100 · **40,881**
11 · **1. FSV Mainz 05** · Opel Arena · 34,000 · **29,096**
12 · **FC Augsburg** · WWK ARENA · 30,660 · **28,172**
13 · **Bayer Leverkusen** · BayArena · 30,210 · **28,428**
14 · **1899 Hoffenheim** · Wirsol Rhein-Neckar-Arena · 30,150 · **28,155**
15 · **VfL Wolfsburg** · Volkswagen Arena · 30,000 · **27,586**
16 · **SC Freiburg** · Schwarzwald-Stadion · 24,000 · **23,959**
17 · **SV Darmstadt 98** · Jonathan-Heimes-Stadion am Böllenfalltor · 17,400 · **16,794**
18 · **FC Ingolstadt 04** · Audi Sportpark · 15,800 · **14,601**

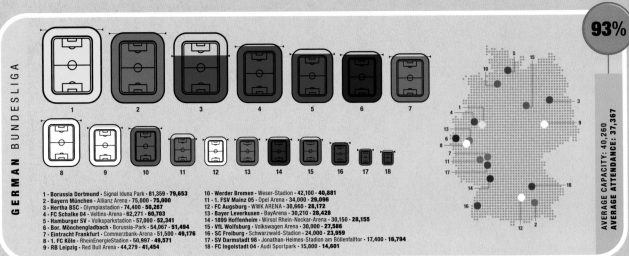

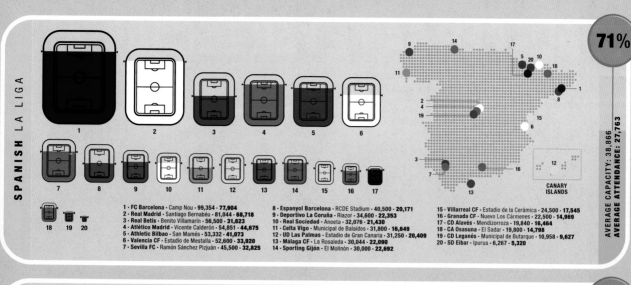

SPANISH LA LIGA — 71%

AVERAGE CAPACITY: 38,866
AVERAGE ATTENDANCE: 27,763

1 · **FC Barcelona** · Camp Nou · 99,354 · **77,904**
2 · **Real Madrid** · Santiago Bernabéu · 81,044 · **68,718**
3 · **Real Betis** · Benito Villamarín · 56,500 · **31,623**
4 · **Atlético Madrid** · Vicente Calderón · 54,851 · **44,675**
5 · **Athletic Bilbao** · San Mamés · 53,332 · **41,073**
6 · **Valencia CF** · Estadio de Mestalla · 52,600 · **33,920**
7 · **Sevilla FC** · Ramón Sánchez Pizjuán · 45,500 · **32,825**
8 · **Espanyol Barcelona** · RCDE Stadium · 40,500 · **20,171**
9 · **Deportivo La Coruña** · Riazor · 34,600 · **22,353**
10 · **Real Sociedad** · Anoeta · 32,076 · **21,430**
11 · **Celta Vigo** · Municipal de Balaídos · 31,800 · **16,649**
12 · **UD Las Palmas** · Estadio de Gran Canaria · 31,250 · **20,409**
13 · **Málaga CF** · La Rosaleda · 30,044 · **22,090**
14 · **Sporting Gijón** · El Molinón · 30,000 · **22,692**
15 · **Villarreal CF** · Estadio de la Cerámica · 24,500 · **17,545**
16 · **Granada CF** · Nuevo Los Cármenes · 22,500 · **14,969**
17 · **CD Alavés** · Mendizorroza · 19,840 · **16,464**
18 · **CA Osasuna** · El Sadar · 19,800 · **14,798**
19 · **CD Leganés** · Municipal de Butarque · 10,958 · **9,627**
20 · **SD Eibar** · Ipurua · 6,267 · **5,320**

CANARY ISLANDS

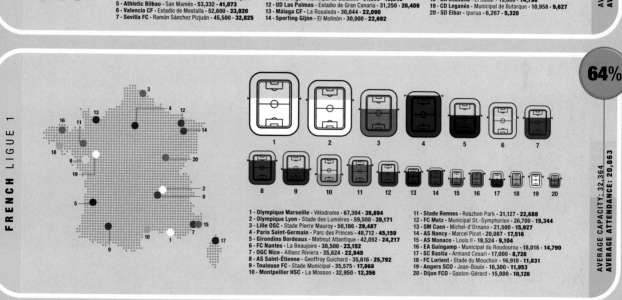

FRENCH LIGUE 1 — 64%

AVERAGE CAPACITY: 32,364
AVERAGE ATTENDANCE: 20,863

1 · **Olympique Marseille** · Vélodrome · 67,394 · **39,894**
2 · **Olympique Lyon** · Stade des Lumières · 59,500 · **39,171**
3 · **Lille OSC** · Stade Pierre Mauroy · 50,186 · **29,487**
4 · **Paris Saint-Germain** · Parc des Princes · 48,712 · **45,159**
5 · **Girondins Bordeaux** · Matmut Atlantique · 42,052 · **24,217**
6 · **FC Nantes** · La Beaujoire · 38,500 · **23,152**
7 · **OGC Nice** · Allianz Riviera · 35,624 · **22,949**
8 · **AS Saint-Étienne** · Geoffroy Guichard · 35,616 · **25,792**
9 · **Toulouse FC** · Stade Municipal · 35,575 · **17,068**
10 · **Montpellier HSC** · La Mosson · 32,950 · **12,356**
11 · **Stade Rennes** · Roazhon Park · 31,127 · **22,688**
12 · **FC Metz** · Municipal St.-Symphorien · 26,700 · **15,344**
13 · **SM Caen** · Michel-d'Ornano · 21,500 · **15,927**
14 · **AS Nancy** · Marcel Picot · 20,087 · **17,516**
15 · **AS Monaco** · Louis II · 18,524 · **9,104**
16 · **EA Guingamp** · Municipal du Roudourou · 18,016 · **14,790**
17 · **SC Bastia** · Armand Cesari · 17,000 · **8,726**
18 · **FC Lorient** · Stade du Mouchoir · 16,910 · **11,831**
19 · **Angers SCO** · Jean-Bouin · 16,300 · **11,953**
20 · **Dijon FCO** · Gaston-Gérard · 15,000 · **10,126**

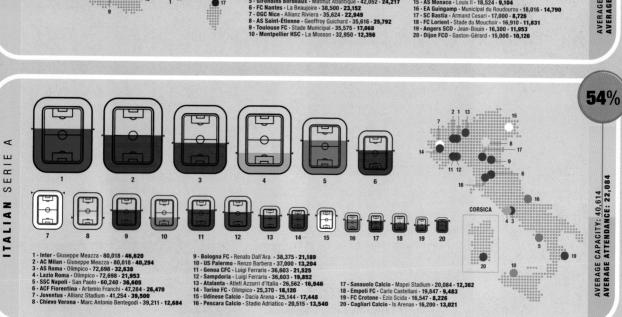

ITALIAN SERIE A — 54%

AVERAGE CAPACITY: 40,614
AVERAGE ATTENDANCE: 22,084

1 · **Inter** · Giuseppe Meazza · 80,018 · **46,620**
2 · **AC Milan** · Giuseppe Meazza · 80,018 · **40,294**
3 · **AS Roma** · Olimpico · 72,698 · **32,638**
4 · **Lazio Roma** · Olimpico · 72,698 · **21,953**
5 · **SSC Napoli** · San Paolo · 60,240 · **36,605**
6 · **ACF Fiorentina** · Artemio Franchi · 47,284 · **26,470**
7 · **Juventus** · Allianz Stadium · 41,254 · **39,500**
8 · **Chievo Verona** · Marc Antonio Bentegodi · 39,211 · **12,684**
9 · **Bologna FC** · Renato Dall'Ara · 38,375 · **21,189**
10 · **US Palermo** · Renzo Barbera · 37,000 · **13,204**
11 · **Genoa CFC** · Luigi Ferraris · 36,603 · **21,525**
12 · **Sampdoria** · Luigi Ferraris · 36,603 · **19,852**
13 · **Atalanta** · Atleti Azzurri d'Italia · 26,562 · **16,946**
14 · **Torino FC** · Olimpico · 25,370 · **18,120**
15 · **Udinese Calcio** · Dacia Arena · 25,144 · **17,448**
16 · **Pescara Calcio** · Stadio Adriatico · 20,515 · **13,540**
17 · **Sassuolo Calcio** · Mapei Stadium · 20,084 · **12,362**
18 · **Empoli FC** · Carlo Castellani · 19,847 · **9,483**
19 · **FC Crotone** · Ezio Scida · 16,547 · **8,226**
20 · **Cagliari Calcio** · Is Arenas · 16,200 · **13,021**

CORSICA

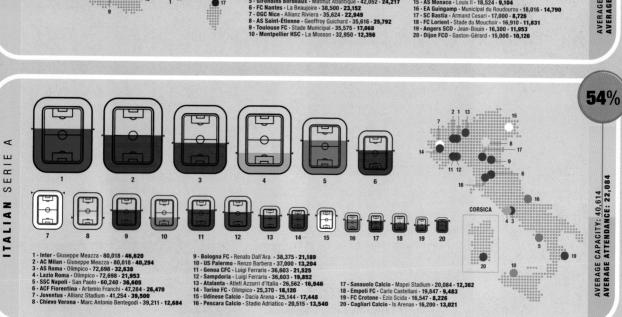

GOALS PER GAME PER DECADE

Watch any major European match this year and you can expect to see around 2.5 goals. The goals-per-game ratio has declined steadily from four per match in the late 1950s to its current level, but has shown signs of rising again in the era of Messi, Cavani, and Aubameyang. You'll need to head to Puerto Rico, Taiwan, or Bermuda to have a good chance of a four goal top-flight match, while games in Tanzania, Lesotho, and Jordan struggle to register two.

German Bundesliga not formed until 1965.

"If you want to have fun, you should go to the circus." With these words Juventus coach Massimiliano Allegri defended his club's safety-first approach. Italian teams' reputation for defensive football is borne out in the tables below as *Catenaccio* and defensive prowess took hold from the 1950s. But there are signs of change—in 2016–17 there were 2.88 goals per game in the league, the highest since 1951, backing up claims of a transformation of Serie A football into an often end-to-end entertaining spectacle.

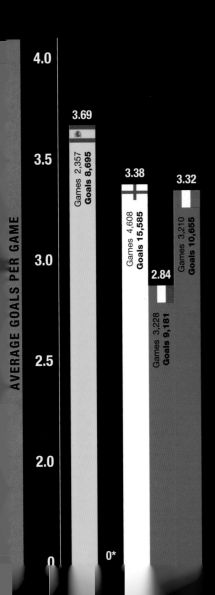

AVERAGE GOALS PER GAME

4.0

3.69
Games 2,357
Goals 8,695

3.5

3.38
Games 4,608
Goals 15,585

3.32
Games 3,210
Goals 10,655

2.84
Games 3,228
Goals 9,181

3.0

2.81
Games 2,408
Goals 6,773

3.16
Games 1,856
Goals 5,868

3.19
Games 4,642
Goals 14,824

2.97
Games 3,522
Goals 10,476

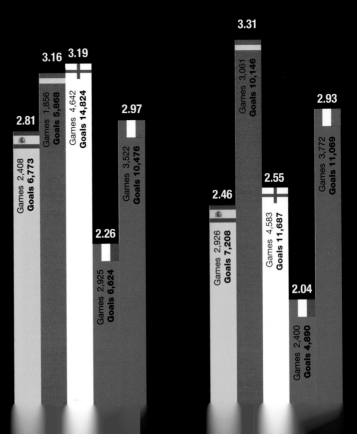

3.31
Games 3,061
Goals 10,146

2.93
Games 3,772
Goals 11,069

2.55
Games 4,583
Goals 11,687

2.5

2.46
Games 2,926
Goals 7,208

2.26
Games 2,925
Goals 6,624

2.04
Games 2,400
Goals 4,890

2.0

0

0*

Robert Lewandowski, the Bundesliga's greatest modern-day goalscorer. The Polish striker has passed 151 league goals for Borussia Dortmund and Bayern München since 2010.

Source: Opta (May 2017)

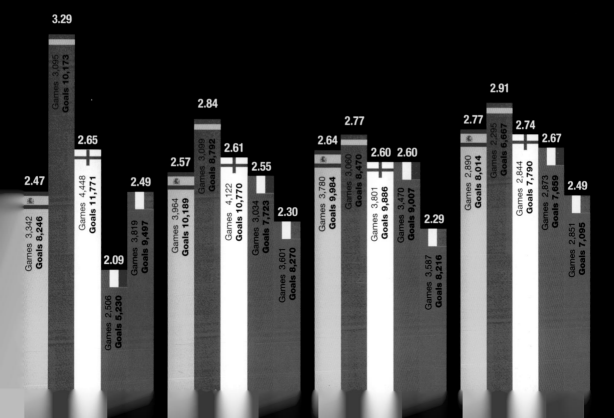

2.47	3.29	2.65	2.09	2.49	2.57	2.84	2.61	2.55	2.30	2.64	2.77	2.60	2.60	2.29	2.77	2.91	2.74	2.67	2.49

Games 3,342 Goals 8,246
Games 3,095 Goals 10,173
Games 4,448 Goals 11,771
Games 2,506 Goals 5,230
Games 3,819 Goals 9,497
Games 3,964 Goals 10,189
Games 3,099 Goals 8,792
Games 4,122 Goals 10,770
Games 3,034 Goals 7,723
Games 3,601 Goals 8,270
Games 3,780 Goals 9,984
Games 3,060 Goals 8,470
Games 3,801 Goals 9,886
Games 3,470 Goals 9,007
Games 3,587 Goals 8,216
Games 2,890 Goals 8,014
Games 2,295 Goals 6,667
Games 2,844 Goals 7,790
Games 2,873 Goals 7,659
Games 2,851 Goals 7,095

LONGEST UNBEATEN RUNS

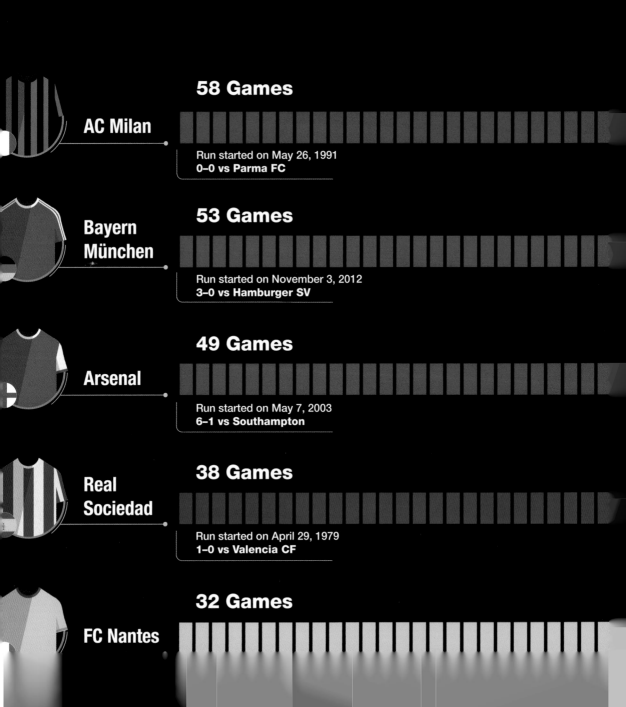

58 Games

AC Milan

Run started on May 26, 1991
0–0 vs Parma FC

53 Games

Bayern München

Run started on November 3, 2012
3–0 vs Hamburger SV

49 Games

Arsenal

Run started on May 7, 2003
6–1 vs Southampton

38 Games

Real Sociedad

Run started on April 29, 1979
1–0 vs Valencia CF

32 Games

FC Nantes

"The Invincibles" was a nickname first given to the 1880s Preston North End team when they won the first "Double", completing the season unbeaten with just four draws. Arsenal would inherit the title in their unbeaten (12-draw) Premier League-winning season of 2003–04. In Europe, Juventus, AC Milan, S.L. Benfica, FC Porto, AFC Ajax, and others have all completed an unbeaten campaign, and in 2017, Celtic's now famous "Infrangibles" became the first Scottish team to manage the feat since the nineteenth century. However, no Ligue 1, Bundesliga, or modern-era La Liga club have yet run the course of the season without defeat.

Source: Opta (May 20

Run ended on March 14, 1993
0–1 vs Parma FC

Run ended on March 29, 2014
0–1 vs FC Augsburg

Run ended on October 16, 2004
0–2 vs Manchester United

Run ended on May 4, 1980
1–2 vs Sevilla FC

Run ended on April 8, 1995
0–2 vs RC Strasbourg Alsace

" It's not impossible [to go through the season unbeaten] as AC Milan once did it but I can't see why it's so shocking to say it. Do you think Manchester United, Liverpool, or Chelsea don't dream that as well? They just don't say it because they're scared to look ridiculous, but nobody is ridiculous in this job as we know anything can happen."

AYING POWER

ion to the top league presents a wonderful opportunity to establish a club in the top
he lucky ones such as TSG 1899 Hoffenheim in the Bundesliga or AC Monaco in
thrive, usually helped by big money backers. Some, like US Pistoiese 1921 (Serie A,
1) or Barnsley (Premier League, 1998–99), are immediately relegated and never seen
More often they are "yo-yo" teams like FC Nürnberg, Middlesbrough, Real Betis, or
1908, doomed to eternally oscillate between promotion and relegation.

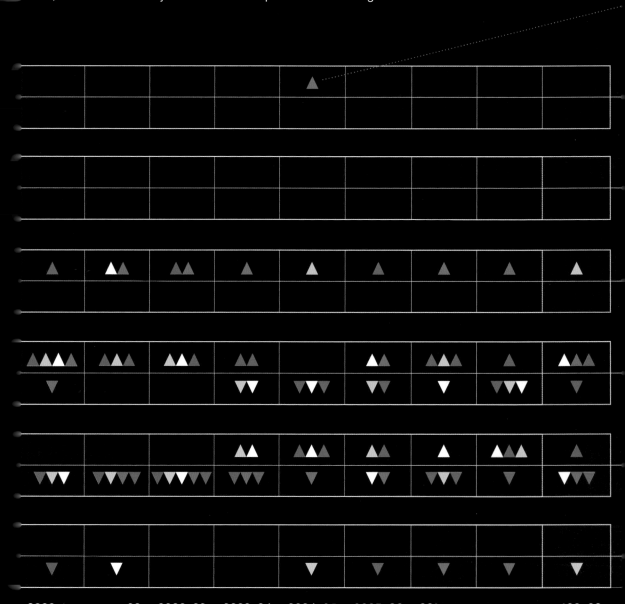

Source: Opta (May 2017)

ENGLISH PREMIER LEAGUE
ITALIAN SERIE A
GERMAN BUNDESLIGA
FRENCH LIGUE 1
SPANISH LA LIGA

This anomaly in the data highlights the May 2006 Italian football scandal, where Italian police implicated many Serie A teams' managers and league referees for their creation of a highly organized match-fixing network.

Against all predictions, there is not one occasion in this time period when all promoted teams are immediately relegated the following season.

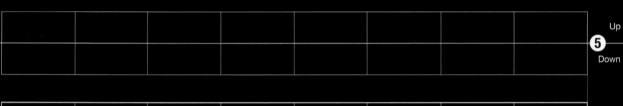
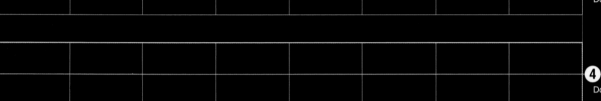
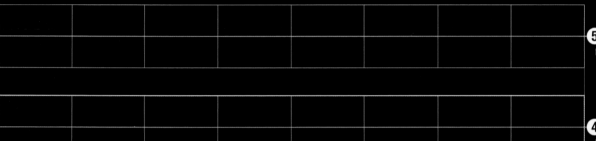
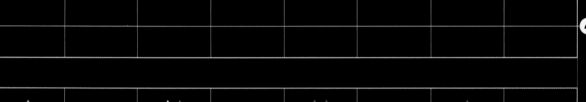
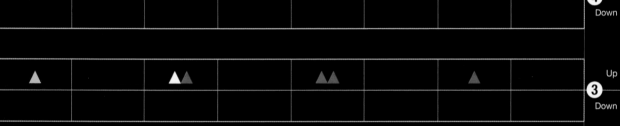

| Up | | | | | | | | | 5 |
| Down | | | | | | | | | |

2009–10   2010–11   2011–12   2012–13   2013–14   2014–15   2015–16   2016–17

FIFA WORLD PLAYER OF THE YEAR WINNERS

n 2010, the Ballon d'Or merged with FIFA's World Footballer of the Year award, the two competitions having run concurrently since 1991. The Ballon d'Or (Golden Ball) is the award given to the soccer player rated by FIFA as the best player in the world. The coach, team captain, and a media representative of every nation selects their top three players (awarded five, three and one point, respectively) from a 23-man shortlist devised by FIFA. The top three players in the world are decided by combining all of the points awarded.

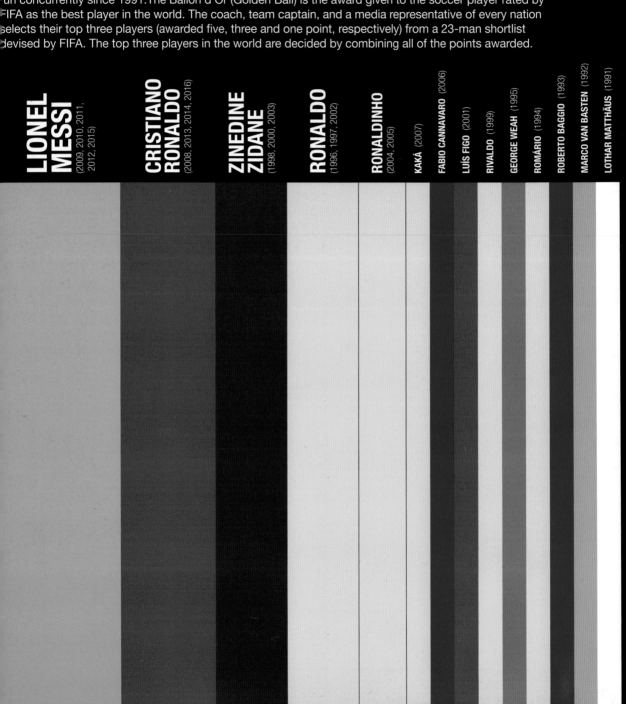

LIONEL MESSI (2009, 2010, 2011, 2012, 2015)

CRISTIANO RONALDO (2008, 2013, 2014, 2016)

ZINEDINE ZIDANE (1998, 2000, 2003)

RONALDO (1996, 1997, 2002)

RONALDINHO (2004, 2005)

KAKÁ (2007)

FABIO CANNAVARO (2006)

LUÍS FIGO (2001)

RIVALDO (1999)

GEORGE WEAH (1995)

ROMÁRIO (1994)

ROBERTO BAGGIO (1993)

MARCO VAN BASTEN (1992)

LOTHAR MATTHÄUS (1991)

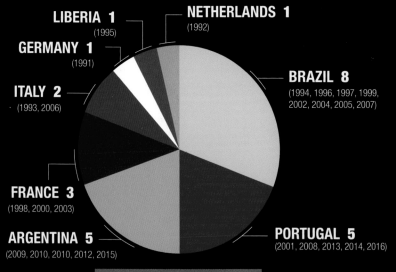

BY NATION

- LIBERIA 1 (1995)
- NETHERLANDS 1 (1992)
- GERMANY 1 (1991)
- ITALY 2 (1993, 2006)
- BRAZIL 8 (1994, 1996, 1997, 1999, 2002, 2004, 2005, 2007)
- FRANCE 3 (1998, 2000, 2003)
- ARGENTINA 5 (2009, 2010, 2010, 2012, 2015)
- PORTUGAL 5 (2001, 2008, 2013, 2014, 2016)

"The only bad thing about Ronaldo's life is Messi. If it was not for him, Ronaldo would be the best player in the world for five years in a row."

Filipe Scolari, former coach of Portugal

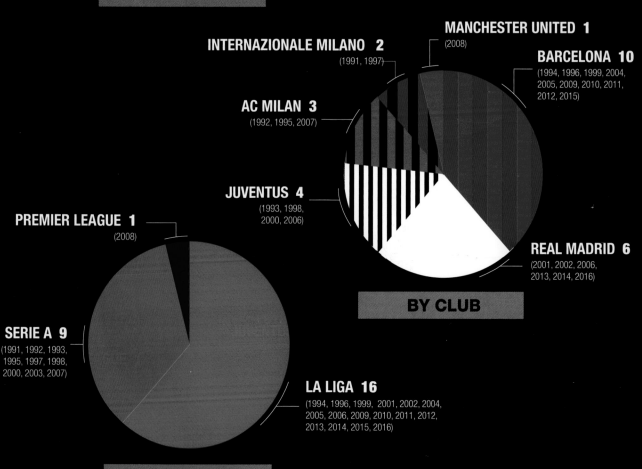

BY CLUB

- MANCHESTER UNITED 1 (2008)
- INTERNAZIONALE MILANO 2 (1991, 1997)
- BARCELONA 10 (1994, 1996, 1999, 2004, 2005, 2009, 2010, 2011, 2012, 2015)
- AC MILAN 3 (1992, 1995, 2007)
- JUVENTUS 4 (1993, 1998, 2000, 2006)
- REAL MADRID 6 (2001, 2002, 2006, 2013, 2014, 2016)

BY LEAGUE

- PREMIER LEAGUE 1 (2008)
- SERIE A 9 (1991, 1992, 1993, 1995, 1997, 1998, 2000, 2003, 2007)
- LA LIGA 16 (1994, 1996, 1999, 2001, 2002, 2004, 2005, 2006, 2009, 2010, 2011, 2012, 2013, 2014, 2015, 2016)

Source: Opta (1991–2017)

THE FLAIR LEAGUE

We all love a wow moment; those demonstrations of skill that are worth the ticket price alone. When it comes to individuals, EA Sports' *FIFA 17* listed its best dribblers as Messi (Barcelona) and Neymar (Paris Saint-Germain). Real Madrid's Ronaldo tops their most powerful shot list, but the top 10 also includes Hull City's Tom Huddlestone, Schalke's Naldo, and Piti from Rayo Vallecano. Take a look at these comparison charts and see where Europe's mazy masters and hot shot kings ply their trade.

Chelsea's often unstoppable Eden Hazard boosted the Premier League's stats by attempting more than 150 dribbles in the 2016–17 season.

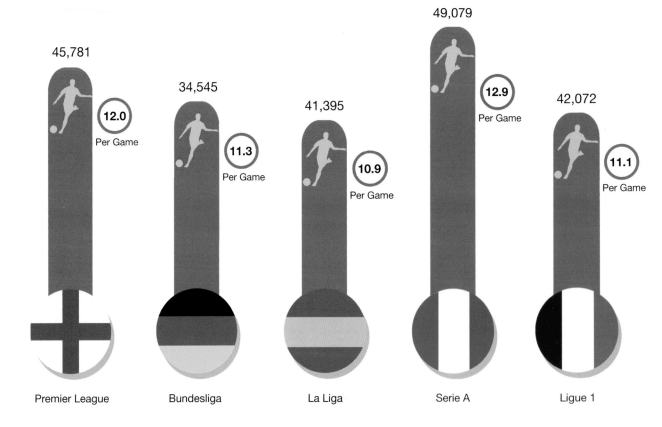

45,781	34,545	41,395	49,079	42,072
12.0 Per Game	11.3 Per Game	10.9 Per Game	12.9 Per Game	11.1 Per Game
Premier League	Bundesliga	La Liga	Serie A	Ligue 1

LONG SHOTS

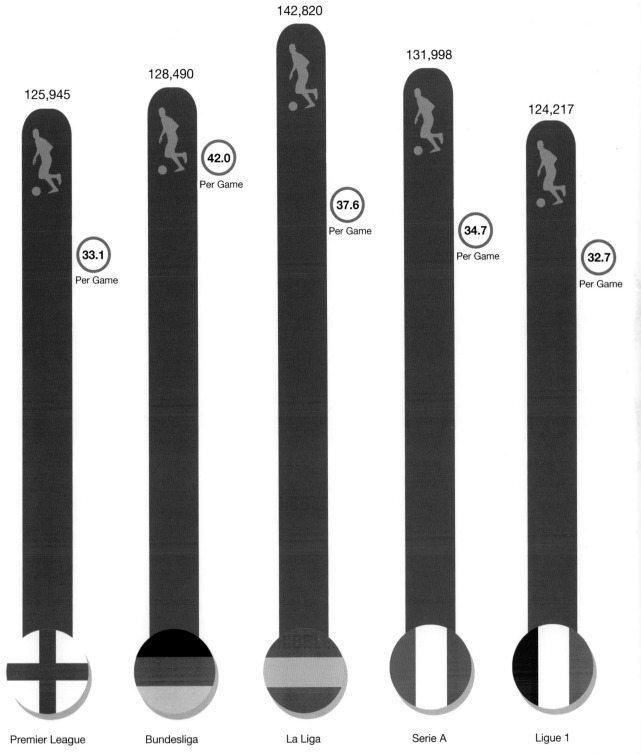

125,945

128,490

142,820

131,998

124,217

33.1 Per Game

42.0 Per Game

37.6 Per Game

34.7 Per Game

32.7 Per Game

Premier League

Bundesliga

La Liga

Serie A

Ligue 1

DRIBBLES

THE FOREIGN LEGION

The quest to build the best team in Europe now involves searching the globe for the best players. While cultural links still explain many of the sources—England picking the best Welsh, Scottish, and Irish players, Germany looking to Switzerland and Austria, with Italy and Spain seeking out South American talent—all major clubs are now prepared to look further afield. Brazil is the leading provider of expatriates to Europe, with French players being most in demand across their own continent.

Source: Opta (August 2016–May 2017)

ENGLISH PREMIER LEAGUE

177 ENGLISH PLAYERS

18.8 AVERAGE APPEARANCES IN SEASON • **3,333** TOTAL APPEARANCES

347 FOREIGN PLAYERS

232 53 44 8 5 5

SPAIN	FRANCE	BELGIUM	NETHERLANDS
36	30	21	20
22.4	18.0	26.3	20.0
807	540	553	399

FRENCH LIGUE 1

303 FRENCH PLAYERS

18.7 AVERAGE APPEARANCES IN SEASON • **5,652** TOTAL APPEARANCES

256 FOREIGN PLAYERS

126 79 42 6 3

GERMAN BUNDESLIGA

216 GERMAN PLAYERS

17.3 AVERAGE APPEARANCES IN SEASON • **3,730** TOTAL APPEARANCES

253 FOREIGN PLAYERS

182 30 21 13 10 1

SWITZERLAND	AUSTRIA	BRAZIL	SPAIN
23	18	16	14
16.8	23.0	17.2	17.6
387	414	275	246

ITALIAN SERIE A

240 ITALIAN PLAYERS

17.9 AVERAGE APPEARANCES IN SEASON • **4,301** TOTAL APPEARANCES

320 FOREIGN PLAYERS

175 99 38 4 3 1

BRAZIL
37
16.0
593

SPANISH LA LIGA

301 SPANISH PLAYERS

19.6 AVERAGE APPEARANCES IN SEASON • **5,904** TOTAL APPEARANCES

240 FOREIGN PLAYERS

106 93 27 10 3 1

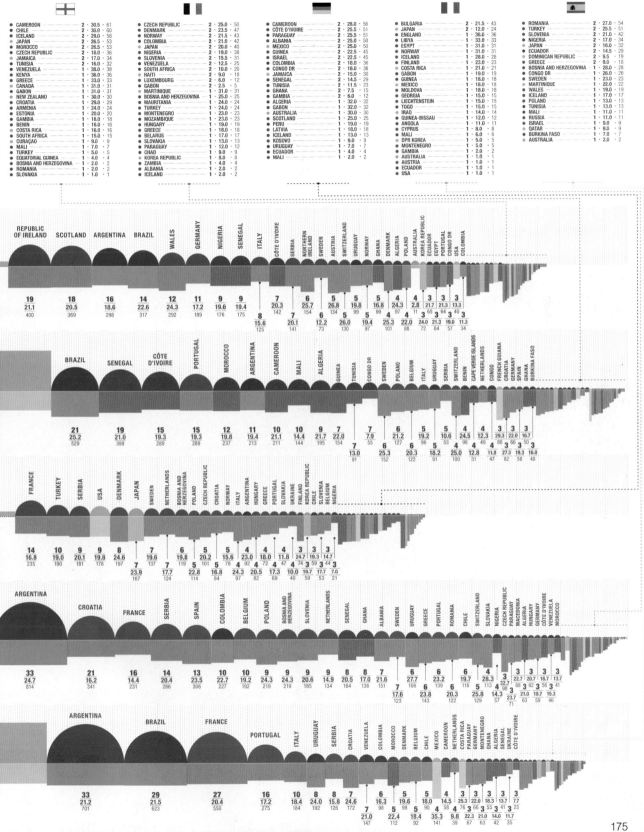

Credits

The publishers would like to thank the following sources for their kind permission to reproduce the pictures in this book.